AN INTRODUCTION TO THE STUDY
OF MEDIEVAL LATIN VERSIFICATION

D1104618

Dag Norberg

AN INTRODUCTION TO THE STUDY
OF MEDIEVAL LATIN VERSIFICATION

translated by Grant C. Roti & Jacqueline de La Chapelle Skubly

edited with an introduction by Jan Ziolkowski

The Catholic University of America Press

Washington, D.C.

Published originally as *Introduction à l'étude de la versification latine médiévale* in 1958 by Almqvist & Wiksell, Stockholm.

LIBRARY OF CONGRESS CATALOGING-IN-PUBLICATION DATA
Norberg, Dag Ludvig, 1909–

    [Introduction à l'étude de la versification latine médivale. English]

    An introduction to the study of medieval Latin versification / by Dag Norberg ; translated by Grant C. Roti and Jacqueline de La Chapelle Skubly ; edited with an introduction by

      Jan Ziolkowski.

      p. cm.

    Includes bibliographical references and index.

    ISBN 0-8132-1335-5 (cloth : alk. Paper) — ISBN 0-8132-1336-3 (pbk. : alk. Paper)

    1. Latin poetry, Medieval and modern—History and criticism.

    2. Latin language, Medieval and modern—Metrics and rhythmics.

    I. Ziolkowski, Jan.   II. Title.

    PA8051 .N59 2003

    871´.0309—dc21

                           2002010003

To my mother and sister
Grant C. Roti

À mon père et mon mari
Jacqueline Skubly

▧ CONTENTS

▣ AN INTRODUCTION TO
DAG NORBERG'S *INTRODUCTION*

For nearly forty years, English-speakers who have wished to study classi-cal meter have relied upon such fine staples as *Latin Metre: An Introduction* by D. S. Raven and *The Meters of Greek and Latin Poetry* by James W. Hal-porn, Martin Ostwald, and Thomas G. Rosenmeyer.[1] Of approximately the same vintage, Dag Norberg's *Introduction à l'étude de la versification latine médiévale* (An Introduction to the Study of Medieval Latin Versification) has also stood the test of time exceptionally well in the more than four decades since 1958. It remains the fundamental starting point for anyone who has questions or seeks information about Medieval Latin metrics. Furthermore, in contrast to the two volumes just mentioned, the *Introduction* has no real competition in any other language. Amazingly, the book has never before been translated from French into another language and indeed has not been reprinted since its first publication in Stockholm.

With the appearance of this translation into English, Norberg's *Introduc-tion* will be given an extended lease on life and will be made accessible to an expanded readership. Every library with a reference collection on medieval studies will want to have a copy of this translation, as will most students and scholars who work with Medieval Latin literature, others who delve into me-dieval music, and many who have an interest in poetry in Romance lan-guages of the Middle Ages. It holds major significance for both Latinists and Romance philologists who hope to gain an understanding of Latin metrics in

1. The original publishing data for Raven's book was London: Faber & Faber, 1965; for the reprint, London: Bristol Classical Press, an imprint of Gerald Duckworth & Co., Ltd, 1998; for Halporn, Ostwald, and Rosenmeyer's book, Indianapolis and New York: Bobbs Merrill, 1963; for the revised edition, Norman: University of Oklahoma Press, 1980, and for the most recent reprint: Indianapolis: Hackett, 1994.

the post-classical period. Linguists, aspiring editors, and lovers of medieval literature will find it indispensable for the data and insights it provides about the history, pronunciation, and accentuation of post-classical Latin. It continues to have particular relevance to the debates that have taken place over the past two decades about the relationship between the early Romance languages and Latin, and about the question of pinpointing the time when Medieval Latin became distinct from the spoken languages that grew out of Vulgar Latin.[2] Finally, anyone—and by no means only musicologists—who desires to explore the intricate interactions between text and music in the Middle Ages would be well advised to consult it.

The reasons for the longevity of Norberg's *Introduction* are not hard to see. It offers clear guidance and many well-chosen examples, drawn from a wide range of texts from late antiquity and the Middle Ages, in a very readable style. A book for both novices and specialists, it can be perused easily from cover to cover, but it can also serve as a reference work. The central theme of the book is the transition from quantitative to accentual Latin poetry. Although such a topic could seem dry and restricted, Norberg's *Introduction* is lively, fascinating, and broad in implications. Furthermore, its terminology and symbolic system, although they have not gone uncontested, have become by far the most common for describing Medieval Latin rhythmic poetry.[3]

Although metrics can seem very abstract, the work of Dag Norberg was not at all detached from the rest of his life's work as a scholar and exercised a catalytic influence upon many students and colleagues. Norberg lived from 31 July 1909 to 20 October 1996.[4] From 1928 to 1948 he first studied and then

2. See Roger Wright, *Late Latin and Early Romance in Spain and Carolingian France*, ARCA 8 (Liverpool: Francis Cairns, 1982), 66–73 ("The Evidence of 'Rhythmic' Poetry") and 177–87 ("Popular Verse?"). Information on Wright's subsequent work in this area can be found in the text and bibliography of his most recent book, *A Sociophilological Study of Late Latin*, Utrecht Studies in Medieval Literacy 10 (Turnhout: Brepols, 2002).

3. For an overview of the different symbolic systems that have been devised, see Edoardo D'Angelo, "Sui sistemi di descrizione strutturale della versificazione ritmica mediolatina," in *Satura. Collectanea philologica Italo Gallo ab amicis discipulisque dicata*, ed. Giancarlo Abbamonte, Andrea Rescigno, Angelo [Rossi], and Ruggero Rossi ([Naples]: Arte Tipografica, 1999), 245–66. The most elaborate alternative to Norberg's system was the one proposed by Dieter Schaller, "Bauformeln für akzentrhythmische Verse und Strophen," *Mittellateinisches Jahrbuch* 14 (1979): 9–21.

4. For information on Norberg's life, see the necrologies by Ritva Maria Jacobsson, "Dag Norberg 31 July 1909–20 October 1996," *Mittellateinisches Jahrbuch* 32 (1997): 1–4, and Pierre Pettitmengin, "In Memoriam Dag Norberg (1909–1996)," *Bulletin du Cange. Archivum latinitatis medii aevi* 54 (1996): 5–8.

taught at the University of Uppsala. From 1948 to 1974 he was a professor at the University of Stockholm. At regular intervals throughout his career, Norberg produced significant contributions to the study of Late Latin and Medieval Latin literature.

His earliest large-scale endeavor during the Uppsala years was two substantial volumes on the *Registrum* of Gregory the Great.[5] Afterward he focused his investigations on syntax in Late Latin and early Medieval Latin, demonstrating in two books (in 1943 and 1944) that many Latin texts had undergone unwarranted emendation by editors who had forced them to conform to a Procrustean bed determined by classical language and style.[6]

Although Norberg never abandoned his researches on Late Latin prose, he directed much of his attention during his Stockholm years to studies on versification. In 1954 he published his first monograph on Medieval Latin poetry of the Merovingian and Carolingian periods, *La Poésie latine rythmique du haut Moyen Âge* (The Latin Rhythmic Poetry of the Early Middle Ages).[7] Less than five years later he came out with the present book, a companion piece of considerable breadth. Not even a decade afterward (1968)—during his long service as rector of the University of Stockholm—he wrote the *Manuel pratique de latin médiéval* (A Practical Manual of Medieval Latin) which has achieved classic status in France and Italy as an initiation into the reading of Medieval Latin texts.[8]

In the later stages of his scholarly life, his scrutiny of both the prose and verse of Late Latin and early Medieval Latin culminated in complete critical editions of Gregory the Great's *Registrum* and Paulinus of Aquileia's poetic oeuvre. With the two massive tomes of the *Registrum* and the two others of

5. *In registrum Gregorii Magni studia critica,* Uppsala universitets årsskrift 4 (Uppsala, 1937) and 7 (Uppsala, 1939).

6. *Syntaktische Forschungen auf dem Gebiete des Spätlateins und des frühen Mittellateins,* Uppsala universitets årsskrift 9 (Uppsala, 1943) and *Beiträge zur spätlateinischen Syntax,* Arbeten utg. med understöd av Vilhelm Ekmans universitetsfond 51 (Uppsala, 1944).

7. Studia latina holmiensia 2 (Stockholm: Almqvist & Wiksell, 1954).

8. *Manuel pratique de latin médiéval* (Paris: A. & J. Picard, 1968). The French text was reprinted in 1980. The Italian translation (first edition, Florence: La Nuova Italia, 1974) was reprinted recently, with a preface by Massimo Oldoni (7–15) and bibliographic updating by Paolo Garbini (239–44), under the title *Manuale di latino medievale,* Schola Salernitana: Studi e testi 1 (Cava dei Tirreni: Avagliano, 1999). A partial translation into English (corresponding to 13–92 of the French edition) by R. H. Johnson is available online (www.orbilat.com/Latin/Medieval_Latin/Dag_Norberg) with the disclaimer "reproduced on Orbis Latinus with no commercial purpose."

Paulinus, Norberg brought his work full circle to the texts that had captivated him recurrently since the 1930s.[9] The bibliography of his works that was published posthumously in 1998 reaches a tally just shy of 140 publications. All the shorter articles he wrote between 1975 and 1995 were reprinted in the volume that includes the bibliography.[10] An earlier book, printed in 1974, contains a florilegium of the notes and essays he had published between 1939 and 1967.[11]

Although much of Norberg's scholarship remains valuable and continues to be cited, the characterization of the *Introduction* as "without doubt the most significant work" in Norberg's research continues to hold true.[12] In 1945 Norberg ceased writing scholarship in German on a regular basis and began to compose his writings predominantly in French. Norberg's choice of language in which to offer his *Introduction* was greeted with admiration and gratitude by Francophone reviewers, who were well aware that he had written earlier studies in Latin and German. The medium of French enabled him to reach a wider scholarly public in Romania—as can be designated the expanse of Romance-speaking countries in Europe—than would have been the case if he had continued to write in German. Yet the very virtue that has facilitated his reception among Italians and Spaniards, to say nothing of Frenchmen, has restricted access to the book in other quarters, as a comfortable reading knowledge of French has become less and less a given for those ever more numerous Anglophone readers who might be drawn to Medieval

9. *S. Gregorii Magni registrum epistularum libri I–VII* and *S. Gregorii Magni registrum epistularum libri VIII–XIV*, Corpus Christianorum Series Latina 140–140A (Turnhout: Brepols, 1982); *L'oeuvre poétique de Paulin d'Aquilée: Édition critique avec introduction et commentaire*, Kungl. Vitterhets Historie och Antikvitetsakademien, Filologisk-filosofiska serien 18 (Stockholm, 1979); and *Contra Felicem libri tres. Paulini Aquileiensis opera omnia, pars 1*, Corpus Christianorum Continuatio mediaevalis 95 (Turnhout: Brepols, 1990).

10. Dag Norberg, *Au seuil du Moyen Âge. II: Études linguistiques, métriques et littéraires 1975–95*, ed. Ritva Jacobsson and Folke Sandgren, Kungl. Vitterhets Historie och Antikvitets Akademien, Filologiskt Arkiv 40 (Stockholm: Almqvist & Wiksell, 1998). The bibliography, compiled by Axel Norberg and Folke Sandgren, runs from pp. 267–79. Many of these studies pertain to metrics, of which special note should be made of "Mètre et rythme entre le Bas-Empire et le Haut Moyen Âge," 81–96; "Carmen oder Rhythmus?" 111–20; and "La versification de Commodien," 171–76.

11. Dag Norberg, *Au seuil du Moyen Âge: Études linguistiques, métriques et littéraires publiées par ses collègues et élèves à l'occasion de son 65e anniversaire*, Medioevo e umanesimo 19 (Padua: Editrice antenore, 1974). Particularly relevant are the studies entitled "L'Origine de la versification latine rythmique," 109–15; "Le vers accentuel en bas-latin," 116–22; and "La récitation du vers latin," 123–34.

12. "L'ouvrage le plus significatif est sans doute *l'Introduction*": in the anonymous "Présentation" that introduces *Au seuil du Moyen Âge* (1974), p. IX.

Latin, even when such prospective readers could aspire to lay their hands upon a book that was printed only once more than forty years ago in a specialized monograph series in Sweden.

Despite a modest title, the book offers brilliant reflections on the evolution of Latin verse technique in the Middle Ages. An introduction in the best sense of the word, it offers balanced attention to both the enduring influence of the classics as purveyed through the schools and the impact of vernacular languages and cultures. Although it claims to be a summary of sorts, it in fact presents an overview of Latin versification from the beginning to the end of the Middle Ages. Of all scholarship on Medieval Latin metrics that was brought into print in the twentieth century, it has been at once the most comprehensive and most enduring. The term *magisterial* has been applied to it more than once.[13] This compliment is deserved, especially when one considers the difficulty, abundance, and variety of the materials with which Norberg had to grapple in order to make any of his broad conclusions hold true.

The opening chapters on quantitative verse (pp. 1–80 of this translation) are restricted to the length necessary to compare the norms of classical quantitative composition with those of Medieval Latin. The chapters deal with prosody and word accent; synaeresis, diaeresis, syncope, prosthesis, elision, and hiatus; assonance, rhyme, and alliteration; acrostics, *carmina figurata,* and other such artifices; and metrical versification. All these *termini technici* could make reading these chapters a daunting experience, but Norberg wears his learning as lightly as he can in contending with such topics. Without being too informal, his own prose style gives the impression of a lucid individual who is conversing, rather than lecturing. The first chapter is particularly helpful as it explains why the accentuation and syllable length of many words in Medieval Latin diverge from the norms of Classical Latin— and why the divergences vary considerably across time and space. Norberg returned to this topic, with a particular focus, in a much later monograph entitled *L'Accentuation des mots dans le vers du latin du Moyen Âge* (The Accentuation of Words in Latin Verse of the Middle Ages).[14] The third chapter

13. When the book first appeared, it was widely reviewed by prominent scholars. For identification of twenty reviews, see Fabio Cupaiuolo, *Bibliografia della metrica latina,* Studi latini 15 (Naples: Loffredo, 1995), 70. The term *magisterial* (or related words) appears in the reviews by R. B. C. Huygens, Louis Nougaret, and Hubert Silvestre which are included in the list just mentioned.

14. Kungl. Vitterhets Historie och Antikvitets Akademien, Filologiskt Arkiv 32 (Stockholm: Almqvist & Wiksell, 1985).

provides a succinct treatment of assonance and rhyme, features that became ever more favored in Latin poetry from the tenth century onward. The chapter on quantitative versification shows what a variety of meters was attested in the Middle Ages, many of them the same as meters found in classical antiquity, but some of them new and others old meters altered through the incorporation of substantially new structures, such as rhyme.

The main thrust in the second half of the book (pp. 81–179) comes as Norberg unfolds his views on the origins and developments of the many different forms of rhythmic poetry. The relationship between Latin quantitative and rhythmic or accentual poetry has long been much controverted.[15] Sweeping aside the generalizations of preceding theories (and the sometimes unfortunate consequences they have had on editorial practices of those who have grappled with Medieval Latin texts), he holds fast to facts as he develops the case—not claiming it as an explanation for all forms of rhythmic poetry—that, partly under the influence of the music, medieval poets often created rhythmic verse by reading ancient meters as prose, without maintaining the lengths of syllables or ictus demanded by classical prosody, but while retaining the number of syllables, placement of caesuras, and cadences before the caesuras and line endings.

In making his case, Norberg avoids espousing any single theory to account for the origins of all rhythmic poetry, as had earlier scholars who—like adventurers in quest of the source of the Nile—had sought to localize the start of rhythmic poetry or of the taste for rhyme in various vernacular languages or in the practices of specific geographical areas, such as Africa or the Orient. In particular he refutes the thesis of Wilhelm Meyer of Speyer (1845–1917),

---

15. A. Etchegaray Cruz, "El tránsito de la poesía latina métrica a la rítmica y algunos problemas conexos," in *Semanas de estudios romanos III–IV 1986: Homenaje a Carlos A. Disandro* (Valparaíso: Universidad Católica, Instituto de Historia, 1987), 259–69; Paul Klopsch, "Der Übergang von quantitierender zu akzentuierender lateinischer Dichtung," in Hildegard L. C. Tristram, ed., *Metrik und Medienwechsel: Metrics and Media* (Tübingen, 1991), 95–106, and, above all, D'Arco Silvio Avalle, "Dalla metrica alla ritmica," in *Lo Spazio letterario del Medioevo*. Medioevo, part 1, "Il Medioevo latino," ed. Guglielmo Cavallo, Claudio Leonardi, and Enrico Menestò, vol. 1, "La Produzione del testo," part 1 (Rome: Salerno editrice, 1992), 391–476. Avalle's contribution is complemented nicely by Mauro Donnini, "Versificazione: le tecniche," in *Lo Spazio letterario del Medioevo. Medioevo 1,* ed. Guglielmo Cavallo, Claudio Leonardi, and Enrico Menestò, vol. 3, "La Ricezione del testo" (Rome: Salerno editrice, 1995), 251–70. However, even when put together as a diptych, these two essays do not form a unity that comes close to replacing Norberg's *Introduction*. (All references to Norberg's *Introduction* will be to this translation.)

who had been the most influential scholar of Medieval Latin meter before him, that held Latin rhythmic poetry to be essentially prose with a set final cadence. (Meyer's three-volume *Gesammelte Abhandlungen zur mittellateinischen Rhythmik* (Collected Writings on Medieval Latin Rhythmic Poetry) [Berlin: Weidmann, 1905–1936; reprinted Hildesheim: George Olms, 1970] provided much of the foundation for the work of other twentieth-century scholars.)[16] At the same time Norberg introduced a new system of signs to indicate accented and unaccented syllables, in place of the symbols taken from classical metrics that Meyer had employed. Equally important, Norberg demonstrates the falsehood of viewing rhythmic poems as having no rules: on the contrary, they operate according to principles, but ones that differ from the norms of quantitative poetry. He points out mistakes in editions by both Meyer and Karl Strecker, another revered founder of Medieval Latin philology.

The chapters on rhythmic poetry conclude with a brief chapter (pp. 156–79) on sequences, tropes, motets, and rondeaux, in which Norberg shows himself alive to the complex relationship between text and music. Frequently the attraction of a preexisting melody caused poets to imitate the number of syllables or accents in a quantitative text as they devised texts in new rhythmic forms to accompany it. To cap the book, there are a conclusion (pp. 180–86), a detailed bibliography (191–98), and six excellent indices (199–217).

Scholarship on Medieval Latin metrics has not ceased to accumulate and even to advance since the publication of Norberg's *Introduction,* as can be verified by consulting any of various bibliographies.[17] But no book has been brought into print that in any way supersedes it. To all appearances, it remains fundamental and not only unsupplanted but even unsupplantable. Paul Klop-

16. For an account of Meyer's activities as a philologist, see Fidel Rädle, "Wilhelm Meyer, Professor der Klassischen Philologie 1886–1917," in *Die Klassische Altertumswissenschaft an der Georg-August-Universität Göttingen. Eine Ringvorlesung zu ihrer Geschichte,* ed. Carl Joachim Classen, Göttinger Universitätsschriften, Serie A: Schriften 14 (Göttingen: Vandenhoeck & Ruprecht, 1989), 128–48. For a quick overview of the scholarship on rhythmical verse that preceded Norberg, see Francesco Stella, "Le raccolte dei ritmi precarolingi e la tradizione manoscritta di Paolino d'Aquileia: nuclei testuali e rapporti di trasmissione," *Studi Medievali,* 3rd series 39 (1998): 809–832 (esp. 809–13).

17. Fabio Cupaiuolo, *Bibliografia della metrica latina;* Jürgen L. Leonhardt, *"Dimensio syllabarum": Studien zur lateinischen Prosodie- und Verslehre von der Spätantike bis zur Renaissance, mit einem ausführlichen Quellenverzeichnis bis zum Jahr 1600,* Hypomnemata: Untersuchungen zur Antike und zu ihrem Nachleben 92 (Göttingen: Vandenhoeck & Ruprecht, 1989); and the section on metrics in the annual bibliography, *Medioevo Latino.*

sch's slim volume in German, which appeared fourteen years later, seems to have been envisaged as a shorter textbook for university students and scholars.[18] Yet, studded with many parenthetic notes and statistical tables, it is not what could be termed colloquially "an easy read." Although it cannot compete in clarity, detail, or sweep with Norberg's *Introduction,* it constitutes an important source of information on quantitative meters, especially dactylic meters.[19]

For English-speakers the most useful treatment may be the appendix titled "Metre" in A. G. Rigg's *A History of Anglo-Latin Literature;* but these sixteen pages, despite the wealth of information they record, are limited to Anglo-Latin verse of the later Middle Ages and make no claim to be more than a checklist.[20] Indeed, they acknowledge unambiguously Norberg's *Introduction* as the standard on the subject. Such acknowledgment has been a feature of virtually every discussion of Medieval Latin metrics in the past forty odd years.

Much effort since Norberg has centered upon developments in particular metrical forms, sometimes as they took place in specific geographical regions. For example, Dieter Schaller has written valuable articles on heptasyllabic and hendecasyllabic verse in the early Middle Ages;[21] Michael W. Herren on heptasyllabic, octosyllabic, and hendecasyllabic verse in Hiberno-Latin and Insular Latin;[22] and Michael Lapidge on Anglo-Latin Adonics and octosyllabic verse.[23] Jesús Luque Moreno studied the trochaic septe-

---

18. Paul Klopsch, *Einführung in die mittellateinische Verslehre* (Darmstadt: Wissenschaftliche Buchgesellschaft, 1972).

19. For a close critique of Klopsch's book in comparison with Norberg's, see Dieter Schaller's review in *Gnomon* 49 (1977): 80–83.

20. See A. G. Rigg, "Metre," in A. G. Rigg. *A History of Anglo-Latin Literature, 1066–1422* (1992), 313–29.

21. Dieter Schaller, "Der alkäische Hendekasyllabus im frühen Mittelalter," in *Studien zur lateinischen Dichtung des Frühmittelalters,* Quellen und Untersuchungen zur lateinischen Philologie des Mittelalters 11 (Stuttgart: Anton Hiersemann, 1995), 252–69 (original pagination in *Mittellateinisches Jahrbuch* 19 [1984]: 73–90), with supplementary notes on 427–28, and "Die Siebensilberstrophen 'de mundi transitu'—eine Dichtung Columbans?" in *Studien zur lateinischen Dichtung,* 236–51 (236–37 supplement Norberg, *Introduction,* 127–28, 142).

22. See Michael W. Herren, "Hibernolateinische und irische Verskunst mit besonderer Berücksichtigung des Siebensilbers," in Hildegard L. C. Tristram, ed., *Metrik und Medienwechsel—Metrics and Media* (Tübingen, 1991), 173–88; "The Stress System of the Hiberno-Latin Hendecasyllable," *Celtica* 21 (1990): 223–30; and "The Stress Systems in Insular Latin Octosyllabic Verse," *Cambridge Medieval Celtic Studies* 15 (1988): 63–84. All three of these studies have been reprinted in Michael W. Herren, *Latin Letters in Early Christian Ireland* (Aldershot, Hampshire: Variorum, 1996).

23. Michael Lapidge, "The Authorship of the Adonic Verses 'Ad Fidolium' attributed to

nary.[24] Scevola Mariotti, Manlio Pastore Stocchi, and, above all, Peter Stotz have plumbed the challenging depths of Medieval Latin sapphics and related forms.[25] Norberg himself published a substantial study of Latin iambic and trochaic verses, both quantitative and rhythmic, and another smaller one of Terentianean verses.[26] Of the many scholars who have written on hexameters, Paul Klopsch, Janet Martin, Franco Munari, Giovanni Orlandi, and Neil Wright deserve special mention.[27] Other fine work on meters has resulted from the close study of individual authors.[28]

Some forms that Norberg treated in a matter of a few pages have become

Columbanus," *Studi Medievali*, 3rd series 18 (1977): 249–314 (especially 253–271), and Michael Lapidge, "Theodore and Anglo-Latin Octosyllabic Verse," in *Archbishop Theodore: Commemorative Studies on his Life and Influence*, ed. Michael Lapidge, Cambridge Studies in Anglo-Saxon England 11 (Cambridge: Cambridge University Press, 1995), 260–80, rept. in Michael Lapidge, *Anglo-Latin Literature 600–899* (London and Rio Grande: Hambledon Press, 1996), 225–45 (to connect with Norberg, *Introduction*, 118–19).

24. Jesús Luque Moreno, "El versus quadratus en los tratados de métrica antiguos y medievales," *Florentia Illiberritana. Revista de estudios de Antigüedad clásica* (Granada) 6 (1995): 282–329, and "Metricólogos tardíos y medievales ante un verso 'vulgar'" in *Latin vulgaire—latin tardif*, vol. 4, 179–90.

25. Scevola Mariotti, "Strofe saffiche e pseudosaffiche ritmico-quantitative," in *Scritti medievali e umanistici*, ed. Silvia Rizzo, 2nd ed., Storia e letteratura 137 (Rome: Edizioni di storia e letteratura, 1994), 19–32; Manlio Pastore Stocchi, "Su una saffica 'barbara' mediolatina," *Metrica* 1 (1978): 173–86; and Peter Stotz, *Sonderformen der sapphischen Dichtung. Ein Beitrag zur Erforschung der sapphischen Dichtung des lateinischen Mittelalters*, Medium Aevum 37 (Munich: Wilhelm Fink Verlag, 1982). All three of these studies amplify Norberg, *Introduction*, 77–78, 95–97, and 124. Stocchi questions Norberg's interpretation of rhythmic verse as imitating the structure of quantitative poetry.

26. Dag Norberg, *Les vers latins iambiques et trochaïques au Moyen Âge et leurs répliques rythmiques*, Kungl. Vitterhets Historie och Antikvitets Akademien, Filologiskt Arkiv 35 (Stockholm: Almqvist & Wiksell, 1988), and "Le vers térentianéan," in *La critica del testo mediolatino*. Atti del Convegno (Firenze 6–8 dicembre 1990), ed. Claudio Leonardi, Biblioteca di Medioevo Latino 5 (Spoleto: Centro italiano di studi sull'Alto Medioevo, 1994), 173–84, reprinted in Dag Norberg, *Au seuil du Moyen Âge. II*, 255–66.

27. Janet Martin, "Classicism and Style in Latin Literature," in *Renaissance and Renewal in the Twelfth Century*, ed. Robert L. Benson and Giles Constable, with Carol D. Lanham (Cambridge, Mass.: Harvard University Press, 1982), 537–68 (esp. 551–63); Franco Munari, ed. *Marco Valerio: Bucoliche*, 2nd ed. (Florence: Felice Le Monnier, 1970), LXIV–LXXVIII; Giovanni Orlandi, "Caratteri della versificazione dattilica," in *Retorica e poetica tra i secoli XII e XIV*, Atti del secondo Convegno internazionale di studi dell'Associazione per il Medioevo e l'Umanesimo Latini in onore e memoria di Ezio Franceschini, Trento-Rovereto, 3–5 ottobre 1985 (Perugia and Florence: Regione dell'Umbria-La Nuova Italia Editrice, 1988), 151–67; and Neil Wright, "The Anglo-Latin Hexameter: Theory and Practice c. 600–c. 800," Ph.D. diss. (Cambridge University, 1981).

28. Andy Orchard, *The Poetic Art of Aldhelm*, Cambridge Studies in Anglo-Saxon England

the topic of entire books and monographs. Such is particularly the case with forms that Norberg touched upon briefly at the end of the book, such as the sequence and the trope; the latter form became the focus of an entire research team that Norberg promoted.[29] Likewise, forms that he covered in succinct chapters early in the *Introduction* have been explored considerably further; for instances, a number of valuable articles have been written on the history of pattern poetry and acrostics.[30] In one instance, the *conductus,* a form that Norberg mentioned only once near the end of the *Introduction,* has become the topic of entire books by Christopher Page and Joseph Szövérffy.[31] The most extensive results are likely to come in connection with the Corpus of Latin Rhythmical Texts (4th–9th Century), under the direction of Francesco Stella and others.[32]

---

8 (Cambridge: Cambridge University Press, 1994); and Jean Soubiran, "Prosodie et métrique des Bella Parisiacae urbis d'Abbon," *Journal des Savants* (1965): 204–331.

29. Books that warrant mentioning are Richard L. Crocker, *The Early Medieval Sequence* (Berkeley and Los Angeles: University of California Press, 1977); F. Liberatore Fiorani, *Lirica mediolatina: sequenza e tropo* (Rome: Edizioni dell'Ateneo & Bizzarri, 1977); and *La tradizione dei tropi liturgici,* Atti dei convegni sui tropi liturgici, Parigi (15–19 ottobre 1985)-Perugia (2–5 settembre 1987) (Spoleto: Centro italiano di studi sull'Alto Medioevo, 1990). For guidance about more recent developments, see Gunilla Björkvall and Andreas Haug, "Sequence and Versus: On the History of Rhythmical Poetry in the Eleventh Century," in *Latin Culture in the Eleventh Century: Proceedings of the Third International Conference on Medieval Latin Studies, Cambridge, September 9–12 1998,* 2 vols., ed. Michael W. Herren, C. J. McDonough, and Ross G. Arthur, Publications of the Journal of Medieval Latin 5/ 1–2 (Turnhout: Brepols, [2002]), vol. 1, 57–82. In numerous other publications Björkvall and Haug have offered prolegomena toward what will be a major musical response to Norberg's work and approach.

30. For instance, see Ulrich Ernst, *Carmen figuratum: Geschichte des Figurengedichts von den antiken Ursprüngen bis zum Ausgang des Mittelalters,* Pictura et poesis 1 (Cologne: Böhlau, 1991), and Margaret Graver, "Quaelibet Audendi: Fortunatus and the Acrostic," *Transactions of the American Philological Association* 123 (1993): 219–45.

31. Christopher Page, *Latin Poetry and Conductus Rhythm in Medieval France* (London: Royal Musical Association, 1997), and Joseph Szövérffy, *Lateinische Conductus-Texte des Mittelalters* (Medieval Latin Conductus Texts), Wissenschaftliche Abhandlungen 74/ Musicological Studies 74 (Ottawa: Institute of Mediæval Music, 2000).

32. On the ongoing project, see especially *Poesia dell'Alto Medioevo europeo: manoscritti, lingua e musica dei ritmi latini. Poetry of Early Medieval Europe: Manuscripts, Language and Music of the Latin Rhythmical Texts. Atti delle Euroconferenze per il Corpus dei ritmi latini (IV–IX sec.), Arezzo, 6–7 novembre 1998 e Ravello, 9–12 settembre 1999,* ed. Francesco Stella, Millennio Medievale 22, Atti di Convegni 5 (Florence: SISMEL-Edizioni del Galluzzo, 2000), and *Poetry of the Early Medieval Europe: Manuscripts, Language and Music of the Rhythmical Latin Texts. III Euroconference for the Digital Edition of the "Corpus of Latin Rhythmical Texts 4th–9th Century,"* ed. Edoardo D'Angelo and Francesco Stella, Millennio Medievale 39, Atti

Medieval Latin philology took root in Germany in the decades around 1900, with the appointment of Ludwig Traube (1861–1907) to a chair in Munich in 1880 and with the activities of scholars such as Wilhelm Meyer and Paul von Winterfeld (1872–1905). But the field has spread to many other countries, first elsewhere in Europe, later as a transplant in North America, and now also in Asia. The achievement of Norberg may be seen in a national context, in that his work belongs to a tradition of Latin philology that began in Sweden at the latest with the publication by Einar Löfstedt of his *Beiträge zur Kenntnis der späteren Latinität* (Contributions to the Knowledge of Later Latin) (Uppsala, 1907) and that has continued through the activities of the Corpus Troporum under the direction of Ritva Jacobsson (one of Norberg's first doctoral students) into the most recent initiatives of Gunilla Björkvall, Gunilla Iversen, and others.

To name all the *eruditi* who have participated in this heritage would require a paragraph-long roll call—and even that would not be adequate, since the tradition of a Latin philology fiercely attentive to the post-classical and also the non-classical can be seen more broadly as Scandinavian, with the inclusion not only of Danish and Norwegian but also of Finnish scholars alongside the many Swedes whose researches were shaped by their exposure to Dag Norberg's teaching. If Norberg were now assessing the grounding and growth of his own scholarship, he would be alert to the local characteristics that colored it, but he would recognize in all the books and articles (whether in Latin, German, French, or Swedish) a unifying devotion to the Latin language that transcended any national boundaries. His lifetime was devoted to a language that knew few borders in the Europe of late antiquity and the early Middle Ages. Although no longer the lingua franca it was once upon a time, Latin still has a role to play in binding together a Europe that now shares a common currency for the first time—just as it served discreetly as a rallying point for those like Dag Norberg, Ernst Robert Curtius, and Erich Auerbach in the decades of the Second World War and its immediate aftermath.[33] On a humbler scale, Late Latin and Medieval Latin may serve a noble

---

di Convegni 12, Corpus dei ritmi latini (secoli IV–IX) 2 (Florence: SISMEL-Edizioni del Galluzzo, 2003).

33. On Ernst Robert Curtius, see Jan Ziolkowski, "Ernst Robert Curtius (1886–1956) and Medieval Latin Studies," *The Journal of Medieval Latin* 7 (1997): 147–67. On Erich Auerbach, see Jan Ziolkowski, "Foreword," in *Erich Auerbach, Literary Language and Its Public in Late Latin Antiquity and in the Middle Ages*, Bollingen Series 74 (Rept. Princeton: Princeton University Press, 1993), ix–xxxix.

purpose even now in drawing together a small but influential set of students and scholars from throughout the world to investigate a language, a literature, and a tradition that have been in continuous use for roughly two and a half millennia. For the sense it brought to the operations of poetry within one millennium of that continuum, Dag Norberg's *Introduction* deserves hearty applause and renewed attention.

Jan Ziolkowski
Harvard University

■ TRANSLATORS' PREFACE

A few technical comments need to be made about the translation itself. We have added a Glossary of Terms, which is not in Norberg's book; the definitions in the Glossary of Terms are based on those given in the second edition of the *Oxford English Dictionary* and on the definitions provided by James W. Halporn, Martin Ostwald, and Thomas G. Rosenmeyer, *The Meters of Greek and Latin Poetry,* rev. ed. (Norman: University of Oklahoma Press, 1980). English readers might also consult D. S. Raven, *Latin Metre* (London: Faber and Faber, 1965) and M. L. West, *Greek Meter* (Oxford: Oxford University Press, 1982). For rhetorical figures refer to Richard A. Lanham, *A Handlist of Rhetorical Terms,* 2nd ed. (Berkeley: University of California Press, 1991), and Heinrich Lausberg, *Handbook of Literary Rhetoric: A Foundation for Literary Study,* trans. Matthew T. Bliss, Annemiek Jansen, and David E. Orton, ed. David E. Orton and R. Dean Anderson (Leiden: Brill, 1998). Norberg frequently uses the terminology of Louis Nougaret, *Traité de métrique latine classique* (Paris: Éditions Klincksieck, 1955), especially in chapter five; we have occasionally tried to clarify these uses with comments in brackets.

The indexes refer only to the work of Norberg, but computer search of technology has allowed us to include additional names and many more page references. For the spelling of names we have depended on *The Dictionary of the Middle Ages, The Catholic Encyclopedia, The Oxford Dictionary of the Christian Church,* F. J. E. Raby's *A History of Christian-Latin Poetry from the Beginnings to the Close of the Middle Ages,* 2nd ed., and *A History of Secular Latin Poetry in the Middle Ages,* 2nd ed.

We have modernized Norberg's documentation style to a certain extent, sometimes expanding the information in his references. Any confusion here should disappear by consulting the editions he cites. We have also silently corrected a few documentation errors.

Norberg refers to the *Analecta Hymnica* (abbreviated *AH*) by volume number followed by a colon with either hymn number (here indicated by the abbreviation *no.*) or page number (here a numeral not preceded by *no.*). Parenthetic references after the volume and hymn or page signify strophe number (and sometimes verse number as well).

For the benefit of English readers who are just beginning work in Medieval Latin verse, we have translated the Greek, German, and French quotations and many of the critical Latin comments. We thank Gary Meltzer who reviewed our translations of Greek phrases, and Doris Cooper and Heiko Bosler, who helped us refine our translations of the various German quotations. Nicole Van Vorst Camilleri clarified for us Norberg's phrase *mesure d'attaque* (measure of attack), which we have translated "anacrusis"; and David McCarthy produced the music graphics on p. 155.

We thank David McGonagle and Susan Needham of The Catholic University of America Press for overseeing the project and Sarah Donahue for a meticulous reading of the manuscript and for either providing or critiquing our Latin translations, but most of all we thank Jan Ziolkowski for his warm encouragement, support, and extensive, painstaking efforts to make a translation into an up-to-date version of Norberg's fundamental work.

Metrics is one of those subjects that generate a great deal of controversy, and the interpretation of Medieval Latin verse is particularly controversial. Latinists are inclined to consider it more or less like Classical Latin verse; Romance language specialists see it as merely Romance-language verse in disguise. Others rely on modern versification or on general metrical considerations and can thereby convince themselves of connections that are entirely hypothetical and improbable. The very reading of verse is keenly debated, and it is not unusual for scholars to accuse one another of lacking an understanding of the rhythm and meter. In this debate it is too often the case that pronunciation habits and personal prejudices serve as the basis for interpretation. Thus an English scholar recently expressed his astonishment regarding St. Augustine's well-known hymn against the Donatists: "There are so many surprising mispronunciations in this poem." The modern scholar who expresses himself in this way is evidently accustomed to scanning classical verse; he cannot imagine that St. Augustine could have written anything without following a regular accentuation: *própter hóc Domínus nóster,* and so forth. When the facts *(dóminus!)* contradict his theory, he asserts, without looking further, that St. Augustine is at fault because he has not correctly accented the Latin words. But clearly it is the modern theory that should be revised. This example illustrates well the difficulties that we encounter trying to free ourselves from prejudices in the field of metrics. It should also serve as a warning to us to limit ourselves, as much as possible, to setting out the facts, without too much theorizing.

This warning is all the more justified when it comes to Medieval Latin verse because we have to deal with a field that has been little investigated. What I can contribute here is only a brief overview which aims merely to provide an introduction to the study of Medieval Latin verse. This aim has obviously influenced the plan of the present work. Compared to the new verse, called rhythmic, quantitative verse has been discussed rather briefly. On the other hand, I could not leave it out entirely because of the close relationships between the different verse forms. In addition, I had to emphasize the time periods in which the new verse forms were elaborated; for this reason the highly developed and varied poetry of the late Middle Ages has been given only a relatively limited space.

To avoid any misunderstanding we have used the signs __ and ◡ exclusively to indicate long and short syllables. If the quantity is not important, an accented syllable is indicated by ´˜ if it has a primary accent and by ˜̀ if it has a secondary accent; a syllable that is not accented is indicated by ˜ . The letters *p* and *pp* indicate that the final cadence before the caesura or at the end of the line is paroxytone or proparoxytone. We thus indicate a rhythmic verse of eight syllables such as *Oculi somnum cápiant* by *8pp;* a verse of fifteen syllables with a medial caesura such as *Apparebit repentína* ‖ *dies magna Dómini* by *8p + 7pp;* a verse of six syllables, the final cadence of which can vary, by *6* alone. For the abbreviations *AH = Analecta Hymnica, PLAC = Poetae Latini Aevi Carolini,* and the like, refer to the bibliography.

It was Wilhelm Meyer of Speyer who laid the foundations for the study of Medieval Latin verse. Today, a good number of his theories are out of date and, besides, in many cases at least, it is also possible to give a more exact analysis of the poetic forms. Nevertheless, his works in this field continue to be of fundamental importance, and I pay my respects here to his insight and to the pioneering work that he accomplished.

AN INTRODUCTION TO THE STUDY
OF MEDIEVAL LATIN VERSIFICATION

ONE ▨ PROSODY AND ACCENTUATION

It is obviously impossible to formulate rules of prosody that would be generally valid for the quantitative poetry of the Middle Ages. The authors, in principle, were bound to models that, for them, were classical; some authors were successful, others were less so. But on this point we ought to note that they were imitating not only Virgil, Ovid, and the other poets of the golden and silver ages, but also Late Latin poets such as Juvencus, Prudentius, and Sedulius. In this last poet one finds, for example, *iŭge, mănavit, trĭduum, ecclĕsia,* and it is thus quite natural that these words should be treated prosodically in the same way throughout the Middle Ages. Some forms as unclassical as *pāter, stātim, quōque, āc, forĭs,* existed at the end of antiquity. Consequently, they appear from time to time in the course of the Middle Ages. Also, they give rise to some analogical forms or to some more or less random confusions, such as *gratĭs* (common during the entire Middle Ages) or *măter* (*Ruodlieb,* 10:39). For the details, I refer the reader to the few studies that exist.[1] Here we will study only certain cases which have a more general range.

From an example like *Terga fatigamus hasta, nec tarda senectus,*[2] the rule was formulated that a consonant followed by *h* could form a long syllable—a

---

1. See Christensen, 71–75; Meyer, *Ges. Abh.,* 1:76; Müller, 380–429; Munari, *M. Valerii Bucolica,* 43–49; Pannenborg, 190; Sedgwick, "The Style and Vocabulary," 360; *idem,* "The Bellum Troianum," 50–51; Thurot, 426–40. One also finds some valuable pieces of information in several editions. Leo, Vollmer, and Ehwald, for example, have dealt with the prosody of Fortunatus, Merobaudes, Dracontius, Eugenius of Toledo, and Aldhelm, *MGH, Auctores antiquissimi,* 4:422–27; 14:441–43; 15:754–55; Strecker has annotated the texts that he published, *PLAC,* 5:8, 80, 95, 110, 146, 177, 227, 253, 262; 6:17, 122, 135. See also the editions of Hrotswitha by von Winterfeld, 543; of *Ruodlieb* by Seiler, 155; of *Ysengrimus* by Voigt, xxvi; of *Ecbasis cuiusdam captivi* by Strecker, 52; of Conrad of Megenberg by Scholz, 101.

2. Virgil, *Aeneid* 9.610.

rule that the grammarians taught at the end of antiquity as well as in the Middle Ages,[3] and a rule that many poets put into practice, for example, Dracontius, Fortunatus, and Hrotswitha, while others like Nivardus of Ghent in *Ysengrimus* (12th cent.) moved away from it. Of course, one finds this phenomenon not only in poets who were using hexameters but also elsewhere, for example, in the poem *De eversione monasterii Glonnensis* written in quantitative iambic dimeters in the middle of the ninth century,[4] where we read *Omnis canāt harmonia* (3, 2); *Auxīt honorem largius* (8, 1); *Bellum fuīt horridius* (12, 2); *Dantūr honores impio* (14, 2); *Quidam fuīt hoc tempore* (16, 1).

It is hardly necessary to point out that quite a few authors lengthen a final short vowel if the following word begins with *st, sp,* or *sc,* and that they scan, as for example Sedulius, *sanctusquē spiritus* (5:403) or *namquē stulta potens* (2:229). But it is characteristic of certain authors, like Aldhelm, who want to avoid this phenomenon, that they sometimes neglect to allow *st, sp,* and *sc* to make a previous vowel long by position, even inside a word, and that they scan, for example, *tĕstantur, gĕstat, rĕstat, prĭsci.*[5]

It seems that John Scottus Eriugena in the middle of the ninth century has borrowed from some ancient author the practice of letting the final -*s* become mute after a short vowel. He writes, for example, *mentibŭs nota prius* (3:62), *aedibŭs constructis* (70), and *omnibŭs Christigenis* (4:46).[6] The same metrical oddity is found in the song *De figuris vel schematibus,*[7] written around A.D. 400, where one finds a series of hexameter endings of this type: *reflectimŭs dicta* (13), *convertimŭs verba* (16), *opponimŭs quaedam* (22).

Some forms such as *adhĕrent, desĕvit,* and *illĕsus* are utterly appalling to the classicist; and yet, as I have shown,[8] they are found already at the end of antiquity and are the result of the fact that *ae* was actually pronounced at that time as a short *e.* One could gather together a large number of examples of this phenomenon throughout the entire Middle Ages. Luxorius (or Luxurius), for example, used the form *quĕsumus* in the Asclepiadean verse *contingat, quesumus, numina, quod cupis;*[9] Aldhelm scans *ĕgrescit* and *ĕgrotum;* and

---

3. See Müller, 14, 19, 391.   4. *PLAC,* 2:147–49.

5. See the edition of Ehwald, 755, and Müller, 386–91.

6. *PLAC,* 3:533–34.

7. *Anthologia Latina,* 1:485. See also Müller, 428.

8. *La poésie latine rythmique,* 26, where I also gave some examples from the Middle Ages. See also Müller, 445, and Nicolau, *L'origine,* 71.

9. *Anthologia Latina,* 1:314, 7. See also *PLAC,* 6:161: *Nomina nostra tibi, quesumus, sint cognita* passim.

Conrad of Megenberg in the fourteenth century scans *coëterne, pěnitisset,* and *adhěrebo,* to give only a few selected examples.

The quantity of some final vowels created a few special difficulties. From the time of the classical period the treatment of final *-o* is unpredictable,[10] and it naturally became still more unpredictable in the Middle Ages. Thus Hrotswitha allows herself not only *sedulŏ, creditŏ,* and the like, but also *ullŏ modo, in monstrandŏ;* and the same attitude was adopted in the twelfth century by Marcus Valerius and a few centuries later by Conrad of Megenberg. However, some authors, such as Nivardus of Ghent, always preserve the *ō* in the ablative, even the ablative of a gerundive.[11] With regard to the final *ē* there are many like Fortunatus and Hrotswitha who follow the model of *beně* and *malě* and scan *piě, congruě,* and the like in the same way. Analogously, other authors shorten the long *-e* of the imperatives of the second conjugation.[12] The endings *-ī* and *-ě* in the dative and the ablative singular of the third declension are exchanged freely by quite a few authors, following the requirements of the meter. Thus Alcuin writes *vestrae pietatě remisi* (13:9),[13] and Hrotswitha, *Hinc genitorě tuo maneat per saecula cuncta gloria* (Maria, 891). St. Isidore shortens even the long *-a* of the ablative of the first declension when, for example, in *Versus in bibliotheca* he writes,

> Ecce Iuvencus adest Seduliusque tibi
> Ambo lingua pares, florentes versibus ambo,[14]

and one finds the same thing in Aldhelm and in several other poets from the beginning of the Middle Ages.

Of course, a final short vowel is also sometimes lengthened. Thus Eugenius of Toledo seems capable of lengthening almost any final vowel according to the requirements of the meter. See, for example, his *Oratio,* lines 15–16:

---

10. See R. Hartenberger, *De o finali apud poetas Latinos ab Ennio usque ad Iuvenalem,* dissertation (Bonn, 1911).

11. See the editions of Hrotswitha by von Winterfeld, 546; of Marcus Valerius by Munari, 46; of Conrad of Megenberg by Scholz, 102; of *Ysengrimus* by Voigt, xxvi.

12. Some examples are found in the indexes and in the work of Müller, 418–19.

13. *PLAC,* 1:237. See Traube, *Karolingische Dichtungen,* 28, note 1, at the bottom of the page; Strecker, *PLAC,* 5:111; the comments by Winterfield and by Scholz in the editions of Hrotswitha and of Conrad of Megenberg.

14. Migne, *PL,* 83:1107.

Nil turpē cupiam, faciam vel proloquar umquam
Te mens desĭderet, linguā canat, actiŏ promat.[15]

Those who go the farthest are the authors who venture into what Meyer
called "Scheinprosodie" [pseudo-prosody],[16] that is, they do not differentiate
between vowels long by nature and short vowels, but they only avoid using
vowels long by position as short vowels. It is in the work of Alvarus of Córdoba that one finds the crudest examples of this metrical anomaly. See, for
example, the beginning of song seven, *PLAC*, 3:130:

Tu, Christē dominē rerum, quem lingua celebrat . . .
Angelicā cūī turbā virtute beata
Laudibus obsequium solbit fulgentĭ decore, . . .
Quem lux aura dies recinet vel hestus et ignis,
Flumina nix glacies ventūs et hunda resōnat,
Omnigenā rerum dominum prex digna venērat:
Tu misero clemens metricas rēsolbe camenas,
Carmine ut pulcro valeat concīnere laudes.

The cases in which not only the quantity but also the place of the accent
differs from Classical Latin are particularly interesting. In these cases we can
also include rhythmic poetry in the scope of our study. Regarding the latter,
Wilhelm Meyer was of the opinion that "die Betonung des Lateinischen zu
allen Zeiten im wesentlichen die gleiche war, kleine Dinge abgerechnet" [the
accentuation of Latin in all time periods was practically the same, with some
small exceptions].[17] But things are not quite that simple; even if one confines
oneself to cases in which the shifting of the accent is confirmed by the Romance languages, by metrical poetry, and finally by the statements of the
grammarians or by other objective criteria, the wealth of words is very extensive, especially among the poets of the early Middle Ages.

The Romance languages assume, as we know, a pronunciation *muliērem,*
pariētem, and *filiōlum* in Late Latin.[18] We can confirm that poetry at the end
of antiquity was also familiar with this pronunciation. Thus, Dracontius em-
ploys *muliērem* exclusively with a long penult; *ariētem* already exists in the

15. *MGH, Auctores antiquissimi*, 14:233.
16. See Meyer, *Ges. Abh.*, 2:13 and 122.
17. Meyer, *Ges. Abh.*, 1:180.
18. See, for example, Bourciez, *Eléments de linguistique romane,* 38–39; Meyer-Lübke,
Grammaire des langues romanes, 1:522–23.

work of Statius, *Thebaid* 2.492; in *Instructiones* 2:26, 6, Commodian has a hexameter ending *filiōli magistro*. In the Middle Ages the form *muliērem* is normal in the quantitative poetry; it is found, for example, in the Sapphic verse of Matthaeus Ronto (d. 1443): *huius ac alme mulieris eque.*[19] One also finds *muliérem* frequently in rhythmic poetry, for example, in the work of Wido of Ivrea (11th cent.) in the line *Salve decus muliérum.*[20] The other types of words that we mentioned appear only rarely and are in general treated in the classical way. However, Fortunatus speaks in *Carm.* 8:3, 43, of a *Liliōla;* St. Paulinus of Aquileia uses as the ending of a hexameter *flore viōlae;* in the well-known rhythmic hymn *Urbs beata Hierusalem,* one reads this in strophe 5: *qui compage pariétis;* in a sequence, Adam of St. Victor writes *pàriétum pária,* words which correspond to *vírtus ét constántia* in the parallel strophe.[21]

Certain other less-observed phenomena are also related to the linguistic usage that we have been discussing. In a collection of Italian hymns of the eleventh century there is a hymn of St. Paul written in classical iambic dimeters in which strophe 3 begins in this way:

> Olim lupus nigredine
> Horror fuĕrat pessimus.[22]

Is *fuērat* really possible here? I think we can say yes, since in a Mozarabic hymn in honor of St. Jerome and written in rhythmic iambic senarii (5p + 7pp) I find the accentuation *fuéro* before the caesura in strophe 9:

> Coepit testari: Si umquam hunc legere
> Ausus fuéro,   te negavi, Domine.[23]

The accent shift in Spanish, where the Latin *fúeram* became *fuéra,* with the accentuation indicated above, shows us that this accentuation is acceptable and that it is not based on barbaric ignorance but on a linguistic reality.[24] By analogy with *fuera,* the Mozarabic poets also accented the literary word *puerum* on the penultimate. In two different hymns written in rhythmic Sapphics (5p + 6p) we find, on the one hand, the verses,

---

19. *AH,* 48: no. 442 (1.3).   20. *AH,* 48: no. 87 (2.1).
21. *PLAC,* 4:913 (18); *AH,* 51: no. 102 (5.2); 55: no. 31 (3.3).
22. *AH,* 14: no. 95.   23. *AH,* 27: no. 126 (9).
24. See Meyer-Lübke, *Grammaire des langues romanes,* 1:527.

> Hostiam qui se   tribus cum puéris
> Obtulit sacra   stipitis in ara
>   Regi polorum,

and, on the other hand, the verse,

> Teufilo mittit   niveum puérum.[25]

Analogously, *puērum* is found in a hymn written in quantitative Sapphic verse where one reads, *Cuius devotum animum puēri* and *Gurgite ductum Placidum puērum.*[26]

For the changing of *diēi* into *diĕi* we must look for another explanation. The *Thesaurus Linguae Latinae* recognizes the new form only in the work of Fortunatus, *Vita S. Martini* 3, 433, but it is found frequently during the Middle Ages, for example, in the verses of Ambrosian hymns: *Labore fessos diĕi* and *Omnique fine diĕi.*[27] In a poem with a rhythmic form of 8p + 7pp, *díei* led also to the accentuation *seríei:*

> Sed excepta quarta parte   noctis atque díei,
> Quae dierum superesse   cernitur seríei.[28]

The alternation *diēi-diĕi* is probably related to the corresponding uncertainty in the use of the forms *fidēi* and *fidĕi*. The first of these forms, which exists in the work of Ennius, Plautus, and Lucretius, was in fact revived in the Late Latin period and in the Middle Ages, particularly in the poetry of the hymns, where it is found several times.[29] However, the influence of the analogy extended even further. On the basis of *fídei, díei*, one also often accented *díerum, díebus*, an accentuation used even by poets such as Paulinus of Aquileia and Pacificus of Verona.[30] In an analogous way, *speciēbus* appears in a rhythmic poem (8p + 7pp) in which a person from Milan is bragging about his hometown around the year 738:

---

25. *AH*, 27: nos. 94 (10) and 110 (7).   26. *AH*, 14: no. 53 (3.1 and 6.2).
27. *AH*, 51: nos. 20 (3.3) and 32 (4.3).   28. *PLAC*, 4:683 (4).
29. See *AH*, 51: nos. 16 (7.2), 18 (2.4), 66 (1.2).

30. See the hymn of Paulinus, *PLAC*, 4:540 (7.2, 8.2, 9.2); the poem *Spera caeli duodenis* of Pacificus, ibid., 693 (2.1), and furthermore 470 (66.3); 645 (9.1); 651 (16.2); 664 (1.3); 677 (23.1, 25.1); 680 (49.2); 681 (64.1); 683 (3.1, 10.1); 684 (12.2, 15.1); *PLAC*, 6:203 (3.3); *MGH, Scriptores*, 14:195 (249.1).

Rerum cernitur cunctarum   inclita speciebus
Generumque diversorum   referta seminibus.

The rhyme shows that Dümmler was wrong to change the order of the words
into *speciebus inclita*.[31] The accentuation *speciebus* also exists as well in Paulinus in his rhythmic poem about St. Lazarus.[32] As for the quantitative poetry,
I will merely point out two verses of a poem on the model of Prudentius' *O
crucifer bone, lucisator* in Alcmanian verses in the Carolingian period:[33]

Quattuor hic decies diēbus
Noctibus et totidem gradiens.

There was also an accent shift in words in which the penult is a short
vowel followed by a mute + a liquid. The classical accentuation *íntegrum*
was replaced in the spoken language of the Roman Empire by *intégrum*, as
Romance languages show (Ital. *intéro,* esp. *entéro,* Fr. *entiér),*[34] and thus
one often finds *intégrum* in the rhythmic poetry of the Middle Ages.[35] But
since words of this type could be handled in various ways even in classical
poetry, it is possible that, in this case, the model of the classical poets had
the greatest influence. Be that as it may, the displacement of the accent
brought about another phenomenon typical of some versifiers of the Middle
Ages whose grasp of the language was less secure: they said *intégrum,* but they
knew that the word could be scanned classically *intĕgrum;* from there it was
a small step to change, for example, *theātrum, arātrum, candelā-brum,
lavācrum, dolābra, salūbris, delūbrum*—words in which the penult is long
by nature—into *theătrum, arătrum, candelăbrum, lavăcrum, dolăbra, salŭbris, delŭbrum,*[36] a change clearly reflected in the rhythmic poetry,[37]

31. *PLAC,* 1:26; see Traube, *Karolingische Dichtungen,* 121.
32. *PLAC,* 6:218 (65.2).   33. *PLAC,* 6:139 (10.1).
34. See, e.g., Seelman, 52.
35. See, e.g., *tenébras PLAC,* 4:777 (60.2) and 820 (129.1).
36. See Leo, in the index of Fortunatus; von Winterfeld, in the index of Hrotswitha; and
Voigt, *Ysengrimus,* xxvii. Candidus, who lived at Fulda in the ninth century, writes sometimes *salūbris* (e.g., *PLAC,* 2:104, v. 6), sometimes *salŭbris* (ibid., 102, v. 33); the latter form is
also found in some Sapphic verses, *AH,* 14: nos. 3 (5.1) and 34 (8.3).
37. See, e.g., *théatra, AH,* 22: no. 6 (2.3); *MGH, Scriptores,* 12:416 (41); *áratra,* ibid., v. 42;
AH, 48: no. 80 (7.4); *candélabrum, AH,* 11: nos. 111 (2.2) and 274 (4.4); 13: p. 109, responsoria in
2 nocturno 1.2; 48: no. 229 (1.1); *PLAC,* 4:664 (8.2); *lávacrum, PLAC,* 4:594 (9.3); *AH,* 10: no.
105 (1a); 48: no. 135 (1.3 and 3.3); 22: nos. 156 (2.2), 416 (7.3), 430 (8.4); *sálubris, AH,* 11: no. 453
(6.3); *délubrum, AH,* 12: no. 148 (4.2); 22: nos. 133 (5.3) and 430 (3.3).

although here some false speculations of the grammarians also played a role.[38]

More numerous and more important are the cases where the accent of compound words is shifted from the prefix onto the principal element. What is happening here is a kind of reconstruction belonging first to the spoken language where, for example, *rénegat* is replaced by *renégat* (Ital. *riniéga*, Sp. *reniéga*, Fr. *reníe*).[39] Quantitative poetry, because it is more dependent on classical models, does not provide as many examples of this shift as does the rhythmic poetry of the early Middle Ages, where they are numerous. When, for example, we read in a hymn from Spain the verse *Crux nos tunc alma protegat ‖ et ab ira eruat*, we can be certain that the writer accented *protégat*, because he uses only paroxytones before the caesura (8p + 7pp).[40] It is not only in verbs that such a reconstruction takes place; this is illustrated by a few strophes of another Mozarabic hymn where it is clear that the writer has accented *innócens* and even *mortiférum* (the rhythmic structure is 7p):[41]

> Quieti tempus adest
> Quo fessa membra quies
> Obtineat innócens
> Et Christo vígilèt mens

38. Cp. Lupus of Ferrières, *Correspondance*, ed. L. Levillain, I (Paris, 1927): 48 (letter 5): *Quin etiam in eiusmodi dictionibus, ut est aratrum, salubris et similia, quae non modo positione sed etiam natura paenultimam videntur habere productam, magna haesitatio est, in qua me adhuc laborare profiteor, utrumnam naturae serviendum sit; utrum paenultima, ut est, longa pronuntietur, an, propter illud quod Donatus ait: "Si penultima positione longa fuerit, ipsa acuetur (ut Catullus); ita tamen si positione longa, non ex muta et liquida fuerit, nam mutabit accentum (ut faretra)," in natura simul et tali positione productis, communis syllaba naturae praeiudicet et accentus in antepaenultimam transferatur.* [But, indeed, even in words of this kind, such as *aratrum, salubris,* and so forth, which not only by position but also by nature seem to have a lengthened penult, there is great indecision, on which I confess that I labor still, (trying to decide) whether indeed (the pronunciation of the syllable) ought to obey nature; whether the penult should be pronounced long, as it is, or, because of what Donatus says—"If the penult is long by position, it will be accented (as in *Catullus*) but only if it is long by position, not from a mute and a liquid, for that (the mute and the liquid together) will change the accent (as in *faretra*)"—(the penult in these words) being long by nature and at the same time by such position, the syllable common to both should take precedence over nature, and the accent be transferred to the antepenult.]

See also Sedgwick, "The Style and Vocabulary . . . ," 361; Thurot, 421.

39. See, e.g., Seelmann, 58–64.

40. *AH*, 51: no. 78 (17).

41. *AH*, 27: no. 73. This hymn is a rhythmic imitation of Prudentius, *Cathemerinon*, 6, *Ades, pater, supreme.*

Pelle a nobis, Deus,
Rogamus, omne taetrum,
Anguis prisci malignum
Virusque mortiférum.

Furthermore, I need only mention Strecker's index, *PLAC,* 4:1163, where one finds a multitude of accentuations of the type *deprémit, indúit, invócans, retúlit, tradédit, eténim, invícem.*[42]

I must also make a few observations about the endings of certain verbs. In the manuscript of a hymn written in rhythmic iambic senarii (5p + 7pp), we find the verse *Sed mox correctae* ‖ *per ipsam credidere.*[43] Since the verse should end with a proparoxytone, it seems that the author accented *credídere.* The same curious accentuation of the ending of the perfect appears in the rhythmic asclepiad (6pp + 6pp) *Putant sacrilegum* ‖ *quidquid obtulere,*[44] where the rhythmic rules require the accentuation *obtúlere,* and in the trochaic rhythmic septenarius (8p + 7pp) *Cohors una omnis turma* ‖ *ei presentávere.*[45] As all of these examples are taken from poems written in Spain, it seems that perhaps in a local school they confused the endings of the perfect *-ēre, -ērunt,* and *-ĕrunt.* The last of these endings, on the one hand, had gained acceptance in literature; on the other hand, it was a part of the spoken language, as is shown, for example, by the Italian *díssero* and the Old French *distrent,* both derived from the Latin *díxerunt.* So we should not be surprised to find the ending *-ĕrunt* quite frequently in the rhythmic poetry of the early Middle Ages.[46]

Near the end of the seventh century, a Spaniard, probably Sisebert of Toledo, wrote a poem in rhythmic hexameters, *Exhortatio poenitendi,* which has been published by Strecker.[47] Verse 80 ends with the words *nitore capere;* the infinitive was changed by Hanssen to *captare,* by Meyer to *habere,* but Strecker rightly retains *capere,* making reference to the Spanish *caber.* The

42. In a rhythmic poem from Italy, the poet even accented *coniúge,* as I have shown in *Archivum Latinitatis Medii Aevi* 22 (1952): 10.

43. *AH,* 27: no. 111 (10.4). The editor has changed the order of the words and has written *credidere per ipsam.*

44. *AH,* 27: no. 120 (11.2).

45. *Revue bénédictine* 36 (1924): 19, line 12, third column.

46. Strecker gives many examples derived from poems written principally in Italy, *PLAC,* 4:1163. The same accentuation is found in the poems written in Spain; see, e.g., AH, 27: no. 108 (3) *merúerunt, accéperunt, césserunt;* ibid., no. 150 (9.3) *dúxerunt,* (12.1) *díxerunt.*

47. *PLAC,* 4:762–68.

fact that in Spanish the ending of the infinitive -*ĕre* was completely replaced with the ending -*ēre* left some other traces in the Latin rhythmic poetry. Thus Agobard of Lyon writes this in a poem that Traube published: *Arcent delicta* ‖ *scandere excelsa*.[48] This is how the manuscript reads, but in Traube it is changed to *ascendere celsa*, since the accentuation ~ ́ ~ ~ ́ ~ is obligatory in the second part of the verse (5p + 6p). But Agobard was Spanish by birth and for him the accentuation *scandére* is just as admissible as the accentuation *construére*, which is found in a few passages of a Mozarabic hymn with the rhythmic form 8p + 7pp:[49]

> Nuntius venit de Indos   quaerere artificem
> Architectum, construére   regium palatium ...
> Huius opus construére   praecipit apostolum.

It seems that we can show parallels between this case and an instance of *canére* that appears in a poem in rhythmic hexameters from Spain where the endings of two verses have *canére decrevit* and *canére te debet*.[50] Here, Meyer wanted to change the order of the words, which would have been a mistake. But one could perhaps consider *canére* as a change of conjugation, since *caneo, canebo,* and some other second-conjugation forms of this verb are found in texts that came from various Romance-language countries.[51] One must likewise attribute to a confusion of conjugation forms like *míscitur, hérere, morítur, patímur, siníte*.[52] Some of these confusions come from the influence of the spoken language, others from false analogical formations, while still others are purely literary. This is the case when Johannes Franco (14th cent.), the learned author of hymns, juggles different accentuations of *oritur, moritur, potitur,* and *metitur* in the following strophe:[53]

> Ut mystice sol óritur
>   Quo Christus sol orítur,
> Deifice non móritur
>   Qui, carne dum morítur,

48. *Karolingische Dichtungen,* 154 (10.1).   49. *AH,* 27: no. 173 (3.2 and 7.3).
50. Meyer, *Ges. Abh.,* 3:191 (55 and 57).
51. I gave several examples in *La poésie latine rythmique,* 9, where I also pointed out the accentuation *cadére* (Ital. *cadere,* Old Fr. *cheoir*) in a rhythmic poem.
52. See *AH,* 27: no. 86 (6.1); *PLAC,* 4:583 (4.3); 509 (17.2); 468 (46.1); ibid., 6:213 (27.3).
53. *AH,* 29:192. Here it is a matter of a pun of the same kind that appears in Ovid, *Metamorphoses,* 13:607, *et primo similis volŭcri, mox vera volŭcris.* See Müller, 30.

Pacifice non pótitur,
  Locusta sed potítur,
  Nec bruchi vice métitur,
  Quod Nahum sic metítur.

This last example obviously reminds us that we must not underestimate the importance of the school or of the grammarians in the propagation of certain accentuations. When, for example, we find in the rhythmic poem *De ratione duodecim signorum* repeated instances of final proparoxytone cadences—with the exception of some instances of *díebus*, which I discussed above, and some of the word *adséverant*—we should not attribute it to a chance mistake by an author who might not have known how to construct the verse correctly or might have been mistaken about the accentuation of the word.[54] The author is, in fact, Pacificus of Verona,[55] and he knew full well his reason for accenting *adséverant* in the same way as Sisebert of Toledo wrote *perséverans* a century before in his *Lamentum poenitentiae*.[56] In both cases what we see operating is a grammatical tradition that was still current in the Carolingian period and that found expression in the following words of Gottschalk of Orbais:[57] *Nec mirum, cum apud nos quoque . . . 'assevero, asseveras,' 'persevero, perseveras,' 'eradico, eradicas,' longa sit naturaliter penultima, et tamen propter eufoniam accentum habet ante penultima* [It is not surprising since among us also . . . the penult is naturally long in *assevero, asseveras, persevero, perseveras, eradico, eradicas,* and yet for the sake of euphony the antepenult has the accent]. In the same way, the grammarians were teaching that one accented *alíquando, néquando, síquando, déinde, próinde, déinceps, álonge, délonge, ábintus, déintus,*[58] and in rhythmic poetry—even that of the late Middle Ages—one occasionally finds some examples of these accentuations.[59]

---

54. *PLAC,* 4:693 (4.2).

55. See my work *La poésie latine rythmique,* 111.

56. *PLAC,* 4:775 (43.2).

57. C. Lambot, *Œuvres théologiques et grammaticales de Godescalc d'Orbais* (Louvain, 1945): 376.

58. Thus Priscian; see Keil, *Grammatici Latini,* 3:82, 22; Gottschalk of Orbais, op. cit., 376; the authors that Thurot cites, 402–5.

59. See *alíquando* in a hymn of Heriger of Lobbes (about the year 1000), *PLAC,* 5:209 (11.2); *próinde* in *Gesta Galcheri, MGH, Scriptores,* 14:196 (257.1); 197 (295.1); *déinceps* Abelard, *AH,* 48: no. 128 (3.2); Walter of Châtillon, *Moralisch-satirische Gedichte,* ed. Strecker, 13, 9, 2 (p. 125); Peter of Blois, *Carmina Burana,* 30, 4, 4. For *álonge,* Walter of Châtillon, *Moralisch-satirische Gedichte,* 7, 17, 3, see Strecker's comment.

The prosodic treatment of words borrowed from Greek in the versification of the Middle Ages should, like so many other questions that we are ex-
ploring here, be the subject of specialized research. For now, I must limit myself to making the reader aware that the Greek accentuation since the end of
antiquity had in a certain number of cases supplanted the Latin accentuation
previously in use.[60] In keeping with the Greek accentuation, St. Paulinus of
Nola writes *abỹssus;* Fortunatus, *emblĕma* and *problĕma;* Aldhelm, *machĕra*
and *papĭrus.* In the same way in both the metrical and rhythmic poetry we
have the early appearance of *éremus, ídolum, parádisus, spéleum, trópeum,*
báptismus, thésaurus, and *sarcofágus.* According to Lupus of Ferrières, *blás-*
phemus is a more correct pronunciation then *blasphémus;* Gottschalk of Orbais says in his grammatical work that *ábyssus, báptisma, bútyrus, rómphea,*
among others, must be accented on the antepenult, even though the penult is
long.[61] In this group must be placed the Greek derivatives in -*ía: sophia,*
philosophia, melodia, theoria, and so on, which in the Middle Ages ordinarily
have a long *i* with an accent on the penult, even though examples of the classical accentuation and prosodic use of all of these words are by no means
lacking.[62]

The prosodic treatment of proper nouns should also be the subject of
special studies. After what we have seen, it should come as no surprise that
Greek proper nouns have often been accented following their Greek accent.
Fortunatus scans, for example, *Euphemīa* (Εὐφημία), Paulinus of Aquileia
accents *Alexándria* (Ἀλεξάνδρεια),[63] and others provide examples of accentuations of *Árrius, Theódorus, Isídorus, Ágatha, Christophórus, Aégyptus, An-*
tióchia.[64] The proper nouns of other languages are treated more or less arbi-

---

I note in passing the forms *gratúitus, clandéstinus, serpéntinus, lúmbricus, méndicus, rúgi-*
tus, múgitus, which one finds often in the Middle Ages. It seems that an Italian school
teacher is responsible for the accentuation *téllurem, AH,* 14: no. 93 (5.2); *PLAC,* 4:543 (10.3),
749 (36.2). For *éxclamo, cónclamo, próclamo* see *La poésie latine rythmique,* 107–8; *próclamant*
is found as well, *AH,* 23: no. 1 (2.4).

60. See Seelmann, 54–70, and Claussen in *Romanische Forschungen,* 15:774–883 (here:
808–22).

61. Lupus of Ferrières, ed. Levillain, 1:64–67; Lambot, 376. See also Thurot, 406–7.

62. See, e.g., Christensen, 73. Strecker has noted many examples of words that preserved
the Greek accent, *PLAC,* 4:1164, and I have provided others, *Notes sur quelques poèmes du*
haut moyen âge, 353–58.

63. Fortunatus, *Carm.* 8:3, 33, and *AH,* 50: no. 104 (8.1 and 10.2).

64. See for *Árrius AH,* 22: no. 32 (2.2); *PLAC,* 4:583 (10.3); for *Theódorus, Versus de Medi-*
olano 19.1 (Traube, *Karolingische Dichtungen,* 121); for *Isídorus, Versus de Verona,* 1.2 (Traube,

trarily. So one reads *Karŏlus* as well as *Karōlus* in the poem *De eversione monasterii Glonnensis; Píppin* as well as *Tarcán* in the poem *De Pippini victoria Avarica;* Fortunatus at one time scans *Abrăham,* at another time *Abrāham;* Hrotswitha, *Ioăchim* and *Ioāchim;* and likewise one sometimes finds in other authors *Marĭa* and *Marīa; Iacŏbus* and *Iacōbus; Gabrĭhel* and *Gabrīhel; Hierusălem* and *Hierusālem.*[65] In rhythmic poetry, the accent is often placed on the last syllable of biblical names, for example, *Abél, Samsón, Moáb, Amón, Iesús.*[66] I cite as an example the second strophe of a well-known song from the festival of the asses at Sens, by Peter of Corbeil:[67]

Hic in collibus Sichén
Enutritus sub Rubén
Transiit per Iordaném
Saliit in Bethlehém
    Hez, Sir asne, hez!

Let me now say a few words about the secondary accent, which plays an important role in rhythmic poetry. One can take practically any strophe from a poem written according to a system of regular accentuation and find in it several examples of secondary accents. Here are the last words of the *Stabat mater:*

Quando corpus mòriétur
Fac ut ánimè donetur
Pàradísi glórià.

It emerges from these verses that proparoxytone words like *glórià* and *ánimè* can have a secondary accent on the last syllable and that words like *mòriétur* and *pàradísi* can have a secondary accent on the first syllable. But how are those words treated in which three or more syllables precede the one that

---

Karolingische Dichtungen, 122); *AH,* 16: nos. 314 (1.1), 315 (1.6), 320 (1.4); *PLAC,* 6:168, (40); for *Ágatha AH,* 27: no. 89 (2.1); for *Christophórus AH,* 27: no. 101 (9.3, 11.3, 15.5); for *Aégyptus PLAC,* 6:465 (19.1); for *Antióchia AH,* 11: no. 387 (3.1); 19: no. 24 (8.2).

65. *PLAC,* 2:147–49; ibid., 1:116 (5.1 and 10.2); ibid., 4:1164, and the *Indices nominum.*

66. *PLAC,* 4:138 (3.1, 6.2); *Carmina Burana,* 50, 5, 3; *PLAC,* 6:210 (1.3); 215 (42. 1); 216 (44.2).

67. *AH,* 20:217; H. Copley-Greene, "The Song of the Ass," *Speculum,* 6 (1931): 534–49. See also what P. Wagner said about the accentuation of the final syllable of Hebrew nouns, *Einführung,* 3:39–40. Thurot showed, p. 400, that the grammarians of the Middle Ages recommended the accentuation *Abrahám, Ihesús,* etc.

carries the primary accent? In other words, in the Middle Ages would a writer accent *èdificáta* or *edìficáta*? For each particular case the accentuation depended on the exigencies of the verse. Since rhythmic verse in most cases imitated trochaic or iambic verse, it was generally one syllable out of every two, counting from the primary accent, that received a secondary accent. Hence in the poem praising Milan and dating from the middle of the eighth century, we find hemistichs like *fírmitèr edìficáta* and *ánte-quàs catàractárum.* Peter of Pisa (8th cent.) writes *dé-permànsióne;* Paul the Deacon, *réx sapìentíssimùs, kòniugàtiónis;* Walter of Châtillon (d. ca. 1180), *èvangèlizántiùm.*[68] It would be easy to collect just about as many examples as one wished on this subject. In relatively rare cases, the writer follows a system of regular dactylic accentuation, and we find the accentuation *èdificáta.* Likewise, in a song about St. Eustace, we find the accentuation *cònsolatóres* and *còmmorarétur,*[69] or even in a rhythmic hexameter of this type:

> Ut tibi tecum, sicut est aequum, còngratulémur,
> Ut sine nebula Christo per saecula còngloriémur.[70]

The verses that I have just cited also show that the secondary accent on the last syllable of proparoxytones *(nébula, saécula)* was not obligatory but optional according to the needs of the verse.

What remains for us in this chapter is to discuss proclitic and enclitic words in verse. A great many metrical anomalies would occur if one did not suppose that classical poets took into account in versification possibilities of the spoken language concerning the proclitic and the enclitic. In other words, what has the appearance, graphically, of forming two words could perhaps form in metrical practice only a single word; this is why Nougaret and Nilsson speak of metrical words.[71] Metrical words are, according to these authors, most often a preposition + the principal word and the monosyllabic forms of the verb *esse* joined to certain antecedents. In a good many cases it is possible that other groups of words were also understood as metrical words. Quantitative poetry, however, provides only a few indications to help

---

68. Traube, *Karolingische Dichtungen,* 119, strophes 1 and 5; *Die Gedichte des Paulus Diaconus,* ed. Neff, 61 (8.2); 9 (4.2); 77 (10.1); Walter of Châtillon, *Moralisch-satirische Gedichte,* ed. Strecker, 107 (11.1).

69. *PLAC,* 4:595 (16.3); 596 (19.1). The rhythmic form of the poem has been analyzed by Meyer, *Ges. Abh.,* 3:280–81.

70. *AH,* 48: no. 288 (30).   71. Nougaret, 5; Nilsson, 50–57.

us decide these matters. I will therefore set it aside here and limit myself to certain essential points concerning rhythmic poetry.

Let us begin with the verb *esse*. As we know, the monosyllabic forms of this verb appear before the caesura and at the end of the verse, even in metrical poems in which one avoids placing other monosyllabic words as the final word.[72] This usage was adopted in rhythmic poetry, where we find many examples beginning with the earliest poems. Thus Auspicius of Toul writes, around 475, *nóvus-èst, vérum-èst, scrípti-sùnt, tíbi-èst, éius-èst* at the end of his verses;[73] and in contemporaneous hymns like *Mediae noctis témpus-èst,*[74] we can point out a great many examples that show that all the monosyllabic forms of *esse*, even the subjunctives,[75] are related enclitically to the preceding word, no matter what part of a sentence the preceding word is. In the cases mentioned, the verb has acquired a secondary accent. In the final cadence ⌣́ ⌣, the verb is naturally completely lacking an accent as in the hemistichs *fílios a quíbus géns-est* and *ínfans créscit cònditór-est.*[76] It seems that even the disyllabic forms of *esse* could be enclitics. Thus this is what one finds in the Ambrosian rhythmic verse (8pp) *Nos vero Israél-sumùs,* taken from the hymn *Mediae noctis tempus est* cited above, or in the Goliardic verse (7pp + 6p) *Quám ut ràperét-eràt ‖ coacta Dione,*[77] to cite only two examples from different periods of the Middle Ages.

The monosyllabic pronouns often have an enclitic position in rhythmic poetry. I will cite here only a few cases of final cadences. Sisebert writes not only *períre-mè* but even *pèrsequí-me* and *vìsitá-me;* in a poem written at the end of the Carolingian period the form *fíli-mi* appears; the Archpoet rhymed *vèreór-te* with *forte;* Walter of Châtillon likewise rhymed *mèliór-me* and *enorme.*[78]

It is quite obvious that monosyllabic prepositions are most often related

---

72. Poets often rigorously avoided monosyllables at the end of a verse. Thus in the 318 hexameters of Symphosius, *Anthologia Latina,* 1:286, I have found only the following cases: *ex me, in me* (4 times); *fas est, non sunt* (3 times); *locuta est,* where the two words are fused by aphaeresis (5 times). Metrical words of the same kind, where the monosyllable exists only for the eye, are found before the penthemimer: *per se* once, *non est* 9 times, *certa est* twice. But one finds here also *est, sum, sunt* without aphaeresis 11 times.

73. PLAC, 4:615 (10.1, 17.2, 15.3, 13.1, 14.3).   74. AH, 51: no. 1.

75. See, e.g., PLAC, 4:464 (13.3) *ista sit.*   76. PLAC, 4:463 (4.4); 478 (9.1).

77. *Jupiter et Danaë,* ed. W. Wattenbach, *Zeitschrift für deutsches Altertum,* 18 (1875): 457–60.

78. PLAC , 4:781 (98.1); 775 (46.2); 780 (82.1); 468 (43.2); the Archpoet, 8:44; Walter, *Moralisch-satirische Gedichte,* 14, 11, 4.

proclitically to the following word. But we should also emphasize that if the principal word [the object of the preposition] is a monosyllabic pronoun, the standard accentuation is *ád-te, ín-quo,* and so on, just to cite a few phrases from the Carolingian period.[79] In rhymed verses one finds, for example, the rhyme *dé-te* and *indiscrete* in the work of the Archpoet, *á-te* and *beate* in the work of Godfrey of Breteuil (d. 1196), *pér-se* and *verse* in the work of John of Garland (13th cent.). And so it is perfectly regular when, in the first strophe of a song about Mary, the poet says, while putting the accent on the preposition:

> Ín te, pér te, dé te, éx te
> Pax venit hominibus,
> Súb te, ób te, praé te, cúm te
> Fax lucet hominibus.[80]

It has not been so well noticed that the same displacement of the accent takes place when the main word [the object of the preposition] is a monosyllabic noun. So an anonymous poet has *á-re* rhyme with *papare* (*Carmina Burana,* 42, 13, 1) and John of Garland writes this, with a tasteful pun:

> Ve dat Eva, set hec Ave
> Per quod salvat nos hec á ve
> Et a mortis iaculis.[81]

In the interior of a verse, one finds, for example, in the work of Conrad of Haimburg (14th cent.), *éx-vi;* in *Carmina Burana, ád-cor* and *ín-spe,* an accentuation that the editors of the two last-mentioned examples did not explain correctly.[82]

If the monosyllabic preposition is followed by a pyrrhic or iambic word, an analogous displacement of the accent can take place in medieval verse. In principle, in this case, what is going on is nothing new but a phenomenon parallel to that which, in a remote period of time, had as its outcome *óbviam, dénuo* (< *dé novo*), *ílico* (< *ín loco*). For example, Fulbert of Chartres (d. 1029)

79. *PLAC,* 6:91 (22. 2); 204 (13.2).

80. The Archpoet, 5:5; *AH,* 20: no. 199 (7b); John of Garland, ed. E. Faye Wilson (Cambridge, Mass., 1946), 106, v. 218; *AH,* 32: no. 81.

81. John of Garland, op. cit., 98, vv. 127–28.

82. *AH,* 3: no. 7 (7.4); *Carmina Burana,* 26, 1, 1 and 22, 6, where the editors speak of a "schweres einsilbiges Wort in der Senkung" [an accented monosyllabic word in the thesis].

treats *pér-fidem* as a metrical word; Heribert of Rothenburg (d. 1042), *ín-cruce;* Herrad of Landsberg (d. 1195), *ín-dies;* Rahewin (12th cent.), *á-deo, áb-eo, ín-ea.*[83] In number 47 of the *Carmina Burana* we find an artistic poetic form that is completely regular from the point of view of the accentuation, but where, according to Hilka and Schumann, strophe 2, verse 8, *in luto et latere* is an exception to the rule. In reality, one should not accent *in lúto,* as these scholars suppose, but *ín-luto,* and thus the only irregularity in the poem disappears.

We know from classical versification that disyllabic prepositions could keep their accent,[84] and it would be easy to cite examples taken from the Middle Ages. It is, however, more important to note that in the Middle Ages these prepositions could also be proclitics in rhythmic verse. The clausula is thus formed by *intér-quos* in *Versus de Asia et de universi mundi rota,* 21, 1; by *apúd-me* in *Passio Christophori,* v. 358. 1;[85] by *penés-te* in the work of the Archpoet, 8, 78, where these words rhyme with *peste.* In examples such as these, however, it might be more correct to say the pronouns are enclitics. No other option exists to explain the accentuation when the main word [the object of the preposition] is polysyllabic, such as in the verse *iús sinè-dispéndio* of Walter of Châtillon or *antè-tribúnal Chrísti* and *híc supèr-apóstolos* in the *Carmina Burana.* In these passages the editors have not understood that the preposition is proclitic, and consequently, they have made a mistake in the accentuation.[86]

Words with particular metrical forms become enclitics more easily than others. I am going to discuss here separately, first, monosyllabic words, and then pyrrhic and iambic words that can lose their own accent when they are preceded by a monosyllable.

In the preceding pages I have already dealt with several groups of mono-syllables without an accent, and I could add still more, such as relative pro-nouns, adverbs, and conjunctions. There are a great many examples in the verses of rhythmic poetry in which not only the final cadence but also all the

83. See *AH,* 12: no. 341 (7.3); 50: nos. 223 (3.1) and 338 (3.2); Meyer, *Ges. Abh.,* 1:260, who confuses, however, the concepts of accent and ictus.

84. See, e.g., Nilsson, 54–55.

85. *PLAC,* 4:554 and 839. I have dealt with the first poem in *La Poésie latine rythmique,* 82–86.

86. Walter of Châtillon, *Moralisch-satirische Gedichte,* ed. Strecker, 112 (9.3) (commentary on p. 110); *Carmina Burana,* 49, 11, 1 and 52, 3, 4, with explications by Hilka and Schumann, 102 and 113.

accents are involved. Thus, in the work of Paul the Deacon, *si* and *qui* are not accented in the verse *Péreàm si quémquam hórum* || *imitári cúpiò, Ávià qui sùnt sequúti* and other such verses. In other cases one can suppose that these words have only a secondary accent as, for example, in this verse by the same author, *Nàm a mágno sùnt dirécta* || *quaè pusíllus détulit.*[87] But then how is one to deal with monosyllables in rhythmic poetry that are emphatic or whose meaning is such that the accentuation seems natural? I cannot give a general answer to this question. When, for example, the author of the old hymn *Apparebit repentina* writes[88] *Èrubéscet órbis lúnae* || *sól et òbscurábitùr*, it seems that by reversing the order of *et sol* he has intended to accent the noun. Many authors completely avoid placing in an unaccented position in the verse monosyllables that are important for the meaning. Others admit exceptions in two places: at the beginning of the verse or in cases where the important monosyllable is preceded by a proclitic monosyllable. Peter of Blois (d. ca. 1204) writes some verses like *Vas Déo dètestábilè*, where the noun *vas* is found at the beginning of the verse, or *Út stes péde stábilè*, a case in which *út-stes* can be considered as a metrical word of the same kind as *ín-hoc* in the same poem.[89] In this way one can also explain the joining together of certain words at the end of the verse, like *néc-thus* rhyming with *rectus, dúm-das* rhyming with *emundas, sé-dat* rhyming with *sedat,* and even the three monosyllables *út-plebs ést, sí-das hís.*[90] There are also, however, certain authors who more or less often place words rich in meaning in an unaccented position in the verse without complying with these restrictions. Thus Walter of Châtillon can write verses like *Véniàt mors, véniàt* || *términus meróri*, where the usage of the word *mors* seems very free (Walter has perhaps set off the word *mors* by accenting *véniàt* against the rhythmic scheme *véniat mórs*). At the end of the verse, he and certain other authors also use as metrical words some groupings like *cùm-suá-vi, lucrúm-fert, sponsé-dos, gèntiúm-di, vás-cor, exsúl-cor, èxemplár-det, èx-partú-ius*, groupings which rhyme with *gravi, confert, fedos, mundi, pascor, dulcor, ardet,* and *cuius.*[91]

87. Paul the Deacon, ed. Neff, 65 (5.1) and 64 (1.2).

88. *PLAC*, 4:508 (5.1).

89. See *Carmina Burana*, the commentary, 48, and song 29 (3.1 and 12).

90. The Archpoet, 9:2, 3; *Carmina Burana*, 19, 5; Alexander Neckham, *AH*, 48: no. 284 (1); Walter of Châtillon, *Moralisch-satirische Gedichte*, 4, 27, 2, p. 70; *AH*, 33: no. 263 (3.13).

91. Walter of Châtillon, *Moralisch-satirische Gedichte*, 11, 13, 4, p. 115; 1, 17, 4, p. 10; 5, 7, 1, p. 75; 16, 30, 1, p. 145; the Archpoet, 3:23, 4; Walter of Wimbourne (14th cent.) *AH*, 50: no. 417 (12.2); ibid., 10: no. 232 (3a.2); 11: no. 47 (6.5).

The use of pyrrhic and iambic words as enclitics includes an additional point that so far has not been sufficiently noticed. The rule that can be formulated on this point is that a group of words composed of a monosyllable + a pyrrhic or iambic word can often form a single metrical word in which the principal accent falls on the monosyllable and the second accent on the final syllable of the disyllable. This practice of bringing together a monosyllable and a pyrrhic or iambic word comes from metrical poetry. We know that a hexameter ending of the type . . . — | ∪ ∪ | —‿ is avoided whereas | — | ∪∪ | —‿ is considered completely regular. One can make the same observation about iambic verse at the end of antiquity. In the hymn *Fefellit saevam* written in iambic senarii[92] St. Hilary ends his verses (except in the case of a proper noun), on the one hand, with polysyllabic words, and on the other hand, with *cum Deo, cum meo, in tuos, cum choris,* and finally with *te caro, cum crucis, mors tua, tum tua, te tibi, quod tenes, hoc Dei, mors tuae,* and *es meae;* that is, the disyllables are always preceded by a monosyllable. In the hymn *Aeterne lucis conditor,*[93] written in iambic dimeters, *et dies, et tuas, sol diem, ne famis, hunc diem* form metrical words which are on on a par with the proparoxytone polysyllables; and it is easy to find a large number of examples of this sort in the metrical poetry of the Middle Ages. Metrical words of this type are also present in rhythmic poetry. At the end of the fifth century, Auspicius of Toul uses in his rhythmic iambic dimeter, among the proparoxytone words at the end of the verse, the metrical word *út-simul;* and it is only a short time later that the hymn *Alma fulget in caelesti* was written, in which we find as verse endings *quód-valèt, ét-piaè, ést-locùs.*[94] Meyer, who was not aware of this rule, thought that these words ought to be accented *quod valét,* and so forth, and he thus wrongly classified this hymn as "Troch. Fünfzehnsilber mit unreinem Schlusse" [Trochaic fifteen-syllable with impure endings].[95] One can show the same thing occurring in the following centuries. Here I will name only Hugh of Trimberg (13th cent.) as an example of an author who applied this rule to the end of his verses; in his *Registrum multorum auctorum,* he always ends the first hemistich with a proparoxytone. Langosch extracts the following from Hugh's poem, calling them (on p. 111) exceptions to the rules of meter: *ut erat* (221), *in sua* (231), *imitatusque fuit* (255), *et ovis* (707), *et amor* (715), and *nec eum* (758). But, as I see it, all we

92. *AH,* 50: no. 2.

94. *PLAC,* 4:617 (34.3); 513 (13.1, 15.1, 22.1).

93. *AH,* 51: no. 7.

95. Meyer, *Ges. Abh.,* 1:208.

have here are combinations of monosyllabic words + ⌣⌣ (for the treatment of *-que* as an independent word see below). Consequently, the quoted cadences are in fact completely regular and ought to be accented *út-eràt,* and so on.

The accentuation |⌣ | ~ ⌣ | also appears normally in the interior of the verse of rhythmic poetry. Thus we read in the poem *De Iudit et Holofernes,* dating from the Carolingian period, verse 8, 1,[96] *Ést-Deùs et nón est fórtis,* because a different accentuation would be the only infraction of the system of accentuation in the entire poem. Still other examples will show the importance of the rule we have recognized, which has escaped the notice of editors and commentators. Thus Strecker claims that Walter of Châtillon's hemistich *cor habens tam cecum* is a poorly written verse.[97] That is not at all the case. One must simply accent correctly *cór-habèns.* Meyer found an entirely regular system of accentuation in the poem *Salve saluberrima.* The only exception that he cites is the verse *cor meum complectere,* where he places the accent on *méum.*[98] One must, however, read *cór-meùm.* In the same way, Meyer speaks of "Taktwechsel" [change in the beat] in verses such as *non velut invitus, os habens decorum, urbs bona flos urbium* in the work of the Archpoet,[99] without noticing that *nón-velùt, ós-habèns, úrbs-bonà* each form a metrical unity. The editors of the *Carmina Burana* have misinterpreted lines 16, 3, 5, *rex sedet in vertice,* 43, 2, 2, *que vix latet katholica,* where they say "schweres einsilbiges Wort in der Senkung" [accented monosyllabic word in thesis], and 42, 8, 3 *si velit causari,* 47a, 2, 6 *aut nichil decreverit,* 52, 1, 3 *qui sibi virilia,* where they speak about the change of rhythm interrupting an otherwise regular system. In fact, all these lines are perfectly regular (*réx-sedèt,* and so on), as are these verses in the work of Peter of Blois: *ín-novà fert animus* and *mé-iuvànt deliciae.*[100] I will add only the first verses of the *Carmina Burana* 111:

96. *PLAC,* 4:460.

97. Walter of Châtillon, *Moralisch-satirische Gedichte,* 8, 19, 1, p. 104.

98. Mone, 233, v. 63. See Meyer, *Ges. Abh.,* 1:261. However, I must note that the two-word combination that I am discussing is not an obligatory rule, but a possibility; see in the same song v. 14, *desíderàt cor méum.*

99. Meyer, *Ges. Abh.,* 1:263 and 270.

100. See the remarks of Hilka and Schumann, p. 48 of the commentary, and what they have said about the versification of Peter of Blois.

O comes amoris, dolor
Cuius mala male solor,
   An habes remedium?
Dolor urget me, nec mirum,
Quem a predilecta dirum,
   En, vocat exilium.

There is no change of rhythm here, neither in the first verse, as Schumann says, nor in the other verses; but the entire poem is composed following an invariable system of accentuation, completely regular, provided that one accents *ó-comès, án-habès, én-vocàt* in the verses cited and *néc-vicèm* in verse 3, 3.[101]

It is rare that one has good reason to suppose that a pyrrhic or iambic word relates enclitically to a polysyllabic word. This fusion is natural, owing to the meaning of the disyllabic word at the ends of verses such as *oculí-mei, sermó-tuùs, verúm-tamèn, pauló-minùs, usqué-modò, ulló-modò, quoquó-modò* (after *quómodò*).[102] Rarer are verse endings like *signá-tulì* which, in the work of Walter of Châtillon, rhyme with *seculi*.[103]

Contrary to the tendency we have just been studying, namely, the joining of some groups of words of a certain metrical form under a common accent—I emphasize that it is matter of a tendency, to meet a need and not to meet an obligatory rule—there is another tendency, also encountered in the rhythmic poetry, to separate enclitic words. And so it is not uncommon for the enclitic *-que* to be treated as an independent word. It is already so treated in the hymn *Alma fulget in caelesti*, where we read in verse 13, 1,[104] *Nóvum mélos qué te córam*. There are examples of this sort throughout the Middle Ages.[105] Analogously, *-ne* is independent in a rhythmic poem of the Carolingian period; the manuscript has these words:[106] *Quibus ille: Sanusne est ‖ pa-*

101. One can also join enclitic words and, to the combination of a monosyllable and a pyrrhic, can add an additional monosyllable, e.g. *vís-tibí-te*, AH, 26:240, words which correspond to *Hìppolýte*.

102. *AH*, 48: no. 56 (10.5); 21:189 (V.17); *Carmina Burana*, 77, 17, 4; *AH*, 39: no. 163 (5a); *MGH, Scriptores*, 12:420 (407); ibid., 14:188 (66.1); pr. 200 (373.2); du Méril, *Poésies populaires* (1847): 248.

103. *Moralisch-satirische Gedichte*, 1, 4, 6.

104. *PLAC*, 4:513.

105. See Meyer, *Ges. Abh.*, 1:261; 2:14; von den Steinen, *Notker der Dichter*, 1 [Darstellungsband]:491; Langosch, 112; my book *La poésie latine rythmique*, 67 and 69.

106. *PLAC*, 4:467 (42.3). I note that hiatus is found very often in this poem, e.g., v. 36.4 *ecce ego*, v. 38.1 *cui illi*, v. 39.1 *tollite ergo*.

ter vester senior? The particle *-ne* is accented, a fact not revealed by the spelling. The metrical context of the word is *sánus né-est*. Of course, one must not change the reading of the manuscript, as Strecker does, to *estne sanus*.

It is quite rare that monosyllablic prepositions are treated as independent words. The quantitative hymn *Factor orbis angelorum* provides some remark-able examples of such treatment.[107] Likewise we find some verses like *Ex sacris auctoritate roborata vatibus* = *ex auctoritate sacris vatibus roborata, Ex cherubim plenitate dicta sunt scientiae* = *dicta sunt cherubim ex plenitate scientiae, Illius per ut ducatum transferamur ad Deum* = *ut per ducatum illius transferamur ad Deum*. From rhythmic poetry we have this verse: *Huius omnes ad electi* ‖ *colligentur dexteram* = *omnes electi colligentur ad dexteram huius*, from the old hymn about the Last Judgement *Apparebit repentina*.[108]

---

107. Mone, 306. In this hymn the verse always ends with a proparoxytone, and it is in ac-cordance with the rules that I have given above that the poet has replaced the proparoxytone with *pér manum, ín deo, ád deum*, and further with *vís capit, dúx datus, íam sui, síc alit.*

108. *PLAC,* 4:508 (8.1).

TWO ▓ SYNAERESIS, DIAERESIS, SYNCOPE, PROSTHESIS, ELISION, AND HIATUS

The different forms of vowel contraction that are standard in the poetry of antiquity still exist in the quantitative poetry of the Middle Ages. We find, for example, *nuptiĩs, eorum* in the work of Aldhelm, *subruentur* in the work of Paul the Deacon,[1] *beluă* in the work of Hrotswitha, *aerea, aureis, prout, quousque* in the work of Walter of Châtillon. On this subject see the information furnished by the works cited on p. 1, note 1. In rhythmic poetry, synaeresis is frequent, especially at the end of antiquity. The oldest example of rhythmic poetry, the abecedarian psalm of St. Augustine, reveals a number of examples of this type: *ecclesiam, gladium, nescio, petiit, fieri, suum*. The Irish hymns also go rather far along this path. In St. Columba's hymn *Altus prosator* one finds, for example, *primordii, principatuum, bestiis, mulierum*.[2] One could cite, although to a lesser extent, analogous cases borrowed from the rhythmic poetry of more recent times. None of them implies anything new, as a rule, nor anything that did not already exist in Virgil. However, it seems necessary to underscore the phenomenon while noting the scholarly treatment of the Goliardic verses of Hugh of Trimberg.[3] Much to my surprise, the learned editor believes he has found the curious accentuation *omníum clèricórum* in *Solsequium*, 1, 7, instead of the six-syllable verse with a final paroxytone cadence (6p). One should, of course, read *ómníum clèricórum*.[4] Equally strange is the editor's adoption of the accentuation *tem-*

1. Paul the Deacon, ed. Neff, 30, v. 63.
2. See Vroom, 22, and *AH,* 51: no. 216.
3. See Langosch, 113.
4. For *omnia = omnja,* Virgil, *Aeneid* 6.33, see the commentary of Norden, and of Müller, 299.

póre and *sequítur* in the *Registrum multorum auctorum,* verse 607 *tempore Theodosii,* and verse 621 *sequitur Phisiologus.* There again we are dealing with completely regular verses (7pp): obviously one should read *témporè Theŏdósii* and *séquitùr Phisjólogùs.*[5] More remarkable is the synaeresis found in this same work, verse 23 *pu͡eri primo discant,* and verse 574 *pu͡eros instruxisse.* The word *puer,* however, is treated in the same way elsewhere, for example, in a rhythmic poem of the seventh century where one should read *audite pu͡eri* (5p) or in a hymn at the end of the Middle Ages written in Ambrosian verses (8pp), one strophe of which begins with the verse *Pu͡er mersus quidam Rhodano.*[6]

Other more striking instances of synaeresis are the monosyllables *qui͡a,* used, for example, by Fortunatus in the pentameter *filius ut dicant quia est creatura Dei,*[7] and *De͡us,* of which I give two examples coming from Italy: *Pudor fidem tuebitur, Fides pudorem, utrumque De͡us* (Ambrosian quantitative verses), and *Quia caritas praeceptis in duobus Constat, quibus De͡us amatur atque homo* (rhythmic verses with the structure 8p + 4p).[8] Some words like *diabolus, Diocletianus, Mediolanum, Dionysius* form a group of their own.[9] In these words, *di* is pronounced as a sibilant, often represented with *z,* for example, in *zabolus* [*z* as in English *zeal*]. Another group is the one formed by *hyacinthus, hierarchia, Hieronymus, Hierosolyma* (compare the spelling *Geronymus* and the like);[10] a third group is the one formed by *Neapolis, Michael, Israel,* and the like.[11] We must also note that proper nouns frequently received a completely arbitrary treatment. In the same poem, or in the work of the same author, one can find at the same time *No͡e* and *Noë, Isa͡ias* and *Isaïas, Isa͡ac* and *Isaäc, Moyses, Mŏÿses, Mŏ͡yses, and Mŏ͡yses.*[12]

As for the contrary phenomenon, diaeresis, forms such as *suëtus, suädeo,*

---

5. *Theudosius* with synaeresis is found even earlier in the work of Claudian (Müller, 316).

6. *PLAC,* 4:657, v. 1, and *AH,* 22: no. 314 (3.1).

7. Fortunatus, *Carm.* 2:15, 8. I have pointed out some examples taken from rhythmic hymns in my article *Contributions à l'étude du latin vulgaire,* 251–57.

8. *AH,* 14:39 (5) and *PLAC,* 4:528 (7.4) (a poem composed by Paulinus of Aquileia, as I have tried to show, *La poésie latine rythmique,* 87–97). See also the hexameters *Deus tibi multiplices transmittat ab ethere grates* and *Deus te septenis faciat splendescere donis, PLAC,* 4:1092, verses 2:3 and 5.

9. See *AH,* 14:37 (2.1); 87 (8.2); *Versus de Mediolano,* 1, 3; 12, 2 and 14, 1 (Traube, *Karolingische Dichtungen,* 119).

10. See *PLAC,* 4:632, (12.2); *AH,* 10: no. 378, *Indices nominum.*

11. Some examples are *AH,* 14: nos. 34 (12.1), 78 (6.1), 45 (5.1).

12. *PLAC,* 4:561 (7.1 and 8.1) and *PLAC, indices nominum.*

suävis, cuï, cuïus, linguä, and the like are, as we might expect, entirely normal in the Middle Ages as in antiquity.[13] Traube reported a large number of cases where *seü, ceü,* and *heü* are disyllabic, and he protested against the changes introduced by former editors.[14] One can even find some seven-syllable verses like *In eüangelio* and *Laüs tibi trinitas* where the verse does not lack any syllable, as the editor claims, or even some verses of eight syllables like *Eüsebiae mentibus* and *Tibi fusas Eütropi.*[15] From *laüs, laüdes, caüsa* it was possible to form *pläüstrum,* as I have pointed out elsewhere.[16] In some isolated cases there is a rather remarkable shift of the accent such as that of *persúädens* in the verse *Erat Ruben persúadens* (8pp), which is found in a poem from Italy dating from the Carolingian period, and *alícuï* in the verse of Theoderich of Trier (d. 977): *Nihil umquam per rapinam* ‖ *tulerant alicui* (8p + 7pp), and in a Goliardic verse (7pp + 6p): *Non erit alicui* ‖ *locus hic patronum.*[17]

I will limit myself to pointing out in passing the presence of some syncopated forms like *avunclus, diablus, didasclus, regmen, regla, insla, Barthlomeus.*[18] Similarly I remind the reader that in the course of the early Middle Ages, when reading verses, one could often place a prosthetic vowel in front of *sc, sp, st* and before *sm* in the word *smaragdus.* In the *Versus de Verona* the second hemistich of verse 20, 1, *Ab oriente habes primum* ‖ *martyrem Stephanum* is obviously lacking one syllable, and Traube therefore added a *nam* before *Stephanum.*[19] However, one can instead simply read *Estephanum* or *Istephanum.* In the same way one must read *Per estellae indicium* in a Milanese hymn, since what we have here is a verse of the type 8pp.[20] An abedecarian song influenced by Paulinus of Aquileia begins its last strophe with *Zmaragdo luces pulchrior omni gemma clarior.*[21] Since this song was written

13. See Müller, 308–10; B. Maurenbrecher, *Parerga zur lat. Sprachgeschichte und zum Thesaurus* (Berlin, 1916).

14. *Karolingische Dichtungen,* 112. One finds some examples from a later period in the work of Du Méril, *Poésies populaires* (1847), 108; *Carmina Burana,* 50, 1.

15. *AH,* 10: no. 414 (10a); 23: no. 256 (4.4); 11: no. 219 (2.1); 12: nos. 200 (1.3) and 199 (1.4); 13:133.

16. *La poésie latine rythmique,* 108. See also *cläüso, AH,* 12: no. 95 (5.1).

17. *PLAC,* 4:641 (7.1) and 5:156 (14.1); Du Méril, *Poésies populaires* (1847), 122.

18. See Traube, *Karolingische Dichtungen,* 119, v. 5, 2; *PLAC,* 4:550 (6.3); *AH,* 27: no. 97 (7.5). I have written on an example which Strecker improperly interpreted and in which one must read *baclum* instead of *baculum, La poésie latine rythmique,* 25. See also the indexes of *PLAC,* 3 and 4.

19. *Karolingische Dichtungen,* 126.   20. *AH,* 51: no. 128 (7.2).

21. *PLAC,* 2:257.

according to a versification that is a rhythmic imitation of the trochaic septenarius, Meyer thought that the poet had missed his beat.[22] Actually, it must be read, *Ezmaragdo luces pulchrîor,* ‖ *omni gemma clarior,* and the verse becomes absolutely regular (8p + 7pp). This prosthesis is particularly common in the rhythmic poetry of Spain or Gaul; I refer the reader to the commentaries of Blume in *Analecta Hymnica,* 27:54, and to the examples that Strecker gives, *PLAC,* 4:1164.

Many interesting questions are related to the use of elision and hiatus in the Middle Ages. As far back as the end of antiquity several poets had attempted, with more or less rigidity, to avoid elision.[23] This holds true not only for hexameters but also for lyric poetry and for hymns. St. Ambrose, for example, makes only one elision in *Aeterne rerum conditor,* one in *Splendor paternae gloriae,* three in *Iam surgit hora tertia,* none in *Deus creator omnium,* and, in the exceptional instance where he allows himself three elisions, in the first strophe of the Christmas hymn *Intende qui regis Israel,* it is because he is quoting from Scripture.[24] Sedulius has only two weak elisions in his long hymn *A solis ortus cardine;* Eugenius of Toledo does not have any in his hymns and very few in his hexameter poems.[25] The other poets of the Middle Ages continue this tradition, avoiding the use of elision in quantitative poems, some avoiding it entirely, as does the author of *Ruodlieb* or Conrad of Megenberg; others, like Hrotswitha, only in part.[26] Of course, there continued to be some poets who, with regard to the use of elision, followed classical models. Such is the case of Nivardus of Ghent in *Ysengrimus* and Walter of Châtillon in *Alexandreis.*[27]

The principle of avoiding elision as well as hiatus put the poets to a tough test. It is understandable that, toward the end of antiquity and especially at

22. Meyer, *Ges. Abh.,* 3:178.

23. See Müller, 335–37.

24. The first strophe of this hymn, which is preserved in the liturgical book of the Milanese church, presented some difficulty because of the elisions. This is why it is deleted in some other churches. But this strophe is an indispensable element in the composition of St. Ambrose' original hymn; and Simonetti is wrong, I believe, to declare it not authentic in his *Studi sull'innologia popolare cristiana,* 385.

25. See the index of Vollmer, *MGH, Auctores antiquissimi,* 14:441.

26. See the index of Hrotswitha, 547–48; the preface of *Ruodlieb,* ed. Seiler, 154; Conrad of Megenberg, the index, 102; Sedgwick, "The Style and Vocabulary of the Latin Arts of Poetry . . . ," 360; Thurot, 444; and the general survey that F. Munari gives, *M. Valerii Bucolica,* 47–49.

27. See Voigt, xxxi–xxxii, and Christensen, 60.

the beginning of the Middle Ages when the general level of culture was relatively low, poets could not quite avoid allowing a hiatus from time to time. St. Ambrose himself did so in a few situations, but the difficulties of putting a Scriptural quotation into a verse of poetry gave him an excuse.[28] Sedulius admits a hiatus before *est* in the verse *Enixa | est puerpera*,[29] and analogous cases can be found in other hymns. St. Hilary of Poitiers goes still further. In the three hymns of his that have been preserved, Meyers counted fifteen hiatuses and twenty-six elisions.[30] Likewise, the author of the hymn *Vox clara | ecce | intonat* [31] allows seven hiatuses in four Ambrosian strophes. In addition to the words quoted above, see the verses *Obscura quaeque | increpat, Quae sorde | extat saucia, Omnes pro | indulgentia, Secundo | ut cum fulserit* and *Mundumque | horror cinxerit.* But after the Carolingian reform, hiatuses were very carefully avoided in quantitative poetry, and they were also forbidden by the theorists of the Middle Ages.[32]

Rhythmic poetry adopts the same attitude toward hiatus and elision as quantitative poetry. This must then mean—since the practice in rhythmic poetry cannot be attributed to an imitation of Virgil or any other classical poet—that elision and hiatus were generally avoided but that these two phenomena could nevertheless occur. As to elision, Meyer denied its existence in rhythmic poetry.[33] In support of his theory, Meyer invokes two arguments. The first is that the rhythmic poets could not have been so inconsistent as to admit at the same time elision and hiatus. That is quite an arbitary assertion and one which is refuted by St. Hilary of Poitiers and other poets who permit both phenomena in quantitative poetry. Secondly, Meyer said that he had never found any rhythmic poem in which an abnormal number of syllables would again become normal if one assumed the existence of an elision. Actually, one can find a large number of rhythmic poems of this sort. At the end of antiquity, for example, we have the two hymns, *Christe precamur adnue* and *Christe qui lux es et dies* mentioned by St. Caesarius of Arles. Both are written in rhythmic iambic dimeters (8pp), and both contain only eight-syllable verses with the exception of these three verses: *Venturam in noctem*

---

28. *AH,* 50: no. 9 (5) *In principio erat verbum* etc. Other cases of hiatus, ibid. nos. 12 (7.3 and 4) and 15 (3.4).

29. *AH,* 50: no. 53 (5.1).   30. Meyer, *Ges. Abh.,* 3:155–57.

31. *AH,* 51: no. 49.

32. See Pannenborg, 188; Munari, *M. Valerii Bucolica,* 49.

33. *Ges. Abh.,* 1:178–79.

suscipe, Claritas tua illuminet, Nec caro illi consentiat.[34] It can hardly be attributed to chance that, in each of the three verses, one can make the number of syllables normal by assuming an elision. Among the songs in the treasure of hymns of the Milanese church are the rhythmic songs *Magnum salutis gaudium, Hymnum dicamus Domino,* and *Mysterium ecclesiae,* in which we should likewise assume the existence of an elision in the verses *Commota in gressum tremuit, Die decursa ad vesperum, Fallaces Iudaei impii,* and *Sanctum portare in utero.*[35] According to the sources, the hymn *Sollemnis dies advenit* in honor of St. John the Evangelist comes from Germany; the Lenten hymn *Summe salvator omnium,* from England. In the first of these hymns, we find the verse *Ultima in cena Domine,* in the second, the verse *Iob in favilla et cinere,*[36] and in both cases we can hardly avoid assuming the existence of an elision since all of the other verses are composed of eight syllables. St. Paulinus is probably the author of the two hymns *Congregavit nos in unum* and *Hic est dies in quo Christi,* in which, as I have observed elsewhere,[37] one finds three elisions; Einhard wrote a song *De passione martyrum Marcellini et Petri,*[38] where the versification, which is regular in other respects (8p + 7pp), requires that one assume the existence of an elision in four places: 4, 2 *Poena inflicta praevaleret* ‖ *Christi fidem tollere;* 22, 1 *Meque humana sine ope* ‖ *atque amminiculo;* 23, 2 *Explorando comprobatis* ‖ *ipsum tibi adsistere;* 54, 3 *Suo iubet saevus iudex* ‖ *tribunali adsistere.* Meyer himself later found a series of hymns of the Visigothic and Mozarabic period in Spain in which one can, without any doubt, assume the existence of elisions.[39] In some of the poems of the Carolingian period published by Strecker, one must also assume elisions.[40] Even in the eleventh century, Heribert of Rothenburg and Odilo of Cluny wrote, in hymns whose rhythmic construction (8pp) is certain, verses such as *Pro sine fine excessibus* and *Ultra angelorum gloriam.*[41]

---

34. *AH,* 51: no. 21 (1.4 and 3.4); no. 22 (3.3). Some cases of hiatus also appear in hymn 22.

35. *AH,* 51: nos. 74 (11.2), 75 (2.1 and 7.1), and 128 (2.4). We find one hiatus in the first hymn (in the doxology), three in the second, and eight in the third.

36. *AH,* 51: nos. 160 (3.3) and 69 (6.4). A hiatus appears three times in hymn 160 and once in hymn 69.

37. *La poésie latine rythmique,* 94, n. 15. I have counted nine hiatuses in each hymn.

38. *PLAC,* 2:126–35.

39. See *Ges. Abh.,* 1:204, 210, and 227.

40. See *PLAC,* 4:605 (2.3 and 6.1); 687–92 (19.1; 27.1; and 44.2); 808, 843, and 870 with Strecker's notes.

41. *AH,* 50: nos. 226 and 229.

These examples, to which it would be easy to add others, show clearly that elision exists in rhythmic poems, often side by side with hiatus. All these examples have been taken from rhythmic poems in which the number of syllables is fixed. However, there are also some other rhythmic poems which present a certain variation in the number of syllables. In such poems, how can we know if there is elision or not? Let us take as an example the song *De Pippini victoria Avarica*, composed in Verona at the end of the eighth century.[42] Each verse is normally composed of eight plus seven syllables. In some verses, however, we find in the first hemistich nine syllables, or in the second, eight syllables. An unaccented syllable is similarly added three times before the first hemistich, for example *Ut | víam eíus còmitáret*,[43] and eight times before the second, for example, *tu | Chríste Déi súbolès*.[44] In these cases it is undeniable that we have a surplus of syllables which we should not try to conjure away. Three times we can assume the existence of a synaeresis of *ei*, of *eo*, and of *ie* in the words: *Dei, Deo,* and *mulieri*.[45] However, three cases remain where we find eight syllables instead of seven: see 11, 2 *cum festucis et foliis,* where the irregularity can be excused by the difficulty of introducing into the verse a fixed technical expression and 12, 1 *parent tibi obsequia,* 15, 2 *usque ad diem actenus,* where we can and where we likewise must, as I see it, assume the existence of an elision. In his study of the rhythmic poems, Meyer has counted without considering the possibility of elision in some verses of this genre. To know if there really is an elision or not can, of course, be difficult for certain verses. However, it emerges from the example that I have quoted that it is necessary, when we study poems where the number of syllables varies, to distinguish the cases in which an elision is plausible. The structure of the verse quite often becomes explicable and appears as relatively regular.

There is also hiatus in rhythmic poetry. At the end of antiquity and in the early Middle Ages, certain writers seemed to be very little concerned about avoiding the juxtaposition of vowels. In the opening verse of his poem *Praecelso | et spectabili,* Auspicius of Toul gives an example of the juxtaposition of vowels (hiatus); and in what follows he gives nineteen more examples. In the hymn *Rex aeterne Domine* we likewise find a final vowel followed by an initial vowel (or *h* + vowel) eleven times.[46] Some other poets, however, follow a

---

42. *PLAC*, 1:116–17.   43. Verses 4.3; 13.2; 15.2.

44. Verses 1.1, 2.3, 3.1, 3.2, 8.2, 9.2, 11.3, 14.3.

45. Verses 5.1, 13.1, and 6.3. For these synaereses, see above.

46. *PLAC*, 4:614–17; *AH*, 51: no. 2.

stricter technique. Thus St. Augustine, in his *Psalmus contra partem Donati,* seems to have always avoided hiatus, except at the medial break.[47] In the Carolingian period Peter of Pisa has likewise avoided hiatus completely in his rhythmic poem to Paul the Deacon, with the exception of one case of hiatus at the medial break.[48] Paulinus Aquileia is equally meticulous in certain poems, as are some later poets such as the Archpoet, Rahewin, and many others.[49] We should note that in rhythmic poetry, in general, poets were not in the habit of avoiding placing a word ending in a vowel + *m* before an initial vowel; a case like *Meum est propositum* ‖ *in taberna mori* was not therefore considered a hiatus. But by contrast, in keeping with the classical practice, poets did often avoid a hiatus between the final vowel and *h* + vowel.[50]

In his manual on metrics Bede sets forth, as do other theorists, a curious doctrine that should be mentioned in connection to what we have been examining. He claims that *es* and *est* are not combined by aphaeresis to the preceding word but that the final vowel of the preceding word is cancelled by elision. He cites as examples *arta via est* and *praesidium est,* which should, he says, read *arta vi'est* and *praesidi'est.*[51] One can see this theory being followed in rhymed poetry. For example, Marbod in his poem in hexameters *Missus ad egregiam Gabriel tulit ista Mariam*[52] constantly used the Leonine disyllabic rhyme which in the quoted verse is supplied by the *-iam* syllables in *egregiam* and *mariam.* Likewise in verse thirty-nine of the same poem, the rhyme must be produced by the syllables *-is est.* The verse is the following: *Si sterilis gravis est, si virgo puerpera visa est.* Marbod therefore never read the last two words *visa'st* but *vis'est.*

47. See my article "Ad S. Augustini Psalmum abecedarium adnotationes."

48. See Neff, *Die Gedichte des Paulus Diaconus,* 60–62. Paul the Deacon himself does not avoid hiatus as rigorously. He responds to Peter in a poem of the same genre and the same length, where we find six hiatuses.

49. For the details see Meyer, *Ges. Abh.,* 1:121, 189, and 275–77.

50. See Meyer, loc. cit.

51. See Keil, *Grammatici Latini,* 7:247.

52. *AH,* 50: no. 300.

THREE ▦ ASSONANCE, RHYME, AND ALLITERATION

We know that in classical poetry assonances and rhymes are more or less accidental or serve to produce a special effect.[1] Classical verse without rhyme also existed in the Middle Ages, practiced by a large number of writers who were closely inspired by the older models. But at the same time a systematic and regular use of assonance was developing and, later, of rhyme, a use which reached its peak in the twelfth and thirteenth centuries.[2]

At the beginning of this evolution is Sedulius, who in his poetry uses the same technique for assonances that he uses in his rhetorical prose.[3] Assonance, which in the earlier poets was an exception, becomes in Sedulius' work a conscious and tangible tendency, and it is found in a great number of his verses.[4] In his *Carmen paschale*, composed in hexameters, there are not only assonances at the ends of verses but even some between words right before the different caesuras and words at the ends of verses; these assonances are often double or multiple, or they form different types of figures. In the hymn *A solis ortus cardine*, written in iambic dimeters, there is not a single strophe without an assonance. For the most part, in the work of Sedulius or elsewhere at the end of antiquity or during the early Middle Ages, it is not a question of pure monosyllabic rhyme but only of assonance, that is, the final syllables have the same vowels while the resemblance between the conso-

---

1. See Marouzeau, *Traité de stylistique latine,* 58–65.

2. Several scholars have studied rhyme, e.g., Norden, Meyer (*Ges. Abh.,* 1:190–96, 277–83; 2:122–26), Polheim, Strecker, Descroix, Dingeldein, Grimm, Huemer, Spiegel, Sedgwick, whose works are found in the bibliography.

3. Rhyme came to poetry from rhetorical prose as Norden has shown. However, for certain works of poetry like those of Commodian and the abecedarian psalm of St. Augustine, one must assume a foreign origin of the technique of rhyme.

4. For the rhymes and assonances of Sedulius, see Gladysz.

nants is unimportant. Thus, in the hymn of Sedulius the words *impie* and *times, saeculi* and *induit, pectoris* and *Dei, puerpera* and *praedixerat, venerant* and *obviam, plurimus* and *febrium, sabbatum* and *angelus* are linked by the similarity of the vowel sounds of the final syllables.

The practice of Sedulius must have had an even greater influence on the later development of rhyme since he was considered a scholarly model and was the object of passionate studies and imitations. In the collection of hymns that we know about through the bishops Caesarius and Aurelian of Arles, which had been used in the south of Gaul at the beginning of the sixth century, there are several songs with a marked tendency toward assonance or rhyme. In the hymns *Deus aeterni luminis, Ad cenam agni providi,* and *Aurora lucis rutilat*[5] assonance even became the rule. It is the same for one of the hymns of Fortunatus, *Vexilla regis prodeunt,* while the other, *Pange lingua,* often has assonances but also allows some unrhymed verses. In the work of King Chilperic, Theofrid of Corbie, and some other writers of Gaul appears the same marked tendency, a tendency which in certain cases goes so far as to become the norm.[6] It is the same in the works of the Spanish lyric poets of the Visigothic period as well as in the work of the Irish, whose hymns contain a great number of songs in pure rhymes.[7]

In the poetry written in hexameters after the time of Sedulius, rhyme was often used by the anonymous author who, under the rule of the Vandals in North Africa, wrote the song *Ad Flavium Felicem de resurrectione mortuorum.*[8] Then, Eugenius of Toledo and his successors in Spain took assonance or rhyme to great lengths. What could be achieved along this line is shown us by the poem *Oratio pro rege,* probably written by Eugenius of Toledo.[9] Here we find not only Leonine verses such as,[10]

Oremus pariter toto de corde rogantes,

5. *AH,* 51: no. 9 (83 and 84). There are certain exceptions in the third verse of the strophe; see below p. 133.

6. See *La poésie latine rythmique,* 33 and 43. One finds a regular use of monosyllabic rhymes, for example, in the song *Qui de morte estis redempti, PLAC,* 4:521–23.

7. The technique of Irish rhyme has been analyzed by Meyer, *Ges. Abh.,* 3:315–23.

8. The rhymes of this poetry have been studied by Miltner-Zurunić.

9. See the edition of Vollmer, 275; *AH,* 50: no. 78.

10. It was around the year 1030 that one began to speak of *versus Leonini;* see Erdmann, "Leonitas . . . ," in *Corona Quernea,* 15–28.

where there is a monosyllabic assonance between *pariter* before the penthemimer and *rogantes* at the end, but also some verses like these:

Et genitum patris totum diffusa per orbem
Ecclesia Christum cognoscit et omnipotentem,

where, on the one hand, the final syllables of the two verses are linked by the rhyme *-em* and, on the other hand, the words before the trihemimeris and the hephthemimer in the first verses and before the penthemimer in the second verse are linked by the rhyme *-um,* or else,

Sideribus variis superum depinxit Olympum
Muneribus sacris mundum ditavit et imum,

where all the words of the first verse are linked by rhyme to the corresponding words in the second verse. In Spain Alvarus of Córdoba and some others also adopted this tradition.[11]

In a different development, the Carolingian renaissance and its efforts to recover classicism brought about at first a retreat from the use of assonance and rhyme. The great poets Alcuin, Angilbert of St. Riquier, Theodulf of Orléans, Rabanus Maurus, Walafrid Strabo, and others followed the models of the golden age, and the six Leonine hexameters of Ælberht (Koaena) of York (d. 781)[12] are an exception. Nevertheless, one can find in limited regions of northern Gaul during the first part of the ninth century a systematic use of Leonine rhymes. It is indeed at this time that the poem of forty-six rhymed hexameters composed by Peter of Hautvillers was sent to Archbishop Ebo of Reims. In this same region, Engelmodus also learned this practice and applied it in two poems of more than a hundred distichs in total; and this was also the case with Gottschalk of Orbais, whose poems can be identified in part by the special technique developed in his rhymes.[13] At the end of the ninth century there are Leonine rhymes to be found at, for example, Reichenau and St. Gall; and in the tenth century, the use of hexameters with Leonine rhymes spread until it becomes one of the characteristics of the me-

11. Mariné Bigorra has studied Leonine rhymes in Spanish inscriptions, 182–84.

12. *PLAC,* 1:201, no. 1.

13. See the article by Strecker, "Studien zu karolingischen Dichtern, V, Leoninische Hexameter und Pentameter im 9. Jh." and also Traube, *PLAC,* 3:710–11; Strecker, *PLAC,* 4:934; Fickermann, *PLAC,* 6:88.

dieval hexameter. There was a certain decline in the practice at the beginning of the twelfth century when a strong movement in favor of classicism caused some poets like Marbod of Rennes and Hildebert of Lavardin to abandon their former attitude.[14] Many followed their example, among them Gilo of Paris, who wrote the first five books of his epic on the first crusade in hexameters with Leonine rhymes, but abandoned the form beginning in book six, saying,[15]

Quod tamen incepi, sed non quo tramite coepi
Aggrediar, sensumque sequar, non verba sonora
Nec patiar fines sibi respondere vicissim.

[I will continue with what I have commenced, but not on the path on which I began, and I will aim for intelligibility, not high-sounding words, and I will not allow the ends (of metrical units) to correspond to each other (in sound).]

However, to describe the struggle between rhymed hexameter and classical hexameter in the late Middle Ages would take us too far afield. Let us then return to lyric poetry, the evolution of which was different in part since lyric poetry was often written in new forms free from the classical models and in which rhyme could never be suppressed.

From the beginning of the Carolingian period rhyme made great technical progress in lyric poetry. Poets were thus no longer content with assonances but started to use more and more pure monosyllabic rhymes. In 892 the rhythmic poem *O tu qui servas armis ista moenia*[16] was composed at Modena, a poem which was as erudite as it was elegant and in which all the verses, with the exception of two—which we will revisit—end in *-a*. Two contemporaneous poems, which were probably composed at Verona, *O Roma nobilis orbis et domina* and *O admirabile Veneris idolum,* offer us a technique using rhymes just as pure.[17] The same is true of a great number of other songs, older or more recent.

The two verses of the poem from Modena that do not end with *-a* are the following:

14. See, for example, Descroix, 62–65.

15. See Pannenborg, 184, who gives a list of unrhymed poems.

16. *PLAC,* 3:703–5.

17. Dreves was therefore wrong to claim in *Ein Jahrtausend lateinischer Hymnendichtung,* 2:347, that these two songs were written around 1100 because of their rhymes. Traube thinks that they were written in the tenth century, *O Roma nobilis,* 306.

Tu murus tuis   sis inexpugnabilis,
Sis inimicis   hostis tu terribilis.

These two verses present rhymes before the caesura, instances of which, before that time, appear only sporadically in lyric forms[18] but which become more and more frequent in quantitative poetry as well as rhythmic poetry. One can find some Asclepiadean rhythmic strophes such as,

Tuba clarifica,   plebs Christi, revoca
Hac in ecclesia   votiva gaudia,
Fide eximia   celebra monita,
     Confitere piacula,[19]

or some Sapphic quantitative strophes like,

Christe, rex regum,   dominans in aevum,
Lumen aeternum   patris atque verbum,
Qui regis cunctum   pietate mundum
     Factor egentum.[20]

The latter strophe was taken from a hymn in twelve strophes whose author was Gottschalk of Orbais, and all of the strophes have one rhyme before the caesura and one at the end of the verse. In strophes 1–3 the rhyme is -um, 4–6 it is -am, 7–9 -em, and 10–12 -or.

Disyllabic (or trisyllabic) rhyme also gains ground. From the Merovingian period on, disyllabic assonance had been used with a certain regularity in some songs composed in Gaul, for example, in the two poems *Audite omnes gentes Et discite prudentes,* where the ends of the verse have the cadence $\stackrel{\smile}{} \sim$, and *Felicis patriae Pictonum praeconanda fertilitas, In qua Christi mandatorum declaratur profunditas,* where the ends of the verse have the cadence $\stackrel{\smile}{} \sim \stackrel{\cdot\cdot}{}$.[21] In the same way a disyllabic assonance or a disyllabic rhyme had been used early in certain Irish hymns where, in the final cadence $\stackrel{\smile}{} \sim \stackrel{\cdot\cdot}{}$, one can even find some examples of trisyllabic rhyme.[22] In the Carolingian period it is, above all, Gottschalk of Orbais who offers us the example of a

18. See what I have said in *La poésie latine rythmique,* 43.
19. *AH,* 27: no. 207 (1).
20. *PLAC,* 3:727–28.
21. *PLAC,* 4:501 and 654.
22. See Meyer, *Ges. Abh.,* 3:316–17.

frequent use of polysyllabic rhyme as we can see in the following strophe, which is quite skillfully constructed:[23]

> Magis mihi, miserule,
> Flere libet, puerule,
> Plus plorare   quam cantare
> Carmen tale,   iubes quale
>   amore care.
>   O cur iubes canere?

In the works of other poets of the Carolingian period we can also notice a certain tendency to use polysyllabic rhymes. However, it is only in the eleventh century, for example, in the works of Wipo or Ekkehard IV of St. Gall,[24] that we find a regular use of pure disyllabic rhymes, a use which became widespread in the course of the following century.

At the same time that the rhymes became richer, poets tried to increase the number of rhymes. This could be done in different ways, one of which can be illustrated by the following strophe:[25]

> Tu thalamus pudoris,
> Tu balsamus odoris,
> Tu libanus candoris,
> Tu clibanus ardoris,

where, in addition to the usual final rhymes, assonances have been added among the other syllables in verses 1–2 and 3–4, constructed in an absolutely parallel manner. Another way consists in accumulating words that rhyme within one and the same verse, as did the unknown author of a hymn in honor of St. Bridget, where one finds the following verses:[26]

---

23. *PLAC,* 3:731. In another song of Gottschalk, ibid., 729, we find some strophes of the type,

> Ex quo enim me iussisti   hunc in mundum nasci,
> Prae cunctis ego amavi   vanitate pasci,

where we can see that the author wants to have the disyllabic rhymes at the end of the verses but contents himself with monosyllabic rhymes before the caesura.

24. *Carmina Cantabrigiensia,* 33; *PLAC,* 5:532–33.

25. *AH,* 10: no. 110 (7b).

26. *AH,* 33: no. 69 (20).

Spes,   res   es   pulcherrima,
Cos,   ros,   dos   gratissima,
Lux,   nux,   dux   prudentiae,
Ius,   tus,   rus   fragrantiae.

One could, moreover, practice a concatenation of rhymes, to which medieval theory gave the name *versus serpentini* (or *decisi*)[27] and which consisted in rhyming, in each metrical member, the last word with the first word of the following member. A poem in hexameters in honor of the Virgin Mary begins in this way:[28]

Ave, porta poli,   noli te claudere mota,
Vota tibi grata   data suscipe, dirige mentem
Entem sinceram,   veram non terreat ater,
Mater virtutum, ...

In hymns a tendency toward the use of serpentine rhyme is apparent as early as the era of old Irish poetry, as one can see from the following strophe:[29]

Martinus mirus *more*
Ore laudavit Deum,
Puro corde cant*avit*
Atque am*avit* eum.

In a hymn to St. Catherine and belonging to the end of the Middle Ages, we read,[30]

Tu es filia novella,
   Cella eloquentiae,
Simplex, clara columbella,
   Stella excellentiae,
Ornans stipem tu agnella,
   Fiscella clementiae.

We encounter rhymes that are still more complicated in the following strophe written by a Scandinavian author at the end of the Middle Ages:[31]

27. See Meyer, *Ges. Abh.*, 1:92; *AH*, 41:166–67 (Appendix nos. 5–6). In French versification these rhymes are called *enchaînées* or *annexées;* see Suchier, *Französische Verslehre*, 159.

28. *AH*, 32: no. 26. One also finds in this poem an acrostic, *Ave Maria.*

29. *AH*, 51: no. 247 (2). See ibid., nos. 233, 247, 249, 251, and 258.

30. *AH*, 33: no. 144 (3).   31. *AH*, 45b: no. 205.

> Olla mortis patescit
> Quam vidit Ieremias,
> Cleri status vilescit
> Spernendo scholae vias,
> Schola nola virtutis
> Tutis clangescit moribus.
> Qui spernunt, cernunt luctum,
> Fructum perdunt cum floribus.

If we observe only the final rhymes, *ababcded,* we do not do justice to the very complicated technique of rhymes in the second part of the strophe where serpentine rhymes appear, on the one hand, between the words of the end and those of the beginning of the verses, *virtutis—tutis, luctum—fructum,* and, on the other hand, in the interior of the verse, *schola—nola, spernunt—cernunt.* The other strophes of the poem show that the poet did not wish, by these rhymes, to break up the metrical unity of the verses.

Aside from this, the most common way of increasing the number of rhymes is to divide verses into small parts consistent with the basic pattern. The rhythmic imitation of the trochaic septenarius (8p + 7pp) is thus divided into three parts (4p + 4p + 7pp), as can be seen in the following strophe, whose author is Bernard of Morlas (12th cent.):[32]

Omni die,   dic Marie,   mea, laudes, anima,
Eius festa,   eius gesta   cole splendidissima.

One can likewise find the rhythmic Ambrosian strophe (8pp) divided in the following way (2p + 2p + 4pp):[33]

Cruci   truci   fles filium
Fixum,   nixum,   iam mortuum,
Sero   vero   in gremium
Captas   aptas   -que rigidum.

We have marked the divisions of each verse above (as if there were caesuras) only by increasing the space after the words that form the rhymes. We could, however, just as reasonably, consider the different parts of the verse, which otherwise form a whole, as entirely independent, each forming a

32. *AH,* 50:427 (no. 323, *Rhythmus* 2.1).
33. *AH,* 12: no. 105.

separate verse. It might, in fact, be better to display free rhythmic strophes as they are in the song below, independent of the metrical models, which can present a very peculiar appearance because of the just-mentioned tendency to use very small rhymed verses:[34]

Digna laude	Quorum coetus
Gaude	Laetus
O Maria	Canit ibi
Quia	Tibi
Sine	Ave
Fine	Suave.
Tu pro reis stas.	Super omnes res
Das	Es
Eis fas	Vera spes
Perfruendi luce	Desperatis mole
supernorum	vitiorum.

In lyric strophes, poets originally had been in the habit of putting together rhymes two by two, *aabb*, and so on, or as groups of three, four, or more, *aaaa* and so on, depending on the number of verses contained in the strophe. It also happened that the same rhyme was used throughout a poem or in groups of verses or strophes (continuous rhyme).[35] Only in isolated cases during the early Middle Ages did writers make use of envelope rhymes of the type *abba* or of crossed rhymes of the type *abab*.[36] The appearance in the twelfth century of more artistically shaped strophic forms makes more fre-

34. *AH*, 1: no. 18.

35. Continuous rhymes, called by Meyer "Tiradenreim" [tirade rhyme], exist already in the *Psalmus contra partem Donati* of St. Augustine, in the work of Commodian in the *Carmen ad Flavium Felicem de resurrectione mortuorum*, and later in the Irish and Mozarabic hymns, and in the work of Gottschalk. They are still found in the following period and toward the end of the Middle Ages; see, for example, Meyer, *Die Oxforder Gedichte des Primas*, 16 and 23, the Archpoet, 8; *AH*, 12: no. 217; 23: no. 56; 33: no. 124. See Meyer, *Ges. Abh.*, 1:193–95; 2:123.

36. From the seventh century comes the famous *Versus familiae Benchuir* (*AH*, 51: no. 260), where we find some crossed disyllabic assonances and, at the same time, continuous monosyllabic rhymes as the first strophe shows:

Benchuir bona regula
Recta atque divina,
Stricta, sancta, sedula,
Summa, iusta ac mira.

quent the use of more complicated rhyme patterns. The strophes that I have just quoted provide an example that one can render by the formula *aabbccd-ddeffgghhiiie,* and we will give still others in the penultimate chapter of this work.

As for the pronunciation of rhyme words, it is necessary first of all to emphasize that in the Leonine hexameter, when it is scanned, the ictus falls on different parts of the syllables of the rhyme before the caesura and at the end of the verse, for example, in the verse *Ista vorax fossá Dominici continet óssa.*[37] In rhythmic poetry the accentuation of the rhyme word is unimportant, as a rule, for monosyllabic rhymes. In the rhythmic verse of Leo IX,[38]

O pater Deus aeterne,   de caelis, altissime,
Respice iacentem multis   perforatum iaculis,
Singultibus in extremis   suspirantem ultimis,

the words *aeterne* and *altissime* and so on rhyme in spite of the cadence before the caesura and at the end of the verse (8p + 7p). For disyllabic rhymes, on the other hand, writers did their best to rhyme words having the same accentuation. That practice brought about crossed rhymes within the same strophe *(ababab),* for example, in St. Thomas Aquinas,

Pange, lingua gloriosi   corporis mysterium
Sanguinisque pretiosi,   quem in mundi pretium
Fructus ventris generosi   rex effudit gentium.

In the rhythmic poems in which only the number of syllables counts and where the writer does not pay attention to the final cadence, we also find, however, disyllabic rhymes between words differently accented, such as *abólita* and *oblíta, córpore* and *sopóre, ínfimo* and *límo, virgíneus* and *réus, trámite* and *ríte, propítia* and *pía,* to take some examples from the song *Super*

<hr/>

37. *Carmina Latina Epigraphica (Anthologia Latina,* 2), 798. But we do not know for certain if poets scanned the hexameter in the Middle Ages. According to Geoffrey of Vinsauf it is necessary to read the verse with the prose accent: *Generaliter sciendum est quod qualiscumque fuerit syllaba in metro, non est aliter accentuanda in metro quam extra metrum, sed semper est accentuanda secundum hoc quod regulae docent accentuum* (Faral, *Les arts poétiques,* 319) [In general, one should know that any syllable in a meter should not be accented in a different way in the meter than outside the meter, but it should always be accented according to what the rules teach about accents.]

38. *AH,* 50: no. 238.

Salve Regina by Jean Tisserand (d. 1494).[39] Sometimes this rhyme technique was also used regularly, with exquisite artistry, as we see in the verses of John of Garland:[40]

Nos trans mundi maria   ducas, o Maria,
Deviis per avia   nobis esto via.

Ordinarily the quantity of vowels does not matter in rhymed poems—the quantity must have corresponded to the Latin pronunciation in the Middle Ages. Some rhyming words such as *căve* and *suāve, tămen* and *iuvāmen, bŏna* and *persōna, pĕte* and *quiēte,* are thus placed very simply on the same level. In hexameters as well, writers also allowed themselves Leonine rhymes of the type *Pergama flere vŏlo, fato Danais data sōlo.*[41]

On the other hand, the quality of the vowels forming the rhyme had to be, as a rule, the same; and in general the exceptions to this rule are exceptions in appearance only.[42] Therefore, we find throughout the Middle Ages that words like *favilla* and *Sibylla, quaero* and *spero, poena* and *catena* rhyme because *y* was pronounced like *i,* and *ae* and *oe* like *e.* At the end of antiquity and in the early Middle Ages, *e* and *i, o* and *u* rhyme, since in the spoken language the pronunciation of these vowels was similar. In the hymns belonging to the end of antiquity, *Ad cenam agni providi* and *Aurora lucis rutilat,* the words *vinculo* and *paradisum, gaudio* and *impetus, viribus* and *miseros, vivere* and *Domini, discipuli* and *propere* form rhymes or monosyllabic assonances. It is the same in the work of Eugenius of Toledo, for example, *suspiriis* and *complacet, delectatio* and *solacium, recogito* and *transeunt;* and it is the same in the work of many other poets.[43] In certain poems these vowels are interchanged, even if they are accented. It is thus that in the poem *Audite omnes*

39. *AH,* 50: no. 428.   40. See Meyer, *Ges. Abh.,* 1:281.

41. There are, however, some versifiers who strictly observe the rule that the second foot of the Leonine hexameter must be a spondee; see Bulst, *Studien zu Marbods Carmina varia,* 182.

42. One finds a special technique in the work of some versifiers who were Germanic in origin, for example, in the work of Hrotswitha. In her work all the vowels rhyme together: *illi* rhymes with *multa, vere* with *illo,* etc. If the rhyme ends with a consonant and if the vowels of the last syllable are different, the consonant or the consonants ought to be the same: *examinans* rhymes with *disponens, sobolem* with *ullam,* and so on. See Polheim, 5–6; Seiler in his edition of *Ruodlieb;* Strecker in *PLAC,* 5:227.

43. Meyer, *Ges. Abh.,* 3:284–300, gives many examples taken from poems composed in Gaul or Italy. But Meyer wrongly claims that the equivalence of vowels *e* and *i, u* and *o* does not come from a "vulgar" pronunciation. It is, for example, significant that this equivalence is found in all Romance-speaking lands but not among the Irish or the Anglo-Saxons.

gentes Et discite prudentes[44] the words *Christi* and *estis, clemens* and *exinaniv-it, fides* and *crudelis* form a disyllabic assonance. Even after the Carolingian reform, one can notice that the pronunciation of a poem's Latin was influenced by the language spoken by the poet. In poems written by French-language authors, consequently, we find rhymes like *gemebundus* and *pondus, audi* and *custodi.*[45]

In poems with pure disyllabic rhymes it is also necessary to take into account the pronunciation of consonants. It is thus completely regular and natural that in the poems of France *poscit* should rhyme with *quo sit, rite* with *sagitte,* to take only two examples.[46] When we find in the work of Bernard of Morlas that *antiquus* rhymes with *inimicus, mecum* with *aequum, agni* with *tyranni, omnes* with *nationes, enixa* with *amissa, mediatrix* with *patris, benedicta* with *vita, ipsi* with *missi, sanctis* with *tantis,*[47] it is likely that in these cases we do not have assonances but pure disyllabic rhymes. It would be important to determine to what extent these types of rhymes or other analogues appear and how they reflect the pronunciation of Latin in the different countries and at different time periods of the Middle Ages.

I will note in passing that quite a few writers do not hesitate to repeat the same rhyme or the same rhyme word. Sometimes we find the same word with several senses; for example, in the following strophe of Peter of Blois:[48]

Nec a verbo aspero
  liberum me *feci,*
Servus si serviero
  vitiorum *faeci.*

Often simple verbs rhyme with their compound form, or even different compounds with each other. Thus the poem that we have just quoted presents, in strophe four, the rhymes *abstulit, contulit,* and *protulit.*[49]

44. *PLAC,* 4:501–3.
45. *AH,* 50: no. 323: p. 447 (50.1); p. 449 (33.1).
46. *AH,* 10: nos. 185 (2b) and 208 (6b).
47. See the poem of Bernard of Morlas, *AH,* 50: no. 323: p. 427 (21.1); p. 437 (20.3); p. 443 (29.1); p. 446 (38.3); p. 447 (2.1); p. 451 (2.1); p. 448 (7.1); p. 453 (5.1); p. 454 (19.1).
48. *Carmina Burana,* 31, 6. The poems in which the writer rhymed only homonyms were called *versus differentiales.* Christian of Lilienfeld gives two examples, *AH,* 41:167–69 (Appendix nos. 7–8).
49. For the same types of rhyme in Old French, see, e.g., Suchier, *Französische Verslehre,* 143–45.

A final, remarkable phenomenon is the elision of the rhymed syllable. Following the model of Virgil, *Aeneid* 3.549, *Cornua velatarum obvertimus antemnarum* (which was believed to be Leonine),[50] one could write verses like these:

Iamque nitore novo ac splendore micabat opimo . . .
Dignus et est vitae hinc laudum per saecla favore . . .
Versatus dudum evasisti culmen ad ipsum . . .
Quam liquido exponi auctori quadrando poposci.

These examples are taken from Gottschalk of Orbais, *Carmen ad Rathramnum*, in which the poet constantly makes use of monosyllabic Leonine rhymes.[51] It is therefore obvious that, in spite of the elision, *novo* rhymes with *opimo*, and so on. It would be easy to give a great many examples of this phenomenon, which is common in poetry in Leonine hexameters in the Carolingian period and which even appears in the work of Walter of Speyer around the year 1000.[52]

We know that the repetition of similar sounds at the beginnings of words plays an important role in the Latin of antiquity.[53] In the Middle Ages the theorists warned against an exaggerated use of alliteration, and so Eberhard writes,[54]

Littera non veniat eadem repetita frequenter
    Et nimis assidue, displicet illa metro.

[The same letter should not be repeated too often
and persistently; that offends against poetry.]

And yet throughout the entire Middle Ages, the poets used it and abused it. However, taste varied according to the writer and the country; and the variation was so great that one can dare to draw certain conclusions from it about the place where a poem was composed. Thus, the *Hymnarium Severianum*, as it is called, contains mainly hymns composed in Italy, and in them the

---

50. See Müller, 573. Lind has shown, *Neophilologus*, 25 (1940), that Reginald of Canterbury borrowed Leonine hexameters from Virgil to adapt to his own needs.

51. *PLAC*, 3:733–37.

52. See Strecker's notes, *PLAC*, 5:8 and 80.

53. See Marouzeau, *Traité de stylistique latine*, 45–50.

54. See Pannenborg, 188.

only cases of alliteration we find are of the type *Pastorque verus populo Summus sacerdos rutilat, Magnus existens medicus,* and it is often difficult to determine if the alliteration is due to chance or, on the contrary, to studied effort. But we find in a hymn in honor of St. Gregory the Great, these three introductory strophes:[55]

> Magnus miles mirabilis
> Multis effulgens meritis
> Gregorius cum Domino
> Gaudet perenni praemio.
>
> Carnis terens incendia
> Corde credidit Domino,
> Contempsit cuncta caduca
> Caritatis officio.
>
> Legis praecepta Domini
> Laetus implevit opere,
> Largus, libens, lucifluus
> Laudabatur in meritis.

The alliteration that was here used to excess diverges so much from what one finds elsewhere in the collection of hymns that one has every reason to believe that these strophes are a foreign contribution. In fact, one finds them word for word in a hymn composed in England in honor of St. Cuthbert,[56] and this leaves no doubt that the hymn was really composed in England. Actually, the Anglo-Saxons had borrowed from their masters, the Irish, a pronounced taste for alliteration. But whereas the Irish had made a completely irregular use of it,[57] the Anglo-Saxons had, in a way, regularized it to the point that they often linked short verses in pairs by means of alliteration.[58] That was the practice in Ambrosian verse, as in the strophes quoted; but it

---

55. *AH,* 14: no. 51.   56. *AH,* 11: no. 173.

57. See Meyer, *Ges. Abh.,* 3:323.

58. One finds examples of this alliteration even toward the end of the Middle Ages, for example, in a hymn in honor of St. Thomas Becket, *AH,* 19: no. 478, of which the fourth strophe is,

> Thoma, tutor et tutela
> Triumphantis ecclesiae,
> Nos tuere, ne plus tela
> Nos transfigant nequitiae.

was also the practice in poems composed in Adonic verse. Germanic poetry must have served as the model. Alcuin in this way constructed strophes of six Adonic verses of the following type:[59]

Esto paratus	Care fidelis,
Ecce precamur	Credule nate,
Obvius ire	Primus amore
Omnipotenti	Atque paterno
Pectore gaudens.	Discipulatus
Pax tibi semper,	Dulcis amore.

From poems of this type, in which a regular alliteration of this kind appears, one can draw certain conclusions about the technique followed by the Anglo-Saxons. It is thus certain that all the vowels alliterated with one another. The bringing together of words like *octonae* and *assi, Idus* and *etiam, item* and *ambiunt, aprilis* and *unus, at* and *aevi*—and even *ultima* and *huius* since *h* was not counted as a consonant—is therefore a completely regular linking of words.[60] Between a *u* vowel and a *u* consonant Berhtgyth at least does not differentiate. She makes *vale* and *ut, ut* and *vallata* alliterate in an Ambrosian poem where the verses are linked in pairs.[61] Curious indeed is the alliteration—its existence can be proven in several poems—between words like *flamine* and *verus, verba* and *fudit;*[62] the Anglo-Saxons obviously pronounced *v* like *f* in Latin words, as was the case again later in Germany.[63] Also very remarkable is the alliteration that can be demonstrated in the work of Alcuin between words like *care* and *certo, curva* and *certe, crevit* and *certe.*[64] It is obvious that Alcuin and his compatriots pronounced *c* like *k* even before an unstressed [*faible*] vowel. It was a use that they had learned in the schools from the Irish, who in their turn had learned their scholarly pronunciation

59. *PLAC,* 1:266. See also ibid., 303.

60. I have taken the examples from the poem which is published in *PLAC,* 6:202, v. 838–93.

61. *MGH, Epist.,* 3:428, 28 and 430, 5.

62. *PLAC,* 4:608 (4.5) and 609 (14.3).

63. See Max Hermann Jellinek, "Über Aussprache des Lateinischen und deutsche Buchstabennamen." *Akademie der Wissenschaften in Wien, Philosophisch-historische Klasse, Sitzungsberichte* 212. Band, 2. Abhandlung (Vienna and Leipzig: Hölder-Pichler-Tempsky, 1930): 6–12; and Ingeborg Schröbler, "Zu den Carmina rhythmica in der Wiener Handschrift der Bonifatiusbriefe," *Beiträge zur Geschichte der deutschen Sprache und Literatur,* 79 (1957): 9.

64. *PLAC,* 1:266, v. 5 and v. 19; 4:608, v. 10.

of Latin at a time when the sound *k* was still preserved in *ce* and *ci* on the continent, or at least in the province of Britain.[65] This is why, in Irish songs, there is alliteration between all the words beginning with *c* in the verses *Et clara caeli culmina* or even *Cinis, cautus castus diligentia.*[66] The pronunciation of *c* seems to have varied in the work of the author who, at the beginning of the Carolingian period, composed the poem *De ratione temporum,* which has been passed down in a manuscript of Mainz. He brings together, on the one hand, words like *zodiaco* and *circumferri, zonae* and *caelum,* but, on the other hand, also words like *Kalendae* and *cernebant, certum* and *qui, crescente* and *cernimus,* and so on.[67] The author was probably himself an Anglo-Saxon. He was at least influenced by Anglo-Saxon teaching, as Strecker has shown; and one must also acknowledge that he worked in France or in Germany where *ce* and *ci,* at that time, were pronounced like *tse* and *tsi.*

In addition to rhyme and alliteration, the poetry of the Middle Ages presents still other rhetorical figures. When Fortunatus, in *Vita sancti Martini,* I, 19, writes *Prudens prudenter Prudentius immolate actus,* he is using a figure learned from rhetoric where it is listed under the term *adnominatio.*[68] Puns and wordplay of this type were in vogue during the entire Middle Ages and were used to extremes even by good writers.[69]

However, they are found especially in the twelfth century and later, when writers had a technical understanding of Latin so advanced that they were carried away with their art of words. The writers who managed to write verses like *Christum pro se prosequentem oravit piaculis* or *Decantemus in hac die Eutropii pii pie pia natalitia,* or even *Mala mali malo mala contulit omnia mundo,*[70] certainly must have considered them a beautiful accomplishment. We do not have studies of the stereotyped formulas that writers used in making such puns, but if they could be produced, they would contribute much to elucidating the art of handling the Latin language in the Middle Ages. I will

65. See Jellinek, op. cit., 12–15.

66. *AH,* 51: no. 235 (8).

67. *PLAC,* 6:186–203, verses 16, 507, 78, 261, 297.

68. In the *Rhetorica ad Herennium,* 4:21 and 29, one can read of wordplay like *Cur eam rem tam studiose curas, quae tibi multas dabit curas,* or *Hunc avium dulcedo ducit ad avium.* The figure *adnominatio* was also recommended in the poetics of the Middle Ages; see Curtius, *Europäische Literatur und lateinisches Mittelalter,* 281 [English trans. by Trask, 300].

69. For Walter of Châtillon, see Christensen, 54–55; for *Carmina Burana,* the commentary of Hilka and Schumann, 3, 33, 46, 82, 93, and 114.

70. *AH,* 10: nos. 415 (8b) and 223 (3a); *Revue bénédictine* 48 (1936): 35.

be satisfied here with quoting an example that is particularly interesting in this respect, one taken from a sequence from Reims:[71]

Salve virgo, vitae via
Mundum mundans prece pia,
   Maria per maria;

Salve viror, quae non vires
Perdis, quamvis viro vires,
   Sed vires virtutibus;

Salve cara, culpa carens,
Sine pari patris parens,
   Per te patent omnia.

Salve viror sine viro,
Viror virens modo miro
   Non naturae viribus.

We can neglect other, less common phenomena. To finish, we add only that one quite often finds some playing with vowels of the type,

O, o, o, a, i, a, e,
Amor insolabile,
Clerus scit diligere
Virginem plus milite.[72]

---

71. *AH*, 10: no. 141.
72. See Spanke in *Studien zur lateinischen Dichtung des Mittelalters*, 171.

FOUR ▨ ACROSTICS, *CARMINA FIGURATA,*
AND OTHER POETIC DEVICES

The Middle Ages inherited from late antiquity its taste for metrical devices.[1] In this chapter I am going to give a quick, general survey of the most standard and the most striking.

One of the most common devices is the practice of making what is called an acrostic with the first letters of each verse or of each strophe. Quite frequently in epitaphs the name of the deceased is given in this way and, in liturgical poetry, the name of the saint whose feast was celebrated. Often an author preserved for posterity his own name by slipping it into his poem in this way.[2] All writers were not as verbose as the Visigothic poet who succeeded in introducing the words *Aeximinus hoc misellus scribsit era nonagentesima septuagesima, cursu nono decimo, kalende aprili,*[3] or even Johannes Franco, who announces to us in his lengthy song on Mary, *I. Franco, scolaster Meschedensis, servitor alme virginis Marie humilis et devotus ista collegit et ea domino Iohanni pape XXII misit.*[4] In these cases and in some others too the use of the acrostic gives us invaluable assistance in determining the name of the author. In some other cases where the author is named quite simply *Iohannes* or *Petrus,* it can be impossible or difficult to identify him. But a systematic study of these acrostics and the clues they provide still can reveal to us quite a few facts about the history of Latin literature in the Middle Ages which have not yet been uncovered.[5]

1. Müller gives, 576–94, a general survey of poetic devices that were used toward the end of antiquity.

2. One finds many examples in the *Carmina Latina Epigraphica* of Bücheler and in *PLAC.* Blume has gathered together the most important examples of liturgical poetry in the preface to *AH,* 29. I have shown that one can still make some finds, *La poésie latine rythmique,* 67.

3. *Revue bénédictine* 36 (1924): 19.   4. *AH,* 29:185–204.

5. See, for example, p. 143 below, where I have been able, through the discovery of the

One could, of course, also use the acrostic for other purposes. Thus, in his short riddles in hexameters, St. Boniface uses the first letters of the verses to give the riddle's answer. Sometimes acrostics are found which spell *Ave Maria* or other prayers; and at other times the acrostics themselves have a metrical form.[6]

It is not always easy to recognize an acrostic. Occasionally, as in the work of Walafrid Strabo in *Visio Wettini,*[7] the acrostic is mixed into the verse in some unexpected places. In this respect, the acrostics of rhymed offices studied by Blume in *Analecta Hymnica,* 29:6–9, present some special difficulties. Furthermore, the acrostic is not confined to the first letter of a verse; it can comprise two or more of the initial letters and even go as far as the second or third word of the verse, or farther. The words *carnem datam vermibus* form in this way the acrostic *ca-da-ver;* we find the name *Maria* in the two verses,

> Mater Alma Redemptoris
> Iubar Aurei viroris.[8]

A special device consisted of making the acrostic double or multiple. In the poem,

> Mater mirabilis, Maria, nomine
> Multum lucidior quocumque lumine,
> Muni me miserum mortis in limine,
> Malignis obvians, tuo iuvamine,[9]

each verse of the first strophe begins with an *m;* those of the second strophe begin with an *a;* those of the third, with an *r;* of the fourth, with an *i;* and of the last, with an *a.* It was even more refined to begin all the words of the strophe with the same letter, as in the poem,

---

acrostic *Suintharic,* to attribute one of the Mozarabic *Preces* to the seventh century. According to Meyer, the editor, they come from the Carolingian period, but see I. Pope, "Medieval Latin Background of the Thirteenth-Century Galician Lyric," *Speculum* 9 (1934): 7.

6. See, for example, *AH,* 3: no. 1; 15: no. 94; 32: nos. 5, 15, 17, etc., and what Blume says in the preface, *AH,* 29.

7. *PLAC,* 2:316–19.

8. See Faral, *Les arts poétiques,* 65, and *AH,* 31: no. 153. William of Deguilleville (d. after 1358) composed some poems where the acrostic comprises all the words of the verse, *AH,* 48: nos. 351 and 357.

9. *AH,* 31: no. 125.

Margarita mundans mentes,	Aula agni, Abel ara,
Mater mitigans maerentes,	Arbor auferens amara,
Mel misericordiae,	Ales alimoniae,

and so on,[10] where the versifier in this way formed the name *Maria.*

The acrostic can even be linked with a telestich or even a mesostich. We have an example of the latter device in the work of Eugenius Vulgarius (10th cent.) whose poem to Pope Sergius III[11] begins with the verses,

Aureus ordo micans cEli de numine fulgeT
Elichias vertex sacRati spermatis omeN
Virtutum paret coluMen, sacratio celebS,

and so on, where the author has in this way succeeded in slipping into the hexameter verse *Aeternum salve presul stans ordine Petri.*[12]

From such a complicated letter game it is not a great step to the *carmina figurata,* which after Porphyrius Optatianus were in great favor among Fortunatus, Boniface, Josephus Scottus, Alcuin, Eugenius Vulgarius, and many other poets of the Carolingian period who amused themselves making poems in crosses and pyramids, and even forming other more-or-less complicated figures.[13]

A particular form of acrostic is that of the songs known as abecedarian, in which the first letters of each strophe or of each verse reproduce the alphabet. St. Hilary of Poitiers, St. Augustine, Commodian, Sedulius, Fortunatus, and others wrote alphabetic songs, and their example was followed during the entire Middle Ages by a large number of versifiers.[14] The letter *k* was in

---

10. *AH,* 31: no. 127. See also ibid., 48: nos. 346 and 347.

11. *PLAC,* 4:413.

12. Müller speaks of telestichs and mesostichs, 579; see also *Reallexikon für Antike und Christentum* (under the words *Acrostichia* and *Carmina figurata*) and the indices of *PLAC,* 3 and 4 (under the word *acrostichides*).

13. Fortunatus, *Carm.* 2:4, 5; 5:6; *Carm. Spur.* 2; *PLAC,* 1:17, 153–59, 225–27, 482, 622; 2:165, 479; 4:422; *PLAC,* 3 and 4, *indices.* See also Curtius, 285–86 [English translation by Trask, 284].

14. See, for example, Müller, 578; K. Krumbacher, "Die Akrostichis in der griechischen Kirchenpoesie," *Sitzungsberichte der philosophisch-philologischen und der historischen Klasse der K.B. Akademie der Wissenschaften zu München* (1903): 551–691; Walpole, *Early Latin Hymns* (Cambridge, 1922), 150; Strecker, *PLAC,* 4:1161; Blume, *AH,* 29:10–11; 51:32–33 (no. 32), 72 (no. 73), 82–84 (no. 78), 212–13 (no. 185), 275–78 (no. 216), 302–4 (no. 232), 314–15 (no. 237), 319–20 (no. 241), 321–24 (nos. 243–44). Even in the fifteenth century Ulrich Stöcklin von Rottach composed several abecedarian songs, *AH,* 6:109–52 (nos. 26–47).

general rendered, in accordance with teaching of the grammarians, by a word beginning with the syllable *ca;*[15] for *x, y,* and *z* one managed with *Xristus,*[16] *Ymnus,* and *Zelum,* but the ingenious versifiers found occasion to shine by using words like *Xilon, Ydrus, Ydraula, Zonton, Ziph,* and so on.[17] The *Y* strophe was sometimes salvaged by the use of *y* in words like *Ymmense, Yma, Yesse,* and *Yesus;*[18] and it is perhaps from the spelling *fYdes* that one can explain a practice, which goes as far back as the beginning of the Middle Ages, that makes the *Y* strophe begin with words beginning with *f,* such as *Fides, Fixis, Fixus, Fit, Fecit, Fusca, Facere.*[19] The *X* strophe sometimes begins with the words *eXultantes, eXul, eXcelsa, eXtolle,* which can be compared to the strophes M and C beginning with *sMaragdus* and *sCelus.*[20] One will notice, moreover, some spellings like *Ec = haec* or *Had = ad, Hortus = ortus,* and in the Mozarabic poems *Berbum = verbum* or *Fesanus = vesanus.*[21]

Another letter game, more difficult and consequently rarer, is provided by Peter Riga in his famous poem in twenty-three parts,[22] in which the first part avoids the letter *a;* the second, the letter *b,* and so on. This game [lipogram], like most of the others, was not an invention of the Middle Ages, and it did not disappear even at the end of the Middle Ages. In his indispensable work for understanding the literature of the Middle Ages, Curtius traced it from Nestor of Laranda in the third century through Fulgentius up to the Spanish literature of the seventeenth century.[23] The contrary phenomenon was called paromœon [παρόμοιον]. The best known example is Hucbald of St. Amand's

15. A few exceptions to this rule are *Kurrunt, PLAC,* 4:475; *Koniugationis,* Neff, *Gedichte des Paulus Diaconus,* 77; *Kyrie, AH,* 6: no. 2 (10); 46: no. 150. I have indicated some other examples in *La poésie latine rythmique,* 29–30, where I have also shown that there are some authors who omitted the strophes K, X, Y, and Z because they did not find introductory words.

16. We know that the Greek abbreviation ΧΡΣ meant the spelling *Xristus.* From it also derives the spelling *Xristallo* in a poem from Verona, *PLAC,* 4:580.

17. See *PLAC,* 4:506–7, 510; *AH,* 6: no. 47; 15: no. 49.

18. *PLAC,* 4:491; *AH,* 9: no. 174 (11b); 15: no. 88 (22); 32: no. 14 (21).

19. *AH,* 27: no. 9 (6.2); 51: no. 78 (22.1), where the editor wrongly changed the text; *PLAC,* 4:500, with Strecker's note, ibid., 1161.

20. *PLAC,* 4:514, 628, 909; 1:82; *AH,* 27: no. 130 (2.5); *PLAC,* 3:404 (3.1). I have discussed *celus = scelus* in my article "Notes sur quelques poèmes du haut moyen âge."

21. *AH,* 23: no. 10 (5); 27: no. 32 (3.1); 51: no. 32 (3.1); 27: no. 9 (1.2), no. 178 (6.1) (see 14: no. 40 [6.1]).

22. Migne, *PL,* 212:32–42.

23. Curtius, *Europäische Literatur und Lateinisches Mittelalter,* 286–87 [English translation by Trask, 282–83].

Ecloga de calvis, in which each of the words of the 146 hexameters that make up the poem begins with the letter *c.*[24]

While on this subject I must also mention the poem of Eugenius Vulgarius *Solo tu nutu natis e diceris unus,*[25] composed in ten hexameters, the first of which comprises twenty-seven letters, the next one twenty-eight, the next one twenty-nine, and so on to the last verse, which has thirty-six letters. *Instar organici psalterii formula haec versuum paret* [This pattern of verses follows the standard of a musical psalter] says Eugenius in a detailed explanation of the varied secrets which his poem holds. A certain Heinrich Egher of Kalkar (14th cent.) amused himself in an analogous way by writing a poem of 150 words in honor of the Virgin.[26] He took this number from the 150 strophes of the rhymed psalter.

The theorists of the Middle Ages gave a good deal of attention to the figure called tmesis. Bede taught that one could write *H i e r o quem genuit s o l y m i s Davidica proles* [Hierosolymus = Jerusalem], and Dicuil quotes as an example the verse *P r i s c i canit pueris haec a n i cuncta libellus* [Prisciani].[27] We find examples of this figure not only in poetry in hexameters but also in other types of verses. The following Sapphic verse belongs to the Carolingian period: *Haec prophetas et p a t r i fecit a r c h a s,* and the name *Ricciovarus* was placed in this way in an Ambrosian verse of the early Middle Ages: *Quem V a r u s saeve R i c c i o Laesit flagello pessimo.*[28] Not only proper nouns or words of foreign origin were treated in this way. Thus Conrad of Megenberg separates in a barbarous way the word *singulares* in the verse *Cleros plurales coges vix s i n que g u l a r e s* and the word *pauperes* in the verse *P a u p e r et e s monachi cupientes pocula Bachi.*[29] Eugenius of Toledo calls on the authority of Lucilius when he writes ten *versus dirupti* of the following type:[30]

24. *PLAC,* 4:267–71; see Curtius, 285 [English translation by Trask, 283–84]. See *AH,* 19: no. 215 (1), where all the words begin with *f,* and 15: nos. 63 and 64, where all the words begin with *p;* 43: no. 371, where in five strophes, the words begin with *l, m, c, f,* and *p* respectively. William of Deguilleville in this way wrote an abecedarian paromœon, *AH,* 48: no. 358; see Abbo of St. Germain-des-Prés, *Bella Parisiacae urbis,* book 3, lines 69–112 (PLAC 4:119–121) where the versifier piled up words beginning at first with *a,* then *b,* and finally by *c.*

Another letter play is found in *AH,* 52: no. 201. There the five vowels *a, e, i, o, u* form the rhymes, each in a strophe of the poem.

25. *PLAC,* 4:438.   26. *AH,* 36:5–6.

27. See Müller, 458.

28. *PLAC,* 2:244 (5.1), and *AH,* 11: no. 411 (2).

29. Conrad of Megenberg, *Planctus Ecclesiae,* v. 918 and v. 1333. For some other examples, see *PLAC,* 3:818, and 4:1164.

30. *MGH, Auctores antiquissimi,* 14:262. See Müller, 458.

O *Jo* versiculos nexos quia despicis *annes,*
Excipe *di* sollers si nosti iungere *visos;*
Cerne *ca* pascentes dumoso in litore *melos.* . . .

In an analogous way the grammarian Virgil composed an Ambrosian rhythmic strophe where the word *laudabilis* is divided into four parts:[31]

Lau contemptus pecuniae
Da in omni molimine
Bi per amorem sophiae
Lis menti fiet peritae.

Writers paid considerable attention to plays on words of different length. Ausonius provides the model of plays upon monosyllables in his *Technopaegnion,* of which all the verses end with a monosyllable. We find the same thing in a poem of Marbod, beginning thus:

Porticus est Rome quo dum spatiando fero me
Res querendo novas, inveni de saphiro vas.
Institor ignotus vendebat cum saphiro thus. . . .[32]

Angilbert begins and ends his verses in the poem below with only monosyllabic words:

Rex, requiem Angilberto da pater atque pius rex,
Lex legum, hoc tribue, ut secum semper maneat lex. . . .[33]

Eugenius Vulgarius, who is especially infatuated with all sorts of devices, even succeeded in writing some verses composed entirely of monosyllables with the exception of the inevitable conjunction *igitur* in his versification exercise: *Si sol est, et lux est, at sol est: igitur lux. Si non sol, non lux est, at lux est: igitur sol,* and so on.[34] In the rhythmic poetry of the Middle Ages, the same play with monosyllables is common; a versifier writes, for example,

Dubitantes de vera re
Velle Deum unire se

31. Virgil the Grammarian, *Epitomae,* 2, 5.
32. See Bulst, *Studien,* 204–5. The Archpoet gives the same structure to his poem *Omnia tempus habent.* See also Meyer, *Ges. Abh.,* 1:79 and 95.
33. *PLAC,* 1:420.
34. *PLAC,* 4:426.

> Beatae genitrici, que
> Peperit sine partus ve,
> Licet Iudei spernant te,
> Nos tamen firma vera spe
> Credimus matrem Dei, ne
> Perdas languentem, sana me,
> Incredulos de vita le,
> Bovem credens, Iudea, semper fle.[35]

He ends the other strophes of his poem in the same way with a monosyllabic word which he sometimes seems to have had some difficulty finding (notice that *le = dele* in the quoted strophe).

There also existed, of course, some wordplay suited to extremely long words. We find a typical example in the following verses:[36]

> Coniuraverunt Constantinopolitani,
> Affirmaverunt Saranabara Toronitenses.

As for *versus rhopalici* of the type *Mars, pater armorum, fortissime belligerator,* in which the words are composed of one, two, three, four, and five syllables, it is enough to refer to the work of Müller.[37]

As early as the end of antiquity writers would also amuse themselves by writing hexameters with a fixed number of words. Thus each one of the verses of the poem *Vandalirice potens, gemini diadematis heres,* in honor of Hilderic, king of the Vandals (523–530), is composed exclusively of five words, and each one of the monostichs which are part of the *Carmina duodecim sapientium* is made of only six words.[38] The verses called *versus rapportati* also quite often contain a fixed number of words, as in the following example:[39]

> Pastor arator eques pavi colui superavi
> Capras rus hostes fronde ligone manu.

The use of *versus rapportati* has its roots in Greek literature of the imperial era; it was very much favored in the Middle Ages, and it left numerous traces

35. *AH,* 20: no. 251 (2).
36. See Wilmart in *Revue bénédictine* 48 (1936): 28, no. 143; and also F. Munari, *M. Valerii Bucolica,* 17–19.
37. Müller, 579–80. 38. *Anthologia Latina,* 215 and 495–506.
39. *Anthologia Latina,* 800.

in literature in modern languages, as Curtius showed when he last dealt with this subject.[40] Some medieval treatises on versification also speak of *Ianuarii versus quorum quaelibet dictio directe et transverse respicit more Ianii* [Janus-style verses, in which each word looks straight ahead and crosswise, in the manner of Janus], of which this is an example:[41]

Virgineum	lumen	te	ditat	nectare	numen
Lumen	solare	genitor	te	comit	honore
Te	genitor	peramat	plasmator	culmine	sacrat
Ditat	te	plasmator	amor	promit	populorum
Nectare	comit	culmine	promit	caelica	turba
Numen	honore	sacrat	populorum	turba	salutat

Some other figures are related to those which we have just mentioned: on the one hand, the verses known as *versus recurrentes* [palindromes], where one can read the letters in both directions, as in the verse *Roma tibi subito motibus ibit amor,*[42] on the other hand, the verses known as *versus retrogradi* or *reciproci,* where the words can be read in one direction or the other, as in the verse *Alme pater, mesto pugili palme dator esto* and where *Esto dator palme pugilo mesto, pater alme* also forms a hexameter (and even a Leonine hexameter).[43] The author of the sequence *Lebuine confessorum* produced a veritable masterpiece in this genre.[44] I will quote only the first strophe:

Lebuine, confessorum
Praecellens flos, qui polorum
    Regna scandis ardua
Linquens orbem, validorum
Cor plenum portasti morum,
    Tu pandis miracula.

If we read the sequence backwards we obtain a poem in hexameters:

---

40. Curtius, *Europäische Literatur und lateinisches Mittelalter,* 288 [English translation by Trask 286–87]. See also *Carmina Burana,* 5, Schumann's commentary, 8.

41. See Dreves in *AH,* 18:7. Another example *AH,* 46: no. 120.

42. See Müller, 580; J. Wagner, 30–31; *AH,* 18:7; *PLAC,* 3:612, v. 61.

43. See Müller, 580–82; J. Wagner, 30–31; Dreves in *AH,* 18:6.

44. The entire text is published in *AH,* 13:9–10.

> miracula pandis;
> Tu morum portasti plenum cor validorum,
> Orbem linquens ardua scandis regna polorum,
> Qui flos praecellens confessorum, Lebuine.

It is customary to call the phenomenon illustrated by the following verses *epanalepsis:*

> Primus ad ima ruit magna de luce superbus,
>> Sic homo, cum tumuit, primus ad ima ruit.

The authority of Sedulius, from whom these verses are taken, that of Fortunatus, of Bede, of Paul the Deacon, and yet others conferred a considerable popularity on this type of versification.[45] In an analogous way, Bede put Ambrosian strophes together in pairs by repeating the first verse at the end of each group of strophes.[46] Other devices of this type consist of repeating in a distich the first word of the hexameter in the pentameter[47] or, in poetry written in strophes, repeating the last word[48] or the last verse of a strophe in the following strophe, as one sees in the short poem below:[49]

> In ecclesia   sol iustitiae
> Sola gratia   *luxit hodie.*
>
> *Luxit hodie*   lumen coelitus,
> Et redemptus est   *homo perditus.*
>
> *Homo perditus*   restituitur
> Liber penitus   et efficitur.

One can compare to this, for example, the verse inversion used by Hugh of Orléans for the alternation of the rhymes in his poem 23. We read in verse thirty-one and the following,

> Sum deiectus in momento
> Rori datus atque vento.

45. *AH*, 50:53–56 (no. 52), 98–100 (no. 79); Fortunatus, *Carm.,* 3:30; Paul the Deacon, ed. Neff, 3. See Meyer, *Ges. Abh.,* 1:94.

46. *AH,* 50: nos. 80 and 81.

47. See Voigt in the preface to *Ysengrimus,* xxxvii.

48. In a rhymed office the antiphons are tied together in this way, *AH,* 18:123. In the Middle Ages one spoke of *versus anadiplositi,* see Meyer, *Ges. Abh.,* 1:93.

49. *AH,* 20: no. 247.

Vento datus atque rori
Vite prima turpiori. . . .

Compare, in addition, verses sixty-nine and seventy: *Pondus fero paupertatis*
et *Paupertatis fero pondus,* and seventy-eight and seventy-nine: *Victum quero*
verecundus and *Verecundus victum quero.*

We find something equivalent to the centoes of the end of antiquity in the
custom of inserting into hymns, at precise places in the strophes, the first
verses of famous hymns. This ordinarily develops as we see in the following
strophe written by Gaetani of Stephaneschi (d. 1343):[50]

O athleta victor, laeta,
    Georgi, fulgens laurea,
Te laudamus, hic ovamus,
    Lux, ecce, surgit aurea.

The last verse is borrowed from a song of Prudentius (Walpole, 121), and in
the same way each strophe of the hymn ends with a quotation. At the end of
the Middle Ages, this is a standard way of composing hymns; and the strophes, as in the above example, are most often composed of four verses with
alternative rhyme descending and ascending, 8p, 8pp, 8p, 8pp, in which the
last verse is borrowed from a familiar old hymn. One sometimes composes
in an analogous way strophes of another form. A Spanish breviary preserves,
for example, a Sapphic poem of which all the strophes begin and end with
one quotation, as we see by the first strophe below:[51]

Conditor alme   siderum qui palme
Sanctis das dona,   nobis et condona
Canere corda   vocibus concorda
    Ut queant laxis.

To conclude, let me point out that poets in the late Middle Ages also composed poems in which the first word of each strophe is borrowed from a
known text. William of Deguilleville, for example, wrote some songs of this
kind using the *Pater noster, Ave Maria,* and *Credo.*[52]

---

50. *AH,* 50: no. 406.

51. *AH,* 16: no. 299. See also ibid., nos. 300 and 301.

52. *AH,* 48: nos. 348, 349, 350, and 352. Dreves has published a collection of songs with
glosses, *AH,* 30:179–305 (nos. 82–167).

FIVE ▨ METRICAL VERSIFICATION

For reasons set forth in the introduction, the summary of quantitative verse that I will give in this chapter will be particularly brief. I will begin by saying a few words to explain the most common and the most important verse even in the Middle Ages, the dactylic hexameter. A few medieval poets know the different rules governing the construction of the hexameter so well that their verses, if they are not rhymed, are scarcely distinguishable from those of antiquity.[1] Other poets, by contrast, are insufficiently aware of the rules. The individual variations are numerous, and obviously we must study the metrics of each writer separately. We can get an idea of these variations by comparing the construction of the endings of the hexameters in the work of some poets of the ninth century. In the work of Heiric of Auxerre, a learned and erudite man who described in 2,928 hexameters the life of St. Germain,[2] we find only 3 cases of *versus spondiaci,* where, in each case, it is a matter of a 4-syllable word at the end of the verse.[3] Heiric, moreover, 35 times has words of 5 syllables or more at the end, and 14 times words of 4 syllables.[4] Only once do we find an isolated monosyllable at the end of the verse.[5] *Est,* which six times ends a verse—four times with elision[6]—is actually metrically dependent; and *quo, qua,* and *non* are also closely tied to the preceding monosyllables at the endings *ex*

Dactylic Hexameter ▨

1. Very classical, for example, are the verses of Nivardus, whose technique in *Ysengrimus* has been analyzed by Voigt; and there are parts of the poetry of Hildebert of Lavardin that for a long time were regarded as ancient.

2. *PLAC,* 3:438–517.

3. 1:126, 444; 2:282.

4. The four-syllable word is a proper noun, 4:413; it is preceded by a monosyllable, 1:36, 106, 339; 6:112, 343, 386, 395, 397, 541, 618; it is preceded by a polysyllable, 1:34, 384; 6:26.

5. 1:56 *alterius res.*

6. 3:327; 4:421; 6:319, 645 after a vowel, and 4:374; 6:96 after a consonant.

quo, si qua, and *nec non.*[7] In all the other cases, Heiric uses the normal end-
ings ‿∪∪ | ‿⌣ and ‿∪ | ∪‿⌣ .[8] It is in a quite different way that Can-
didus of Fulda proceeds in his *Vita Aeigili,* consisting of a total of 796 hexameters.[9] There is no spondaic verse; nine times the words at the end have five
syllables; and four times, four syllables.[10] By contrast, Candidus makes very
free use of monosyllables at the ends of verses. Taking Virgil as a model, he
constructed endings such as *audetque virum vir, procumbit humi mox* and
comminus atque hinc,[11] but starting from there he goes much further and
even ends his verses with *in unum et* and *canoro? At. . . .* In the verse ending
potenti in, the preposition governs a word placed at the beginning of the next
verse.[12] In other words, Candidus tried to imitate Virgil, but he did not observe the limits that Virgil set on his own use of monosyllables at the end of
the verse. Some other poets like Abbo of St. Germain-des-Prés (d. ca. 900)
understood well that it was necessary to avoid monosyllables at the end of
the verse; but, on the other hand, they made use of polysyllables without restriction.[13]

What above all influenced the structure of the hexameter of the Middle
Ages was the regular use of rhymes. The fixed form of
Leonine hexameter (Leonini) ▨ the Leonine hexameter *(Leonini)* caused, for example,
the obligatory use of the penthemimer break:

In terra summus ‖ rex est hoc tempore Nummus.

This caesura is thus the only principal break in the two poems in Leonine
rhymes that Engelmodus wrote, although in the third unrhymed poem he
uses certain variations.[14] In these 178 hexameters the penthemimer appears
in fact 166 times; the triple break (trihemimeris—the break at the third

7. 2:133; 3:191; 6:129.
8. See Nougaret, 42–43.
9. *PLAC,* 2:97–117.
10. 6:1; 10:20; 14:11, 20; 15:22; 16:5; 17:30, 72; 19:19; and 17:55, 57, 67, 87.
11. See 10:14; 17:33; 14:45; 24:12; 8:9; 24:4.
12. See 5:10; 10:58; 14:26; 17:82; 21:35; 10:47; 12:48; 14:52; 12:51; 14:4; 21:25.
13. In the first one hundred hexameters of his *Bella Parisiacae urbis* he uses twenty-four
times a word of four syllables at the end of the verse and fifteen times uses the ending ‿ | ∪
∪ | ‿⌣ *(pollet tibi consors).*
Munari gives a general idea of the structure of the medieval hexameter in *M. Valerii Bucolica,* 52–54.
14. *PLAC,* 3:55–66.

trochee—hephthemimer) appears ten times; the double break (trihemimeris—hephthemimer) appears once, and the double break (trochaic—trihemimeris) appears once [see Nougaret, pp. 28–31].[15] The unrhymed hexameter is, as we see here, quite uniform in its structure, but, even so, much more
varied than the rhymed hexameter.

In other kinds of rhymed hexameters other breaks are obligatory. Thus,
the kind of rhyme which the medieval theorists some-
Versus Trinini Salientes ▨ times call *versus trinini salientes* is standard enough, and
Marbod of Rennes (d. 1123) makes use of it in a well-
known poem which begins in this way:

> Stella maris, ‖ quae sola paris ‖ sine coniuge prolem,
> Iustitiae ‖ clarum specie ‖ super omnia solem.[16]

Here the trihemimeris and penthemimer are the obligatory breaks, and it
seems that the poet does not care whether there is a break in the third foot or
not (see verses like *Supplicium post iudicium removeto gehennae).* The trihemimeris and the penthemimer are obligatory breaks in this type of rhyme:

> Per te de ‖ sede ‖ sophia venit ad ima,
> Hinc rursum ‖ sursum ‖ trahis infima tu, via prima, [17]

where the author, Robert of Anjou (d. 1343), makes fun of the standard rule
according to which monosyllabic prepositions must not be placed before the
break (*te de* rhymes with *sede* in the first verse), and this because of the
rhyme. The same versifier shows in the same poem how one puts together
the rhyme in front of the penthemimer and the bucolic in the verses,

> Hortus conclusus, ‖ perfusus, ‖ messis abundans,
> Fons illibatus, ‖ signatus, ‖ flumen inundans.

He even gives some examples of still more complicated rhymes in the following verses:

---

15. The last two verses are 81 *Hocque deum Saturninum venerata decenti* and 166 *Ag-
minibus felixque frueris luce perenni,* where, however, it is possible to assume a penthemimer
after *felix.*

16. *AH,* 50: no. 302.

17. *AH,* 15: no. 98; see the imitation of this poem, ibid., 32: no. 117.

Tu requies, ‖ species, ‖ saties ‖ et manna saporis,
Nutrix, ‖ adiutrix, ‖ tutrix ‖ in agone laboris,
Tu libanus, ‖ platanus, ‖ clibanus ‖ per flamen ‖ amoris.
Balsamus ‖ et calamus, ‖ thalamus, ‖ spiramen ‖ odoris.

In the first and third verses, the breaks are trihemimeris, penthemimer, and hephthemimer, all embellished with rhymes; in the second and fourth verses the rhymes present the following breaks: a break after the first foot + the penthemimer, and the hephthemimer. All the verses are linked by a final rhyme. To this is added, in the third and fourth verse, a rhyme between *flamen* and *spiramen*, that is to say, after the fifth trochee.

The verses that we have just quoted show that poets did not hesitate, for the sake of rhyme, to disrupt entirely the ancient system of breaks in the hexameter. That happened principally in two sorts of variants. First of all, it was happening in the verses that were called *tripertiti dactylici* and

Tripertiti Dactylici ▨ that are quite frequent. Bernard of Morlas (12th cent.) wrote a famous poem of close to three thousand verses in this pattern:

Hora novissima, ‖ tempora pessima ‖ sunt, vigilemus.
Ecce minaciter ‖ imminet arbiter ‖ ille supremus:
Imminet, imminet, ‖ ut mala terminet, ‖ aequa coronet,
Recta remuneret, ‖ anxia liberet, ‖ aethera donet.[18]

In some verses of this type there are only dactyls, except in the last foot; and each verse is divided into three equal parts. These verses are even more similar to one another in the Adonic hexameter, composed of what

Adonici ▨ are called *Adonici*:

Dextera Christi, ‖ nos rapuisti ‖ de nece tristi,
Plasmata patris ‖ tollis ab atris ‖ laeta barathris.[19]

It is necessary to note that in *tripertiti dactylici* as in *Adonici* the accent coincides most often with the ictus. Here, in fact, it is a question of entirely new verses, which are distinguished from the ancient hexameter by

Versus Citocadi ▨ their structure. It is the same for *versus citocadi*, which one encounters very rarely and in which the hexameter is divided into two similar parts:

18. H.C. Hoskier, *De contemptu mundi by Bernard of Morval* (London, 1929).
19. *AH*, 18:8. See, ibid., 48: nos. 60 and 456.

Felices sint illae ‖ linguae, dicere mille
Quae poterunt tibi laudes: ‖ caeli culmine gaudes.[20]

Theorists of verse do not agree on two points: (1) if the break in the classical period corresponded to a true stop; and (2) to what degree it did so. One fact, however, is certain: the importance of the break as a metrical limit was greater in the Middle Ages than it had been previously. One sees it already in the use of rhyme before the break, and it is even more emphasized by the very common use of a *syllaba anceps* before a break. In this way Benedict of Aniane (9th cent.), in his *Praefatio Concordiae regularum,* which is composed of some sixty-one unrhymed hexameters, used one short syllable instead of a long six times before the penthemimer, five times before the hephthemimer, and two times before the trihemimeris.[21] Certain poets limit this liberty and

20. See Meyer, *Ges. Abh.,* 1:79–92, where the author gives a summary of medieval theory. He has grouped the hexameters according to the number of rhymes in each verse in the following way:

   I. *Caudati* with a single rhyme at the end of the verse, for example,

       Non est crimen amor, quia si scelus esset amare,
       Nollet amore Deus etiam divina ligare.

   II. *Leonine hexameters,* of which I have spoken above.
      Collaterales, two hexameters with crossed rhymes, *abab,* for example,

       In commune precum ‖ demus communia vota,
       Nos velit ut secum ‖ summa pia gratia tota.

      Cruciferi, two hexameters with rhymes in envelope form, *abba:*

       Angelico verbo ‖ castus tuus intumet alvus,
       Ut fieret salvus ‖ homo tentus ab hoste superbo.

      Unisoni with continuous rhymes, *aaaa:*

       Festa sonans mando, ‖ cum funere proelia pando,
       meque fugit, quando ‖ resono, cum fulmine grando.

      Citocadi, see above.

  III. *Trinini salientes,*
      Tripertiti dactylici,
      Adonici, of which I have spoken above.

  IV. Verses with four rhymes.

  V. Verses with five rhymes. See the hexameter of Robert of Anjou above.

21. *PLAC,* 6:167–69. For the use of the *syllaba anceps* in antiquity, see Fr. Vollmer, *Zur Geschichte des lat. Hexameters,* Sitzungsberichte der Bayer. Akad. der Wissenschaften, Philos.-philol. und hist. Klasse, 1917; the medieval usage is discussed by Munari, *M. Valerii Bucolica,* 50.

make use of it only before the penthemimer. We see that Walter of Châtillon, in his *Alexandreis,* uses one short syllable instead of a long several hundred times in this position, but only twice before a trihemimeris, three times before a hephthemimer, and once before a bucolic.[22] As one can expect, the use of *syllaba anceps* before the penthemimer is particularly frequent in Leonine hexameters.[23]

From the end of antiquity on, there is a certain tendency to group hexameters in pairs, following the model of the distich. One sees examples of it already in the work of Commodian.[24] In the Middle Ages, Florus of Lyons (d. 860) brings verses together in pairs in this way in one poem, in groups of four in another poem.[25] Reginald of Canterbury (d. after 1109) brings together groups of three or four.[26] To this one can compare more sporadic attempts to replace the distich by two hexameters + a pentameter,[27] or by three hexameters + a pentameter,[28] not to mention other combinations.

Pentameter As for the pentameter of the Middle Ages, I can limit myself to pointing out that, in most of the poets, one finds many instances of a *syllaba anceps* at the break, and there is often also a hiatus at the break.[29]

Iambic Dimeter The iambic dimeter, which became, thanks to St. Ambrose, the most common verse in hymns, also suffered a few changes of structure. As for the use of disyllabic words at the end of the verse, one can make some interesting observations. Horace in his epodes placed disyllabic words in that position in almost half of his iambic dimeters; this practice is more and more avoided at the end of antiquity. Some poets such as St. Ambrose and Prudentius (4th cent.) are still quite close to the ancient models when they make their dimeters end with a disyllabic word in a third or a quarter of their verses. However, in Sedulius' hymn *A solis ortus cardine* (5th cent.) the figure falls to one ninth: his ninety-two verses end in four cases

---

22. See Christensen, 57–58.

23. See Meyer, *Ges. Abh.,* 1:76, and Seiler, 155, for comment on the *syllaba anceps* in *Ruodlieb.*

24. See Meyer, *Ges. Abh.,* 2:39–43.   25. *PLAC,* 2:524–30 and 559–64.

26. *AH,* 50:370–83 (nos. 287–93).

27. As does Godfrey of Viterbo (12th cent.) in several poems which have been published in *MGH, Scriptores,* 22.

28. Auson., *Epigr.,* 38 (ed. Schenkl, 206), *Anthologia Latina,* 487; *PLAC,* 1:248, 283; 2:222; *AH,* 18:139 and 141; 26:154.

29. See, for example, the remarks of Traube, *PLAC,* 3:817, and of Strecker, *PLAC,* 4:1163.

with a disyllabic word preceded by a monosyllable (for example, *fit Dei*), and in 6 cases by a disyllabic word preceded by a disyllable or a polysyllable. To just about the same time period belongs the collection of hymns known to the bishops Caesarius and Aurelian of Arles (6th cent.). In this collection there are several hymns in which final disyllabic words are entirely, or almost entirely, banished. The same is true for the hymn *Perfectum trinum numerum*.[30] The hymns *Deus qui caeli lumen es*, strophes 1–6, *Aeterne lucis conditor*, *Iam sexta sensim volvitur*, *Deus qui certis legibus*, and *Sator princepsque temporum*[31] seem to present 12 cases, out of a total of 128 verses; but these 12 cases in reality ought to be treated as final polysyllables. In fact, in these 12 cases what we have is a final iambic or pyrrhic word preceded by a monosyllable; and as I have emphasized previously (in Chapter 1), the combination *qui polum, iam tegit*, and the like can form a metrical unit and be treated in the same way as a single word of the type $\_\cup\!\underline{\cup}$.[32] Even in the Middle Ages it is common to avoid disyllabic words at the ends of iambic verses. One cannot find any instance of a final disyllabic word in the hymn of Fortunatus *Vexilla regis* with the exception of the verse *Regnavit a ligno Deus*, which is a quotation from the Bible; nor in the hymn in honor of St. Leucadia that was composed at Toledo, perhaps by Eugenius;[33] nor at all in the *Laudem beati martyris* of Walafrid Strabo,[34] to mention only a few examples. It is, of course, not impossible to find in all the poetry of the Middle Ages some iambic dimeters of a more classical construction. And so in his hymn to St. Benedict, Paul the Deacon[35] uses final disyllables in the same proportion as Prudentius (16 cases in 64 verses, of which only 2 are preceded by a monosyllable).

The second case of structural change about which we wish to speak is the use of the break in the middle of the iambic dimeter. As Meyer has shown,[36] certain poets more or less avoid this break. Thus in Prudentius' *Peris-*

---

30. *AH*, 51: no. 15.   31. *AH*, 51: nos. 5, 7, 16, 18, and 19.

32. It is very interesting to compare how many times the disyllabic word is preceded by a monosyllable in the works of different authors. In Horace 10% of the disyllabic words at the end of the verse are preceded by a monosyllable, and in Prudentius the figure is the same. In the four hymns of St. Ambrose that according to the testimomy of St. Augustine are authentic, about 30% of the disyllables follow a monosyllable; in the work of Sedulius about 35% of the disyllables follow a monosyllable; and in the hymns mentioned above 100%.

33. *AH*, 27: no. 148. J. Perez de Urbel has discussed the question of authenticity in *Bulletin Hispanique*, 28 (1926): 119.

34. *AH*, 50: no. 124.   35. Ed. Neff, 35–37.

36. Meyer, *Ges. Abh.*, 3:15–23. See also Brandes in *Rheinisches Museum* 64 (1909): 59–67.

tephanon, 5, one finds only 7 examples of this break in a song of 576 verses. On the other hand, St. Ambrose and Sedulius, whose example will be followed by most of the authors of hymns, allow the dimeters in 20 to 25 percent of the verses to be broken in this way into two equal parts. In the Carolingian period, the author of *Versus de eversione monasterii Glonnensis* goes even farther in this direction. In almost half of the cases, he uses verses of the type *Dulces modos* ‖ *et carmina Praebe, lyra* ‖ *Treicia,* and Rupert of Deutz does the same at the end of the eleventh century.[37]

Iambic dimeters are often put together in groups of two. Such is the case in the song of Ausonius, *Ephemeris,* 2 (Schenkl, p. 4); and in the works of St. Ambrose and other hymn writers, it is often the case that, in each strophe of 4 verses, there is a longer pause in the phrase after verse 2 than after verses 1 or 3.[38]

Iambic Trimeter ▨ The same changes of structure that are found in the iambic dimeter are also found in the iambic trimeter. One finds again an abundance of final disyllabic words in the work of Ausonius (9 cases in 21 verses in the song 16:16), in the work of Prudentius (45 cases in 220 verses in *Cathemerinon,* 7), or in the song 1:31–33 of Martianus Capella (9 cases in 31 verses). This last poet, however, in his other iambic trimeters, shows some restraint in his use of disyllables at the end of verses (9 cases in 127 verses).[39] In the Middle Ages, in the work of Eugenius of Toledo, for example in songs 14 and 20, we do not find any cases in 64 verses; in the works of Braulio of Saragossa, we do not find any in 80 verses.[40] In the eleventh century Alphanus of Salerno has only 2 cases in 72 verses, and one of those cases is preceded by a monosyllable.[41]

In the work of Martianus Capella, Eugenius, Braulio, and Alphanus the break is always a penthemimer, and it is very rare to find another kind of caesura in the Middle Ages.[42] In general they avoid monosyllables before the break, as at the end of the verse.

37. *PLAC,* 2:147–49, and *MGH, Libelli de lite,* 3:637–39.

38. On this subject, see Meyer, *Ges. Abh.,* 2:119, n. 1, and Becker, *Der gepaarte Achtsilber,* 5–6. However, Meyer was wrong to think that there was an influence from rhythmic poetry. It was, on the contrary, the authors of rhythmic poems who borrowed this grouping of verses from metrical poetry.

39. 2:120, 219–220; 3:289; 4:423; 5:566; 9:913–914; 9:997–1000.

40. *MGH, Auctores antiquissimi,* 14:243 and 247; *AH,* 27: no. 87.

41. *AH,* 22: nos. 321 and 322.

42. One finds some exceptions in the following hymns: *AH,* 27: nos. 29 and 33; 11: no. 161; 16: no. 119.

In hymns that were composed in iambic trimeters, strophes often have 5 verses. One can, however, in rare cases, find strophes of 4 verses.[43]

It is important to point out that at the end of the Roman period several poets, including St. Hilary of Poitiers and Ausonius, wrote archaic senarii in which not only the first, the third, and the fifth iamb, but even the second and the fourth could be replaced by a spondee.[44] The ordinary scheme of the classical iambic trimeter is the following: ◡ _ ◡ _ ◡ ‖ _ ◡ _ ◡ _ ◡ _ ; that of the archaic senarius is ◡ _ ◡ _ ◡ ‖ _ ◡ _ ◡ _ ◡◡ .

One also finds at the end of antiquity two types of iambic dimeters: on the one hand, the classical dimeter of the type ◡ _ ◡ _ ◡ _ ◡ _ ; on the other hand, the archaic dimeter of the type ◡ _ ◡ _ ◡ _ ◡_ , in which the second iamb can also be replaced by a spondee; so in the hymn that we previously discussed *Deus qui caeli lumen es,* in strophes 1–6, the third syllable is long 13 times in 24; in *Aeterne lucis conditor,* 16 times in 24; in *Deus qui certis legibus,* 9 times in 20; in *Sator princepsque temporum,* 7 times in 20; and similar cases are also found later in the Middle Ages.[45]

On this subject I want to point out that it is relatively rare for a long syllable to break down into two short syllables. Still, St. Ambrose gives a few examples of it, such as *Geminae gigas substantiae,* with an anapest in the first foot, or *Omnia per ipsum facta sunt,* with a dactyl in the first foot.[46] But after St. Ambrose and Prudentius one rarely encounters examples of this sort (this is as true for classical iambic verse as for archaic iambic verse).

Although Prudentius, in *Cultor Dei memento, Cathe-*

Catalectic Iambic Dimeter ▨ *merinon,* 6, produced an example of it, the catalectic iambic dimeter, ◡ _ ◡ _ ◡ _ ◡ , appears only rarely. A song of this type is found in the collection of Mozarabic hymns, *Assunt tenebrae primae;* and at Poitiers on Easter Sunday, they sang *Tibi laus, peren-*

---

43. See, e.g., *AH,* 27: nos. 29 and 33; 16: no. 119; 4: nos. 391, 411, and 430; 22: no. 322.

44. This occurs in the poem of Ausonius *Ludus septem sapientium* and in the hymn *Fefellit saevam* of St. Hilary, whose form has been analyzed by Meyer, *Ges. Abh.,* 3:164–65. See also Meyer, *Ges. Abh.,* 2:345.

45. It is important to analyze the quantity of the third syllable in the iambic dimeter, as Meyer has shown, *Ges. Abh.,* 3:325. In *Studi e testi,* 12 (1904): 25, Mercati had attributed to St. Ambrose the hymn *Ignis creator igneus* (*AH,* 51: no. 226). However, Meyer noticed that in this hymn the third syllable is long 18 times in 32 verses, that is to say, that the structure of this hymn is archaic. Since St. Ambrose writes only dimeters of the classical type, he cannot be the author of this hymn.

46. *AH,* 50: nos. 8 (5.3) and 9 (6.1).

nis auctor, Baptismatis sacrator.[47] Only in the first verse of the latter song is
there an anapest in the first foot. But an anapest in this posi-

Anacreontic Meter ▓ tion is the rule in Anacreontic meter, $\cup \cup \_ \cup \_ \cup \_ \cup$,
which was used by Martianus Capella and other authors
writing at the end of the Roman Empire. Later, one finds this verse again in a
song attributed to Prosper of Aquitaine, of which this is the first strophe:

> Age iam precor mearum
> Comes inremota rerum,
> Trepidam brevemque vitam
> Domino Deo dicemus.[48]

In the Carolingian period, Walafrid Strabo and Gottschalk of Orbais imitated this meter in some of their songs.[49]

A very important role was played in the Middle Ages by the trochaic verse
composed of a catalectic tetrameter and often called the

Trochaic Septenarius ▓ trochaic septenarius. With regard to its structure I want first
to emphasize that even in this case the end of the verse was
standardized because poets avoided placing disyllabic words there. A poet
with classical tendencies such as Prudentius writes, for example, in *Cathemerinon, 9, Da puer plectrum choraeis ut canam fidelibus,* final disyllabic
words 21 times (of which 2 are preceded by a monosyllable) in 114 verses. But
in 29 verses of St. Hilary of Poitiers, one does not find a single case, nor in the
23 verses of Ennodius, nor in the 21 verses of Dracontius.[50] The same holds
true in the the Middle Ages. Eugenius of Toledo, Rabanus Maurus, Walafrid
Strabo, and most of the other writers completely avoid the use of final disyllables.[51] The exceptions to the rule are exceptions in appearance only. Such is
the case of verse 8, 2 of the hymn to St. Eulalia by Quiricus of Barcelona (d.
ca. 666) where we have *tam pium* at the end. In one of his songs, Smaragdus
of St. Mihiel (9th cent.) ends verse 7, 3 in the same way by *hos beas,* and verse
8, 1 by *sint dii.*[52] Indeed, as we have emphasized, a monosyllable and a pyrrhic

---

47. *AH,* 27: no. 72; 50: no. 70. See also Sedulius Scottus, *PLAC,* 3:161.

48. This song has been published by Hartel, *CSEL,* 30:344.

49. *PLAC,* 2:412, and 3:733; see also the long poem in a Bern codex, *PLAC,* 4:246–48. For
songs written in Anacreontic meter during the imperial era, see J. Wagner, 12–13.

50. St. Hilary, *Adae carnis gloriosae,* Meyer, *Ges. Abh.,* 3:166; Ennodius, ed. Vogel, 199, 242,
277, 313; Dracontius, *Romul.,* 1. See J. Wagner, 15.

51. See, e.g., Eugenius, song 5, and *PLAC,* 2:235 and 405.

52. *AH,* 27: no. 116, and *PLAC,* 1:619.

or iambic word are often joined to form only one single metrical word carrying only one principal accent.

The trochaic septenarius is divided, almost without exception, into two parts by a break in the middle of the verse. To this break is often added a secondary break after the first dipody in the first hemistich. Ancient comedy was already familiar with the septenarius of this type: *Scis amorem,* ǁ *scis laborem,* ǁ *scis egestatem meam,*[53] where a triple anaphora emphasizes the threefold division of the verse. This phenomenon has been dealt with often, and it has been pointed out that verses of this type enjoyed a great popularity at Rome.[54] After the death of the orator L. Licinius Crassus in 91 B.C., the Romans engraved, for example, the verse *Postquam Crassus* ǁ *carbo factus,* ǁ *Carbo crassus factus est.* A few verses of the same type, borrowed from some songs of the Roman soldiers, have been preserved for us. Here is a specimen:

Caesar Gallias subegit, ǁ Nicomedes Caesarem;
Ecce Caesar ǁ nunc triumphat, ǁ qui subegit Galliam,
Nicomedes ǁ non triumphat, ǁ qui subegit Caesarem.[55]

The last two verses have a secondary break after the first dipody, as does the first verse of the refrain that Martianus Capella repeats in his songs 2:117–25:

Scande caeli ǁ templa virgo ǁ digna tanto foedere:
Te socer subire celsa ǁ poscit astra Iuppiter.

It must be pointed out that in all these verses, which were intended to be sung while on the march or in a chorus, the accents coincide with the ictus.

It is thus natural that the same secondary break was used in the trochaic septenarius of processional hymns of the Middle Ages.[56] It is also natural that the refrains too show this secondary break. Walafrid Strabo wrote some poems in trochaic septenarii in which the secondary break is missing in nearly half of the verses.[57] But in the refrains *Imperator* ǁ *magne, vivas* ǁ *semper et*

---

53. Plautus, *Pseud.*, 695.
54. See Eduard Fraenkel, "Die Vorgeschichte des Versus Quadratus," *Hermes* 62 (1927): 357–70; Schlicher, 33–38; Herman Usener, "Reim in der Altlateinischen Poesie," Chap. 24 in *Kleine Schriften,* 4 vols. (Leipzig: B. B. Teubner, 1912–13; reprint, Osnabrück: Proff & Co. KG, 1965), 2:255–58.
55. Suetonius, *Divus Iulius,* 49.
56. See, e.g., *AH,* 51: nos. 77, 132, and 167–169.
57. *PLAC,* 2:405–6.

feliciter and *Salve regum* ‖ *sancta proles,* ‖ *care Christo Carole,* there is a secondary break, which must not be a matter of chance.

In the rest of Christian poetry, its usage varies. The poets with classical tendencies are obviously not concerned with the secondary break. Thus in the work of Prudentius, *Cathemerinon,* 9, one finds only 34 secondary breaks in 114 verses. The example given by Prudentius is followed by many other writers, among others, authors of hymns of Visigothic Spain, such as Eugenius (8 cases in 30 verses, in song 5) or Quiricus (6 cases in 42 verses). On the other hand, St. Hilary of Poitiers in his *Adae carnis gloriosae et caduci corporis,* and some other writers after him made the break obligatory,[58] which, as we will see later, was of great importance in rhythmic poetry. Venantius Fortunatus adopts an intermediate solution when, in his hymn *Pange lingua,* he uses the secondary break in 21 verses of 30.

Poets normally observe the rule of not placing monosyllables before the medial break or before the secondary break.

Besides the ordinary classical type of the trochaic septenarius _∪_∪_ ∪_∪‖_∪_∪_∪∪, one encounters also, at the end of antiquity and in the Middle Ages, an archaic type in which the first, the third, and the fifth trochee can also be replaced with a spondee _ ∪_ ∪_ ∪_ ∪‖_ ∪_ ∪_∪∪. For example, the hymn of St. Hilary *Adae carnis gloriosae* is archaic: the first foot is a trochee 10 times, a spondee 19 times; the third foot is a trochee 14 times, a spondee 15 times; the fifth foot is a trochee 10 times, a spondee 18 times. The same thing occurs in the hymn *Hymnum dicat turba fratrum,* which dates from the end of antiquity and in which, according to Meyer,[59] the first foot is a trochee 56 times, a spondee 12 times; the third foot is a trochee 61 times, a spondee 7 times; the fifth foot is a trochee 34 times, a spondee 34 times. We find the same structure, to take an example from the Middle Ages, in a hymn *De santo Gisleno,*[60] in which the first foot is a trochee 10 times, a spondee 14 times; the third foot is a trochee 11 times, a spondee 13 times; the fifth foot is a trochee 7 times, a spondee 17 times.

It is interesting to note that in the trochaic septenarius of the archaic type, at the end of antiquity, the rule about dipodies was still being observed[61]

58. See Meyer, *Ges. Abh.,* 3:171.

59. Meyer, *Ges. Abh.,* 2:346–47.

60. *AH,* 12: nos. 219–20. Meyer gives, loc. cit., other examples of this phenomenon in the Middle Ages.

61. See Nougaret, 71: "Demi-pieds purs et demi-pieds condensés" [Pure half-feet and compressed half-feet].

whereas poets in general forgot it in the Middle Ages. For the poets of late antiquity, this rule implied that a spondaic word or a word that ended with a spondee was not supposed to be placed before the fourth nor before the twelfth half-foot (it was impossible to place a word of that form before the eighth since at the end of antiquity poets normally avoided a monosyllable before the medial break which had become obligatory).[62] In other words, one was not supposed to place at the beginning of the verse nor at the beginning of the second hemistich words of the metrical type _ | _ _ or _ _ _. Verses such as the following _ _ _ | ∪_∪_∪ | _ _ _ | ∪ _ ∪∪ were thus prohibited. This rule is rigorously respected by St. Hilary of Poitiers and the unknown author of the hymn *Hymnum dicat turba fratrum*. In contrast, in the hymn *De sancto Gisleno*, composed at the beginning of the Middle Ages, we see that the septenarius begins 4 times with forms like *Indūlgēns culparum actis*, or *Qui vītām duxit pudicus*. At the beginning of the second hemistich the rule is violated 8 times, for example, in the verse *Tam clerus quam praesens vulgus* ‖ *dēvōtī persolvimus* and *Nunctius salutis factus* ‖ *quōs mīsīt coelestibus*.

The last part of the trochaic septenarius has a metrical form entirely similar to the last part of the iambic senarius. After the medial break, namely, after the penthemimer, both verse forms are composed of seven syllables which in archaic poetry present themselves in the following way: _ ∪_ ∪ _ ∪∪. Even in the iambic senarius, we find in the Middle Ages verses such as *Plebs omnis sancta,* ‖ *cōnvēntūs ecclesiae,* containing words which have the metrical form of _ _ _ or of _ | _ _ after the break and in which, therefore, the rule mentioned above is forgotten. We find ourselves here in the presence of a characteristic that differentiated the verse of the Middle Ages from Late-Latin verse, one that was extremely important for the corresponding rhythmic verses.[63]

One curious mistake in interpretation of the metrics of the trochaic septenarius was committed by St. Bede who maintained[64] that the spondee

62. Likewise, the poets who regularly use a secondary break after the first dipody cannot place a spondaic word before the fourth half-foot: _ _ _ | ∪ ‖ ... is an impossible structure because of the monosyllable before the break. St. Hilary of Poitiers can therefore do violence to the rule given above only before the twelfth half-foot.

63. See Meyer, *Ges. Abh.*, 2:345–46, and my article "L'origine de la versification latine rythmique," 86–87.

64. Beda, *De re metrica, Grammatici Latini*, 7:258.

could be placed everywhere except in the third foot, which therefore, according to him, always had to be a trochee. It is, however, interesting to point out that the influence of Bede was such that a good number of poets, among others Rabanus Maurus, Walafrid Strabo, and Hincmar of Reims, adopted this theory and wrote archaic septenarii in which the third foot is always a trochee.[65]

We find another more accidental variant of the scheme of the septenarius in the work of Sedulius Scottus, who attempted to use only trochees, even in the second and sixth foot, where spondees were allowed in the classical form.[66]

To close this section I note that trochaic septenarii are customarily grouped in strophes of two or, more often, three verses.

Phalaecean or Hendecasyllabic Verse 🔲 During antiquity, Phalaecean or hendecasyllabic verse enjoyed a remarkable popularity. It is curious, therefore, that it is rarely found in the Middle Ages. After Prudentius, poets most often group the hendecasyllables in strophes.[67]

Sapphic Verse 🔲 In contrast, Sapphic verse is as common in the Middle Ages as in antiquity. Its structure is ordinarily that which appears in the well-known hymn attributed to Paul the Deacon; here is the beginning:

Ut queant laxis resonare fibris
Mira gestorum famuli tuorum,
Solve polluti labii reatum,
    Sancte Johannes.[68]

Here the fourth syllable is long, and the break always comes after the fifth syllable. Moreover, monosyllables are excluded from the end of the verse and

65. *PLAC*, 2:235, 245, 406; 3:415; and 4:491. See Meyer, *Ges. Abh.*, 2:348–50.

66. See Meyer, *Ges. Abh.*, 2:352. The trochaic septenarii of Sedulius have been published by Traube, *PLAC*, 3:159, 165, 218.

67. The following authors wrote strophes of four Phalaecean verses: Walafrid Strabo, *PLAC*, 2:276, 362, 391, songs in which Dümmler failed to group the strophes, and ibid., 367; Florus of Lyons, *PLAC*, 2:544–45; Wandalbert of Prüm, ibid., 574–75; Ademar of Chabannes, *AH*, 48: no. 7. There are, of course, also, those who, following in the style of Prudentius, *Cathemerinon*, 4, and *Peristephanon*, 6, composed some strophes of three verses; see, e.g., *PLAC*, 4:337 and 433. Heiric of Auxerre has some strophes of 6 verses, *PLAC*, 3:432–36.

68. *AH*, 50: no. 96.

before the break. It is only in rare cases that one has strophes in the Middle Ages such as this one:

> Caritas praeclara tonantis, atque
> Ardor et communio trinitatis
> Cuncta virtus rite regens, potens lex
>   agmina caeli,

where we see a poet of the Carolingian period, on the one hand, not take into account the common system in use for the breaks and, on the other hand, place a monosyllable at the end of the third verse. He saw in the classical models that the position of the break could vary, and he likewise noticed that the third verse could, with the Adonic, form a metrical unity.[69]

Poets do occasionally use the Sapphic verse stichically following the model provided by Boethius, among others.[70]

Adonic ▨   The Adonic, which ordinarily serves as a clausula in the Sapphic strophe, is also used by itself by Martianus Capella and other poets at the end of antiquity.[71] Poets of the Middle Ages often write poems completely in Adonics which can be placed stichically[72] or grouped in strophes of 4, 5, 6, or 7 verses.[73] They are most often constructed as the endings of hexame-

---

69. *PLAC*, 2:244–45. When the poet places a monosyllabic preposition at the end of the third verse, e.g., in strophe 12:

> membra supponit capiti, caput cum
> corpore iungit,

he has followed classical examples such as Horace, *Carm.*, 3:8, 3. See Nougaret, 107.

70. Boethius, *Consolatio Philosophiae*, 2:6 and 4:7; *PLAC*, 4:334; *AH*, 50: no. 260; Liutprand of Cremona, Migne, *PL*, 136:865.

71. See J. Wagner, 19.

72. See *PLAC*, 1:69; 4:425, 431; 5:453, 483; *AH*, 13:160; Benzo of Alba, *MGH, Scriptores*, 11:649; Dudo of St. Quentin, Migne, *PL*, 141:618; Rupert of Deutz, *MGH, Libelli de lite*, 3:629; Gislebert in *S. Anselmi opera omnia*, ed. Schmitt, 5 (1951): 309–10; Hildebert of Lavardin, *Physiologus*, Migne, *PL*, 171:1223; Guibert of Nogent, ibid., 156:720–21; Saxo Grammaticus, 1:4, 3–7; an English poet in Wright, *The Anglo-Latin Satirical Poets*, 2:170–71. See also Traube, *PLAC*, 3:724, n. 1.

73. One finds some poems written in strophes of 4 verses, e.g., *PLAC*, 2:394, 418; 4:1079, 1102, 1106; *AH*, 26:192; in strophes of 5 verses *PLAC*, 4:334; in strophes of 6 verses *PLAC*, 1:266, 303; 2:257, 575; 3:724, 737; 4:608, 421; 6:140; *AH*, 11: nos. 8, 42, 334, 335, and 336; 17:160; 48: no. 10; in strophes of 7 verses *AH*, 12: no. 101; 13: no. 97; Wright, *The Anglo-Latin Satirical Poets*, 166. In the last case, the Adonics form a pseudo-Sapphic strophe; see *AH*, 13: no. 97:

> Tyro beatus   mansit humatus,
> Non putrefactus,   qui bona nactus

ters, that is to say, with a break after the second or the third syllable. However, some poets use forms like *Virginitatis, Purpureus flos,* or *Hinc meruisti.*[74]

Terentianean Verse ▨ Before talking about the ordinary Asclepiads we need to mention a type of verse that appeared for the first time in the work of Terentianus Maurus (around 180 A.D.) and Martianus Capella [75] and that was used as early as the middle of the fifth century by an unknown author who lived in Italy and wrote, among other hymns, the one mentioned by Bede.[76] Here is the first strophe:

Squalent arva soli pulvere multo,
Pallet siccus ager, terra fatiscit,
Nullus ruris honos, nulla venustas,
Quando nulla viret gratia florum.[77]

As the above strophe shows, the new verse is constructed in the following way: _ _ _ ∪∪◡ ‖ _∪∪_ ◡, that is to say that it is composed of a half-Asclepiad + an Adonic. Sometimes one finds a *syllaba anceps* or a hiatus before the break.[78] This type of verse was much in favor in the Middle Ages. It was used, among others, by Rabanus Maurus, Candidus, Wandalbert of Prüm, Sedulius Scottus, Hucbald of St. Amand and many other poets of the Carolingian period,[79] and finally by Alphanus of Salerno, Hildebert of Lavardin, Baudri of Bourgueil, and Alan of Lille and their contemporaries.[80] Baudri (d. 1130) constructed some strophes which are composed of 4 verses of the new type + an Adonic. Another curious stophe made from 2 verses + 2 Adonics is found in a hymn *De sancto Gendulfo*[81] where the first strophe is,

---

Reddit ovantes   et jubilantes
          Se venerantes.

74. *AH,* 17:161.   75. See J. Wagner, 28.
76. *De arte metrica, Grammatici Latini,* 7:255.
77. *AH,* 27: no. 204. It is probably the same poet who composed hymns 203 and 206 of the same collection. They were all written in Italy in the fifth century, as Raby has shown, *Medium Aevum,* 16 (1947): 1–5 (see also hymn 205). But hymns 200, 201, and 202, written in the same verse, come from Spain and belong to the Visigothic or Mozarabic period; their metrics is entirely different and much more rough.
78. See *AH,* 27: nos. 203 (2.1, 3.4, 5.4), 204 (3.4), 10 (2), and 205 (5.1).
79. *PLAC,* 2:204–5, 96, 112, vv. 124–27, 573; 3:158, 169; 4:273; *AH,* 51: no. 171, and moreover, *PLAC,* 4:254–56, 997, 1074; 5:494–95.
80. Migne, *PL,* 147:1256, 1260; *AH,* 50: no. 322; Baudri of Bourgueil, ed. Phyllis Abrahams, 247:356; Migne, *PL,* 210:460–61.
81. *AH,* 43: no. 258 (1).

Inter caelicolas aetheris omnes
Qui summae renites lampadis instar,
   Nostra, beate, nubila pelle.

Most of the time, however, the strophes are composed of 3[82] or 4[83] verses.

Boethius used the same verse again in his song 1:2, but he there allowed himself verses such as *Mens hebet et propria luce relicta, Tendit in externas ire tenebras,* or *Hic quondam caelo liber aperto.* Boethius' verse is therefore constructed in this way: _‿‿ _ ‿‿‿ || _‿‿_ ‿, that is, it is composed of a half-hexameter + an Adonic. The example given by Boethius was followed in the Carolingian period by Dungal among others and later by Erchanbald of Strasbourg, Liutprand of Cremona, Benzo of Alba, Dudo of St. Quentin, Rupert of Deutz, Saxo Grammaticus, and the anonymous authors of a certain number of hymns.[84]

Asclepiad ▨   In the Middle Ages, the ordinary Asclepiad is as common as before; and we find it, on the one hand, in hymns, and, on the other hand, in the works of poets with classical tendencies. The break is almost always fixed after the seventh syllable, as in the work of Prudentius: *Inventor rutili,* || *dux bone, luminis.*[85] In his song *Cathemerinon,* 5, from which the quoted verse is taken, Prudentius places a disyllabic word before the break 36 times, and at the end of the verse 25 times (the poem is composed of 164 verses). In the work of Walafrid Strabo, in a poem of 24 verses, the corresponding figures are 5 and 2; in Alphanus of Salerno, in a poem of 36 verses, the figures are 8 and 12.[86] It would be easy to show that quite a few writers are not afraid to put disyllables in Asclepiad verses before the metrical pause. But there are, moreover, quite a few poets who try, even in this meter, to end before the break and at the end of the verse with trisyllabic or polysyllabic words. Thus the hymn *Assunt, o populi, festa celebria,*[87] in which one never

---

82. *AH,* 4: no. 110; 12: no. 120; 23: no. 278; 51: no. 183; and 52: no. 369.

83. *AH,* 4: no. 453; 11: nos. 26, 117, 174, 184, 209, 370, 452; 12: nos. 142, 223, 301; 14: no. 32; 16: nos. 70, 71, 72, 412; 19: nos. 117, 210, 254, 260, 261, 268, 498; 23: nos. 305, 352, 390; 33: no. 175; 43: nos. 64, 241, 261; 51: no. 126.

84. *PLAC,* 1:412; 5:514; Migne, *PL,* 136:821; *MGH, Scriptores,* 11:668; Migne, *PL,* 141:617, 683–84, 726–27; *MGH, Libelli de lite,* 3:629, 641; Saxo, 1:6, 5; 5:11, 4; *AH,* 11: nos. 108 and 142; 12: no. 402; 4: no. 96; 19: nos. 114, 211, 221.

85. The exceptions are rare: see, e.g., Alphanus of Salerno, *AH,* 50: no. 259 (8) *Extollens Catharinae niveum decus.*

86. *PLAC,* 2:275; *AH,* 22: no. 348.

87. *AH,* 27: no. 127. See on this hymn J. Perez de Urbel in *Bulletin hispanique,* 28 (1926): 220.

finds disyllables, neither before the caesura, nor at the end of the verse, has been attributed to Eugenius of Toledo. The same absence of disyllables can be found in many other hymns or poems from different countries and of different time periods.

The Asclepiad is used stichically or grouped in strophes. The most common is the best known of Horace's strophes, composed of 3 Asclepiads followed by a Glyconic, but sometimes one also finds strophes composed of two Asclepiads, a Pherecratean, and a Glyconic.[88] The third form of the Asclepiadean strophe, which Horace uses in *Sic te diva potens Cypri, Sic fratres Helenae lucida sidera,* where Glyconics and Asclepiads alternate, is used by St. Hilary of Poitiers in the hymn *Ante saecula qui manes,*[89] but later it is found only in isolated cases of authors directly influenced by Horace or St. Hilary.[90] In the poetic preface to his poems Prudentius also created an Asclepiadean strophe, composed of a Glyconic + a minor Asclepiad + a major Asclepiad:

> Per quinquennia iam decem,
> Ni fallor, fuimus, septimus insuper
> Annum cardo rotat, dum fruimur sole volubili.

88. Alphanus of Salerno uses, in his song *Ad Gosfrit,* Migne, *PL,* 147:1258, some strophes of 2 Asclepiads + a Pherecratean. Here is the first strophe:

> Gosfrit pontificum laetitiae penus,
> Perlongus valeas, usque tibi mala
> Possint nulla nocere.

His model must have been,

> Alleluia piis edite laudibus
> Cives aetherei, psallite naviter
> Alleluia perenne,

(*AH,* 27: no. 19) where the Pherecratean *Alleluia perenne* is used as a refrain in each strophe.

89. The versification of St. Hilary of Poitiers is very curious. As Meyer has shown, *Ges. Abh.,* 3:154–57, he often used iambic dimeters of an archaic structure in place of Glyconics; in addition, he often replaced the Asclepiads with iambic senarii or with Alcaic hendecasyllables. We have very few comparable instances. In the work of Ausonius, *Epist.,* 14, the pentameter of the last distich is replaced with an iambic trimeter (see song 66 of Eugenius of Toledo); in the work of Boethius, 3:10, the Sapphics were mixed with Phalaeceans (see also *PLAC,* 4:260, v. 39). One can also compare the mixture of different verses in a hymn by Odo of Cluny (d. 942), *AH,* 50: no. 202, and in the song on the death of Hubert (11th cent.), Du Méril, *Poésies populaires* (1843), 292–93.

90. See Alphanus of Salerno, *AH,* 22: nos. 348 and 412; Rupert of Deutz, *MGH, Libelli de lite,* 3:631; John of Garland, *AH,* 50: no. 380.

Pherecrateans ▨   This strophic form, and others, were used by Wandalbert of Prüm,[91] who also wrote some poems entirely in Pherecrateans, arranged in this way:

Simplex purus et unus
Summae fons bonitatis,
Aevi principioque
Verbo cuncta creante.[92]

Glyconic ▨   Poets had learned from Prudentius, among others,[93] to write poems composed only in Glyconic verses. This is what, for example, Walafrid Strabo, Liutprand of Cremona, Alphanus of Salerno, Rupert of Deutz, and Dudo of St. Quentin did.[94]

Alcaics ▨   Of course poets in the Middle Ages also use Horace's Alcaic strophe.[95] Prudentius, however, used the Alcaic hendecasyllable stichically; and Ennodius made, in his hymn *Quae lingua possit, quis valeat stilus*, Alcaic strophes of 4 verses.[96] In the Middle Ages this was the most common use of Alcaic verse. And so the hymn *Quis possit amplo famine praepotens*,[97] written in the Carolingian period in the south of Italy, where it was

---

91. *PLAC*, 2:603; see also the comments of Strecker, *PLAC*, 4:1162, and Dudo of St. Quentin, Migne, *PL*, 141:704. The same strophe is found again in an antiphon published by Dreves in the following way (*AH*, 28:197):

Praesentis pater inclitus
Mundi de cavea
   liber ad aethera
Paulus transit,
Ubi perfruitur
   perpete gloria.

The learned editor seems to be little interested in the metrics. In any case he did not recognize Prudentius' strophe which ought to be reconstructed in this way:

   Praesentis pater inclitus
Mundi de cavea liber ad aethera
Paulus transit, ubi perfruitur perpete gloria.

92. *PLAC*, 2:619–22. Other examples are pointed out by Strecker, *PLAC*, 4:1162. See also Saxo Grammaticus, 3:9, 18.

93. Prudentius, *Peristephanon*, 7, and *Contra Symmachum*, 2, *praef.* See also J. Wagner, 16; Müller, 115.

94. *PLAC*, 2:360; Migne, *PL*, 136:834; *AH*, 22: no. 414; 50: no. 257; Migne, *PL*, 147:1262; *MGH, Libelli de lite*, 3:632–33; Migne, *PL*, 141:683, 689, 717.

95. It is used, for example, by Rupert of Deutz, *MGH, Libelli de lite*, 3: 633–36.

96. See Prudentius, *Peristephanon*, 14, and *AH*, 50: no. 61.

97. *AH*, 50: no. 97.

very widely known, is visibly influenced by Ennodius. The hymn in honor of St. John the Baptist *Almi prophetae progenies pia* also enjoyed a certain fame in Italy, in Spain, and in France; and I could also cite many other hymns in the same meter.[98]

Other medieval versifiers composed some poems solely in Alcaic decasyllables. In this way Saxo Grammaticus wrote (I, 8, 18),

Quid moror in latebris opacis
Collibus implicitus scruposis. . . .

When one studies the Latin metrics of the Middle Ages, one often notices that a particular verse form is more or less popular in accordance with the popularity of a certain song. We have a typical example of this *Alcmanian Verse* in the catalectic dactylic tetrameter (Alcmanian verse) used by Prudentius in his well-known hymn *Germine nobilis Eulalia*, each strophe of which is formed of 5 verses.[99] The poem of Prudentius was imitated by Walafrid Strabo, by Gottschalk of Orbais, Ademar of Chabannes, Alphanus of Salerno, and quite a few others.[100] However, the hymn whose first strophe I give here, was also very widespread:[101]

Martyris ecce dies Agathae
Virginis emicat eximiae,
Qua sibi Christus eam sociat
Et diadema duplex decorat.

The author of this hymn, who must have lived in the Carolingian period, is dependent on Prudentius; but he has introduced strophes of 4 verses. His hymn and this form of strophe were afterwards constantly imitated, among others by Peter the Venerable (d. 1156) in *Magdalenae Mariae meritis Magna dies micat et celebris.*[102] When the same meter is used in poems other than the hymns, the dactyls are occasionally replaced by spondees.[103]

98. *AH,* 27: no. 137; see also 22: nos. 175 and 336; 23: no. 295; 27: no. 145; 51: no. 211.

99. *Peristephanon,* 3. Prudentius used the same verse in the hymn *O crucifer bone, lucisator, Cathemerinon,* 3.

100. *PLAC,* 2:246, 369; 3:728; *AH,* 48: nos. 5 and 6; Migne, *PL,* 147:1235. See also *PLAC,* 6:137–40; *AH,* 11: no. 465; 16: nos. 182, 404, 415; 33: no. 277; 22: no. 333.

101. *AH,* 51: no. 134.

102. *AH,* 48: no. 259. See ibid., 11: nos. 212, 213, 478; 16: nos. 84, 421; 19: no. 322; 22: no. 349; 23: no. 224; 43: nos. 203, 396, 466; 51: nos. 157, 193, 212; 52: no. 187.

103. See Dudo of St. Quentin, Migne, *PL,* 141:618, 683, 699; Saxo Grammaticus, 1:6, 2.

Other quantitative verses are relatively rare in the Middle

Archilochian Meter ▦ Ages. It is clearly in accordance with Horace, *Solvitur acris hiems*, that Fulbert of Chartres (d. 1028) wrote his song:

> Sanctum simpliciter Patrem cole, pauperum caterva,
> Quantumque nosti, laudibus honora.[104]

The poem of Boethius *O stelliferi conditor orbis* inspired an anonymous poet of the Carolingian period when he wrote the song *O*

Anapestic Verse ▦ *sidereae conditor aulae,* which is also in anapestic dimeters.[105] Prudentius had written in catalectic anapestic dimeters his famous hymn *Deus, ignee fons animarum* that Berno of Reichenau (d. 1048) imitated when he wrote *Omnis chorus ecclesiarum.*[106] Saxo Grammaticus even used some choriambic tetrameters *Solus in octo pariter spicula mortis egi,* some minor Ionics *Mala soli, gravis uni manet omnis domus orbis,* and, furthermore, he constructed a strophe comprising a Glyconic, an Asclepiadean, an iambic dimeter, and an Alcaic decasyllable:[107]

> Quae coniunx fore daemonum
> Possit monstrigeni conscia seminis
> Suumque giganti fero
> Consociare velit cubile?

One finds in the work of Fulbert of Chartres a strophe made of two catalectic dactylic tetrameters and two acatalectic anapestic dimeters + a refrain:[108]

> Carus abunde, Caraune, nites
> Idque vocamine significas:
> Lyricos ideo tibi versiculos

---

104. *AH,* 50: no. 220; three Archilochian verses form a strophe in the work of Ademar of Chabannes in the poem *Quam pia digne Deo praeconia rite sunt supremo, AH,* 48: no. 8. See also Dudo of St. Quentin, Migne, *PL,* 141:728, 736.

105. Boethius, *Consolatio Philosophiae,* 1:5; *AH,* 51: no. 105. See also *AH,* 12: no. 182; Alphanus of Salerno, *AH,* 50: no. 262; Rupert of Deutz, *MGH, Libelli de lite,* 3:628.

106. Prudentius, *Cathemerinon,* 10, *AH,* 23: no. 23. For the use of this meter in the imperial era, see J. Wagner, 17. In the Middle Ages, Radbod, Eugenius Vulgarius, Liutprand of Cremona, and Dudo of St. Quentin, among others, used the catalectic anapestic dimeter; see *PLAC* 3:161; 4:165 and 415, 421, 424, 433; Migne, *PL,* 136:832; 141:691, 722.

107. Saxo Grammaticus, 1:4, 16; 5:11, 4 and 1:4, 9–10.

108. *AH,* 50: no. 218.

Canimus hilares et amore pio,
Tu, pie martyr, posce nobis veniam.

Heiric of Auxerre forms another quite curious strophe with an Adonic, a catalectic dactylic trimeter, a Pherecratean, and a Glyconic:[109]

Scandere puppim
Transque meare salum
Coetum discipulorum
Quondam Christus ïusserat.

This strophe was imitated by Dudo of St. Quentin,[110] who in his *De moribus et actis primorum Normannie ducum* gives us some excellent examples of the way in which some poets, imitating Martianus Capella and Boethius, were juggling different verses, interspersed with narratives in prose.

But we can not study here the more or less fortuitous combinations that the writings of the Middle Ages present, and so I will end by saying a few words about the rhymed offices, a subject which scholars have totally neglected to study from the metrical point of view. An examination of the forms of these offices would be very fruitful. The oldest rhymed offices are often a mixture of prose, of quantitative poetry, and of rhythmic poetry, the whole being composed of a disconcerting variety. So the rhymed office of St. Alban contains, as well as one part in prose, several rhythmic songs and some others in quantitative hexameters, in Sapphic verses, in Glyconics, in anapests, and other songs that the editor did not analyze.[111] Here, for example, is a song from this office:

In terris adhuc
mundanum lucrum
Spernere coeperat
Albanus martyr,
Pietatem sectans
sumptus pauperibus

---

109. *PLAC,* 3:474–76.
110. Migne, *PL,* 141:657; Traube has shown, *PLAC,* 3:816, that this strophe was derived from the first verses of song 732 in the *Anthologia Latina,* a song which was composed only to give examples of different Latin verses.
111. *AH,* 13:27–30 (no. 7).

Dabat, credens,
    in coelis sibi compensandum
    Vitae munere perpetim.

The metrical form of the song does not stand out at all when presented in this way. We are, in fact, in the presence of a song composed alternately of Sapphics (on a spondaic base) and Glyconics; and the metrics confirms, moreover, a change of text that it is necessary for us to introduce in the first verse. The song should be, in fact,

In terris adhuc \<positus\> mundanum
    Lucrum spernere coeperat
Albanus martyr, pietatem sectans
    Sumptus pauperibus dabat,
Credens in coelis sibi compensandum
    Vitae munere perpetim.

We find the model in the *Consolatio Philosophiae,* 2:3, of Boethius:

Cum polo Phoebus roseis quadrigis
    Lucem spargere coeperit.

SIX ▨ THE BEGINNINGS OF RHYTHMIC
VERSIFICATION: RHYTHMIC VERSIFICATION
AND METRICAL POETRY

Quantitative verse is based on the opposition in length between long and short syllables. In the classical period the principle was natural since when pronouncing words one made a distinction between long and short syllables. However, during the imperial era the Latin accent changed and, after having been musical, or at least basically musical, it became mainly a stress accent even among cultured people. At the time of St. Augustine, according to Augustine himself, the difference between long and short syllables had completely disappeared.[1] Poets obviously continued to write quantitative verse at the end of antiquity and during all of the Middle Ages, but it was through learned studies that they acquired with difficulty knowledge about the quantity of syllables. Quantitative verse, therefore, no longer had a natural base in the spoken language, and it is easy to understand how a new principle of composing verses appeared, determined by the stress accent of words. Since Bede, we have become accustomed to calling the new poetry, which no longer took into account the quantity of syllables, rhythmic poetry.[2]

1. Augustine, *De Musica*, 3:3, 5, Migne, *PL*, 32:1118: *Nam iudicium aurium ad temporum momenta moderanda me posse habere non nego, quae vero syllaba producenda vel corripienda sit . . . omnino nescio* [For I do not deny that I can have the judgement of my ears on intervals of time that are to be regulated; but, in fact, which syllables should be lenthened or shortened . . . I do not know at all]. Nicolau has studied the development of the Latin accent in two notable works, *L'origine du cursus rythmique et les débuts de l'accent d'intensité en latin*, 65–82; and *Les deux sources de la versification latine accentuelle*, 57–58. The new stress accent even transformed the metrical prose, as H. Hagendahl, among others, has shown, in *La prose métrique d'Arnobe* (Göteborg, 1937).
2. The word *rhythmus* was often used by the grammarians of antiquity, but in a different

So far the facts are sufficiently clear, and scholars are in basic agreement.[3] However, when it is a matter of analyzing and determining the principles of the new rhythmic poetry and explaining in more detail its origin, opinions differ completely. The most common conception is that rhythmic poetry conveys the system of quantitative poetry by replacing the syllables that carry the ictus (the "beat" of the verse) with accented syllables and the syllables that do not carry the ictus with unaccented syllables. This conception is based on verses such as *Apparebit repentina dies magna Domini,* where the quantity does not visibly play any role but where the accents present themselves in the following way ´ ˘ ´ ˘ | ´ ˘ ´ ˘ ‖ ´ ˘ ´ ˘ ´ ˘ ´ which corresponds to the trochaic septenarius _˘_˘ | _˘_ ˘ ‖ _˘_ ˘_˘_. However, those who are inclined to adopt this theory immediately encounter one difficulty: in rhythmic poetry at the end of antiquity and in the early Middle Ages, it is quite common for the accent not to agree with the ictus. St. Augustine writes in this way in what must correspond to trochaic verses in his *Psalmus contra partem Donati:*

> Propter hoc Dóminus noster   voluit nos praemonere
> Comparans régnum caelorum   retículo misso in mare.

And in what corresponds to iambic verses, we find some verses such as these:

> Óculi somnum capiant,
> Cor semper ad te vigilet;
> Déxtera tua protegat
> Fámulos qui te diligunt.

Strangely enough, certain scholars believe that St. Augustine, in the verses quoted, really followed the accentuation *Domínus, regnúm* and *reticúlo* or that the anonymous author of the hymn read *ocúli, dextéra,* and *famúlos.* Some scholars have also attempted to justify this non-Latin accentuation. Vroom, who has studied the *Psalmus* of St. Augustine,[4] comments that the

---

sense; see Meyer, *Ges. Abh.,* 3:126–38. Bede seems to have been first to identify the rhythm of a verse with the ordinary accentuation of its words.

3. There are, however, some scholars who seem to think that the Latin accent had always been a stress accent and that quantitative metrics was only an exterior covering imported from Greece. See, e.g., Suchier, "Der französische Vers und das frei akzentuierende (bedingt-wägende) Verssystem," *Romanische Forschungen,* 68 (1956): 27–73.

4. See Vroom, 25–27 and 39–40.

song must have been sung to a melody of the same kind as those to which one sang the biblical psalms. He compares it with a French song beginning with the words *La vierge Marie* and where the rhythm of the melody, which in the text can be marked in the following manner, *lá viergé Marie,* is incompatible with the accent of the words. Vroom thinks that it was the same for Latin rhythmic verse. This comparison, however, is incorrect even from the musical point of view. The melody to which one sang the biblical songs in the ancient Church was, so to speak, plastic and followed the number of syllables and the ordinary accentuation of the words, whereas the melody to which one sang *La vierge Mari*e was syllabic and rhythmic. Anyway, Vroom's theory is unacceptable since it confuses musical rhythm and verse accent, which are two quite different things.

Other scholars thought that the tonic accent was so weak in a word like *Dóminus* that in versification it allowed a certain displacement to which the German scholars have given the name "schwebende Betonung" [gliding accent]. This theory has often been pushed to the extreme. During the last century, Huemer gathered together from rhythmic poetry a large number of examples in which, because of this imprecise accentuation, the accent had been, in his opinion, displaced and became, for example, *sanctá, trinítatis, spirítus,* and the like.[5] This conception of Latin accentuation in rhythmic poetry still finds quite a few defenders. Thus Langosch thinks that Hugh of Trimberg accented *unúm, tempóre, omníum, doctoríbus.* But the evidence that he adduces is not very solid.[6]

5. Huemer, *Untersuchungen über die ältesten lateinisch-christlichen Rhythmen,* 24. If one speaks about an accentuation *Domínus* in Latin rhythmic poetry, one obviously thinks that this poetry is "streng-akzentuierend" [strictly accented] and not "frei-akzentuierend" [freely accented], to use the terminology of Suchier, *Französische Verslehre,* 10–11.

6. Langosch wants to prove his theory by starting with the accentuation of final verse cadences, 110–22. By doing this he found a few disyllabic words before the break in Hugh's Goliardic verse (7pp + 6p) which proves, according to him, that Latin disyllables can be oxytones. But in all these cases it is a matter of a monosyllable + an iambic or pyrrhic word, a group of words which often form, as I have shown in the first chapter, a single metrical word: *ín-suà, út-eràt* and the like. The sole exception is the verse *Deum trinum et unum (Vita beatae virginis Mariae,* 42), where it is a matter of a fixed formula that Hugh has not succeeded in adapting to the verse. Likewise, Langosch found before the break the accentuation *Bérnhardus,* and he draws the conclusion that a Latin word that has the form of a molossus can be accented $\stackrel{\_}{\_} \_ \_$. In fact, the accentuation of proper nouns of barbaric [non-Latin] origin is free in the Middle Ages (see above, pp. 12–13), and one can conclude nothing from it. The accentuation of the following verses is entirely absurd: *Tempóre Thèodósiì, Sequítur Phìsiólogùs, Omníum clèricórum.* One must, of course, read with synaeresis *Témporè*

This theory has also been the object of lively criticism, particularly by Meyer. He assumed that in the Middle Ages Latin was accented in the same way as in antiquity (which, on the whole, must be true, but not entirely, as I have shown in the first chapter); and he found that in rhythmic verse the accents are in general fixed before the break and at the end of the verse; they have to be either $\acute{\sim} \sim$ or $\acute{\sim} \sim \acute{\sim}$. Only the syllables before the final cadences were counted, according to Meyer; and they were completely assimilable to prose from the rhythmic point of view. "Ich habe stets als Ergebnis meiner Untersuchungen behauptet: die Zeilen der lateinischen und griechischen rythmischen Dichtung sind Prosa mit einer bestimmten Schlusscadenz" [I have always maintained as a result of my investigations that the lines of Latin and Greek rhythmic poetry are prose with a definite closing cadence], Meyer states in one of his last works.[7] Taking this idea as a basis, Meyer carefully worked out a special system for rendering the characteristic of a rhythmic verse, for example, a rhythmic imitation of the trochaic septenarius is designated by $8 \acute{\sim} \sim + 7 \sim \acute{\sim}$ (or $8 \_\cup + 7 \cup\_$, using the signs that in this work have been reserved for the quantitative poetry in order to avoid confusion). German Latinists who are specialists in the Middle Ages adopt, in general, this system as well as the theory of Meyer. Since it is often important to indicate if the final word of a verse is paroxytone or proparoxytone, I myself, for practical reasons, use a parallel system, designating the verse mentioned by 8p + 7pp (= a hemistich of 8 syllables with a final paroxytone cadence + a hemistich of 7 syllables with a final proparoxytone cadence).[8] But the idea

---

Thevdósiì, Séquitùr Phisjólogùs Ómnjum clèricórum. The other arguments of Langosch are not any more convincing.

7. *Ges. Abh.,* 3:12.

8. In a Latin proparoxytone word, a secondary accent can be placed on the last syllable; but, as we emphasized in the first chapter, the secondary accent is not obligatory in this position. A word like *temere* can be accented *témerè* or *témere.* It is therefore false to assume that the last cadence of a rhythmic verse is always $\acute{\sim} \sim$ or $\sim \acute{\sim}$; it can also be $\acute{\sim} \sim \sim$. See, e.g., song 3 of the Arundel lyric collection (Meyer, 12):

Que dum temere
   Totam tradidit
Se sub Venere,
Venus ethere
   Risus edidit
Leto sidere.

Meyer indicates this verse with $5 \cup\_$, that is to say, he scans *Qué dum témerè tótam trádidì* and so on. I prefer reading without secondary accents *Qué dum témere Tótam trádidit.* In

that the syllables before final cadences could have any rhythm whatsoever clashes with several facts and must be revised. Rhythmic verse had, instead, as I am going to show, exactly the same accents as the corresponding quantitative verse.

Just as theories of the nature of rhythmic verse vary, so do conceptions of scholars about the origin of the new versification. Meyer thought that rhythmic verse came to the Romans from the Semitic peoples through the Greeks as intermediaries. This hypothesis, which has never had many followers, has been definitively refuted by Dihle.[9] Nicolau thought that the technique of accentual verse had been developed in African schools in the course of the fifth and sixth centuries, and he finds confirmation of this in the rhythmic poem of Fulgentius the grammarian that he considers to be the oldest example of this new versification.[10] Nicolau obviously was not at all familiar with the sources. He is unaware of, among others, Auspicius of Toul and the rhythmic hymns of southern Gaul. Other scholars grapple with the expression "popular poetry" and think that in the people there survived hidden sources of poetic inspiration that had not been touched by the seeds of the degeneration of the Greco-Latin civilization, sources which revealed themselves at the end of antiquity.[11] To support this theory, one scholar cites some soldiers' songs of the imperial period, without taking the trouble to observe that, in so far as they are satisfactorily transcribed, these songs are, in fact, quantitative verse.[12] We find ourselves then in the presence of a Romantic theory of the

---

any case, it is more prudent to omit the secondary accent when it is a matter of indicating a rhythmic verse and to speak only of paroxytone and proparoxytone endings (indicated by *p* and *pp* in this work).

The system that Romance language specialists used to describe a verse rests on the hypothesis that the syllable or the syllables after the last accent do not count. This is a principle completely foreign to Latin verse, which ought therefore to be described according to other methods.

9. Dihle, "Die Anfänge der griechischen akzentuierenden Verskunst."

10. Nicolau, "Les deux sources de la versification latine accentuelle."

11. For example, Gaston Paris in *Lettre à M. Léon Gautier;* Vossler, *Die Dichtungsformen der Romanen,* 30; Verrier, *Le vers français,* 1:19.

12. See the analysis that Schlicher gives of these songs, 33–38. There are also some quantitive songs that are the subject of discussion in *Ars Palaemonis, Grammatici Latini,* 6:206: *Rhythmus quid est? Verborum modulata compositio non metrica ratione sed numerosa scansione ad iudicium aurium examinata, ut puta veluti sunt cantica poetarum vulgarium.* [What is rhythm? A harmonious arrangement of words brought into balance so as to suit the discernment of the ears, not by a metrical principle but by a well-proportioned change in pitch, as are, for example, songs by poets of the common people.] These words have too often been

same type as those which were common in the history of nineteenth-century literature.

The question posed by the nature and origin of the rhythmic poetry is therefore still far from being resolved. This problem has often been attacked by starting from general theories. Following the methods of current research, we will leave aside, as much as possible, the theories and explanations and limit ourselves to analyzing and determining the facts. By so limiting ourselves, we will, among other things, avoid admitting *a priori* that all rhythmic poetry can be confined under one single formula. It can no longer be right to start from the experiences that we have from modern verses and their metrical interpretations. The Romans did not have the slightest idea of modern versification. For the Romans the basis was quantitative poetry, and they started from there when they tried to make verses according to the new principles. This is why, in the explanation that follows, I will first explain the link that exists between rhythmic verse and quantitative verse; and then in subsequent chapters I will deal with the phenomena that cannot be traced back to ancient quantitative poetry.

First of all, I want to make some preliminary remarks about the nature of the documents that we have examined. At the end of antiquity and the beginning of the Middle Ages, rhythmic poetry was considered to be inferior to quantitative poetry. Thus St. Augustine says of his *Psalmus contra partem Donati*, which is the oldest example of rhythmic poetry written in Latin that has been preserved: *non aliquo carminis genere id fieri volui, ne me necessitas metrica ad aliqua verba, quae vulgo minus sunt usitata, compelleret*[13] [I did not want it to happen in any kind of song that metrical need should force me toward some words which are less used by the people]. In an analogous way Master Stephen, who composed in 698 the rhythmic poem on the synod of Pavia, apologizes for his form:[14]

Mihi ignosce,   rex, quaeso, piissime,
Tua qui iussa   nequivi, ut condecet,
Pangere ore   styloque contexere
Recte, ut valent   edissere medrici.
Scripsi per prosa   ut oratiunculam.

---

misinterpreted, recently by Vossler, *Die Dichtungsformen der Romanen*, 160. See Meyer, *Ges. Abh.*, 3:122–45.

13. Aug., *Retractationes*, 1:20.
14. *PLAC*, 4:731, strophe 18.

[I ask you to pardon me, most devout king, I who have been unable in a fitting way to compose with my mouth (the things) you have bidden and to link them together rightly in writing, as prosodists are able to do in detail. I have written in prose, as a short speech.]

In the ninth century, Milo of St. Amand expresses the desire that, if his hexameter composition cannot carry the name *carmen*, one might concede to it, however, the right to be called *rithmus*:[15]

Quodsi, ut credo, nequit carmen iam iure vocari,
Sit satis huic saltem censeri nomine rithmi.

[But if, as I believe, it cannot rightly be called a poem,
let it at least suffice for it to be called a *rhythmus*.]

Alvarus of Córdoba, who is very proud of his talent for writing in metrical verses, says, *pedibus metricis rithmi contemnite monstra*[16] [shun the monstrosities of rhythmic form when (composing) in metrical feet]. All of these expressions—we will later come back to the interpretation of them—show that the rhythmic form was considered low and prosaic in comparison to the quantitative form which alone merited the name of *carmen*.

This attitude then is probably one of the essential reasons why the rhythmic poetry of the Late Empire and the early Middle Ages has been preserved for us only in a fragmentary state. We must not, therefore, lose sight of the fact that many phases of the development of the new versification may have escaped us.

Moreover, not all of the preserved documents can be used in the study of the characteristic traits of rhythmic poetry. Quite a few rhythmic poems are, in fact, from the point of view of form and content, of such a low level that it is impossible to find fixed rules. Such are, for example, the hymn of King Chilperic and some other songs of the Merovingian period of which I have spoken in another work.[17] Chilperic and some other versifiers sometimes blend diverse poetic forms, and they sometimes express themselves in a completely prosaic form. In the preceding centuries we likewise notice in a large number of inscriptions that some ignoramuses not only mangled the quantitative hexameter from the metrical point of view, but they also neglected

15. *PLAC*, 3:674, v. 1036.
16. *PLAC*, 3:129, v. 21. See also ibid., 1:79 *Alfabetum de bonis sacerdotibus prosa compositum.*
17. *La poésie latine rythmique du haut Moyen Âge*, 31–40, 52–53, 70, n. 20.

the breaks, and in some places there are too many feet, in other places too few. Among the inscriptions one can pick out examples of all of the intermediate states between hexameters containing some technical faults and prose containing some traces of metrical organization. If one begins with documents this crude, one cannot get a good idea of the laws of Latin metrics, nor can one study the principles of rhythmic poetry in works that are characterized by barbarism and the absence of rules.

Make no mistake about what I have just said concerning the prosaic form of rhythmic poetry, and do not assume that it lacks rules. St. Augustine, Master Stephen, and others distinguish between, on the one hand, the *carmen,* composed of *pedes metrici,* which one learned with difficulty in the school of that time period, and on the other hand, rhythmic poetry, which was much simpler; but they do not say that the structure of rhythmic verse does not matter. Too many scholars are guilty of an error of interpretation by believing that a poem in hexameters became a poem in rhythmic verse if it contained quite a few metrical mistakes. These faults indicate only a lack of refinement, that is to say, a lack of order and system. A rhythmic poem is, however, a poem in which the ancient system is replaced by a new system, not a poem in which the absence of rules and barbarousness are its characteristics. We cannot, therefore, support the theory of Mariné Bigorra, who, in his remarkable studies of inscriptions in original verses from Spain, designates as "rhythmic" verses that the versifiers did not carry out successfully.[18] We also do not agree with those who consider Commodian to be representative of the new rhythmic poetry. The many traces of quantity that we find in his verses indicate that he intended to write in ordinary hexameters but that he failed in his undertaking. If we are right on this point, then Commodian no longer represents a new system but rather the absence of system and the presence of barbarousness. But because this is not the subject of our study, we will leave aside Commodian and the other versifiers of his caliber.

I will now provide a systematic general survey of the different ways of imitating quantitative poetry in rhythmic poetry.

---

18. See Mariné Bigorra, *Inscripciones Hispanas en verso,* 165–66.

IMITATION OF THE STRUCTURE

When in 814 Emperor Louis the Pious visited Orléans, Bishop Theodulf wrote in his honor a poem in quantitative Sapphic verse, of which this is the first strophe:[19]

> En adest Caesar pius et benignus
> Orbe qui toto rutilat coruscus,
> Atque prae cunctis bonitate pollet
>   Munere Christi.

Four years later the Emperor visited Tours, where he was also honored with a poem, perhaps also composed by Theodulf or, in any case, by a man who was familiar with the first poem. These are the first strophes of *Sapphic verse 5p + 6p* ▨ the song of 818 (Sapphic verse 5p + 6p):

> Terra marique   victor honorande,
> Caesar Auguste   Hludowice, Christi
> Dogmate clarus,   decus aevi nostri,
>   Spes quoque regni,
>
> Quamvis adventus   sit ubique tuus
> Laude perenni   rite celebrandus,
> Cui totus orbis   voto, fide bona
>   Cuncta precatur.

Clearly what we have here is a Sapphic strophe constructed on the model of the preceding one. However, the author has not at all attempted to imitate the quantity of the syllables, and there can therefore be no question of a quantitative poem. Nor has he tried at all to replace with accented syllables the long syllables sounded at the ictus. Such a process would not have been inconceivable and would have produced verses of the following type: *Cáritàs praeclára tonántis átque Árdor ét commúnio trìnitátis.*[21] But the author has read the quantitative poem with its prose accents: *En | ádest* (or *én-adest*) *Caésar || píus | ét | benígnus, Órbe | qui tóto || rútilàt corúscus,* and the like while carefully observing where the ends of the words were found.[22] Then he

19. *PLAC,* 1:529.   20. *PLAC,* 1:578.
21. *PLAC,* 2:244.
22. Several scholars have interpreted the rhythmic verse in a similar way, including

wrote some verses with the same accents but without taking into account the quantity: *Térra | maríque || víctor | honoránde, Cui | tótus | órbis || vóto | fíde | bóna,* and the like. The result was an accented or rhythmic verse of which the accents were entirely fixed following the two types ⌣ ⌣ ⌣ ⌣ ⌣ || ⌣ ⌣ ⌣ ⌣ ⌣ ⌣ or ⌣ | ⌣ ⌣ ⌣ ⌣ || ⌣ ⌣ ⌣ ⌣ ⌣ ⌣ , the latter verse beginning with a monosyllable. From the quantitative Sapphic ⌣́⌣ ⌣́ _ _ ⌣́ || ⌣⌣⌣́⌣ ⌣́ ⌣ , the author of the rhythmic verse therefore has taken neither the quantity nor the ictus but the repetition of the words and the prose accents or what we call here in this section *the structure of the verse.* In Sapphic quantitative verse, the break in the Middle Ages is normally set after the fifth syllable: it is the same in the rhythmic verse. In quantitative verse one avoids monosyllables before the break and at the end of the verse; since in these two places of the verse the penultimate syllable is long, it is necessary to place there paroxytone words: the rhythmic verse has, therefore, at the corresponding places the cadence ⌣́ ⌣ . Because of the metrical scheme, the quantitative verse cannot begin with a word of three syllables of the type ⌣ _ ⌣; words of three syllables of the type ⌣ ⌣́ ⌣ are therefore also avoided at the beginning of the rhythmic verse. The rhythmic poems that in this way strictly imitate the structure of a quantitative verse form we call *verse entirely imitating the structure.*[23] However, there are verses which imitate the structure only partially, that is to say, in which the authors have allowed themselves some liberties before final cadences. In a Sapphic hymn dating from the Carolingian period we see that about one third of all the trisyllabic words placed at the beginning of the verse have the form ⌣ ⌣́ ⌣ , as in the verse *Festínus post haec || angelus adiunxit.* It is the same in the work of John of Jenstein, the archbishop of Prague (d. 1400).[24] In a Mozarabic hymn in honor of St. Agatha,[25] the trisyllables at the beginning of the verse are paroxytones just as often as proparoxytones, that is to say, on this point the author has not at all attempted to imitate the structure. In the same hymn the structure of the second part of the verse is also neglected before the final cadence, and it often presents the form ⌣ ⌣́ ⌣ | ⌣ ⌣́ ⌣ , for example, in the strophe

---

Schlicher, whose thesis contains a number of interesting points of view that have unfortunately been ignored by the scholarly world.

23. See, e.g., in the hymns, *AH,* 14: nos. 16, 54, 86; 27: nos. 94, 129; 51: nos. 61, 95, which go back to the early Middle Ages. To a more recent period belongs the hymn *De caelesti Ierusalem* of Joachim of Flore, *AH,* 46: no. 180.

24. See *AH,* 23: no. 10, and 48: nos. 408–411. 25. *AH,* 27: no. 90.

Additur poena   crudelis et saeva,
Virginis sacrae   torquetur mamilla,
Diuque torta   abscindi praecepit
     Ubera sacra.[26]

All that remains of the structure of quantitative verse is the number of syllables, the fixed break, and the fixed cadence before the break and at the end of
the verse. However, it is relatively rare to find such freedom in the great
quantity of hymns and songs written in rhythmic Sapphics. Only in these extremely rare cases does Meyer's rule that the accentuation before the final cadence is free reveal itself as valid.

     I note in passing that, just as some quantitative Sapphic poems exist
where the verses are arranged stichically, one can also find some rhythmic
Sapphic poems without Adonics.[27]

Adonic 5p ■   With regard to rhythmic Adonics (Adonic 5p), "entirely imitating
the structure" implies, in a corresponding way, that initial words of
three syllables must not be paroxytones (to a word of the type $\_\cup\cup$ can
correspond only $\overset{\backsim}{}\ {\sim}\ {\sim}$). One finds an entire imitation of the structure in a
large number of poems.[28] In the Sapphic hymn I discussed above, which
dates from the Carolingian period, we find, however, one Adonic of the type
Nobíscum Deus, and John of Jenstein as often begins his Adonics with a word
of the type ${\sim}\ \overset{\backsim}{}\ {\sim}$ as with a word of the type $\overset{\backsim}{}\ {\sim}\ {\sim}$. We can make the same
observation about poems which are written entirely in rhythmic Adonics. In
quite a few the imitation of the structure is strict;[29] in the others it is only
partial. One can find strophes such as these:

---

26. In this strophe the Sapphic verse almost always has the rhythm $\overset{\backsim}{}\ {\sim}\ {\sim}\ \overset{\backsim}{}\ {\sim}\ \|\ {\sim}\ \overset{\backsim}{}\ {\sim}\ |\ {\sim}$
$\overset{\backsim}{}\ {\sim}$. Agobard of Lyon (9th cent.) took such pleasure in this rhythm that he used it in all the
strophes of a song which begins in this way:

     Árvae políque   creátor imménse
     Quí tuum glóbum   diménsus es pálmo,
     Tellúrem cúnctam   pugíllo conclúdis,
       Fave placatus.

Here it is only the beginning of the verse that is treated with a certain liberty ($\overset{\backsim}{}\ {\sim}\ {\sim}$ or ${\sim}\ \overset{\backsim}{}$
${\sim}$); all the other accents are fixed. See Traube, *Karolingische Dichtungen,* 152–55.

27. See *AH,* 43: no. 53.

28. See, e.g., *AH,* 14: nos. 16, 54, 86; 46: no. 180; 51: nos. 61, 95.

29. See, e.g., *AH,* 25:172, where the Adonics are arranged stichically; 51: no. 90, where 6
Adonics form 1 strophe; 43: no. 391, where 10 Adonics form a strophe; 23: no. 444, where 7
Adonics form a pseudo-Sapphic strophe:

Extrema die
Extincto sole
Excelsus subens
Evadat mala,
Extendens plumis
Evolat summis,

of which only the last verse is a verse entirely imitating the structure.[30]

Let us now examine the rhythmic imitation of the verse so much in favor in the Middle Ages and of which the scheme is the following:

Asclepiad 6 + 5p ▨ ———— ∪∪— ‖ —∪∪—◡ (Asclepiad 6 + 5p). According to Meyer we ought to end up with a rhythmic verse of 6 syllables with the final cadence $\acute{\sim} \sim \acute{\sim}$ + 5 syllables with the final cadence $\acute{\sim} \sim$.[31] This theory is, however, false. Poets who, in rhythmic verse, wanted to imitate the aforesaid quantitative verse found in the same poem verses of different structures like *Squálent árva sóli* ‖ *púlvere múlto* or *Fraudátum móriens* ‖ *lábitur hérbis* or even *Iústi supplícii* ‖ *víncla resólvat*. They did not scan these verses but read them with prose accents, and then they reproduced what they had heard. Heribert of Eichstätt (d. 1042), who composed a rhythmic poem in honor of St. Willibald,[32] wrote, without making any distinctions among them, verses such as *A te bóna flúunt,* ‖ *ád te recúrrunt, Anglórum ínsulae* ‖ *félix alúmne, Iésu vivéntium* ‖ *fóntem aquárum*. The first part of the verse which is always composed of 6 syllables can therefore have the final cadence $\acute{\sim} \sim \sim$, but it can also have the final cadence $\acute{\sim} \sim$ if the final word is disyllabic. If the first word of this part of the verse is trisyllabic, it must clearly be paroxytone (if the syllables ———— at the beginning of the quantitative verse form a single word, this word must present the rhythmic type $\sim \acute{\sim} \sim$). The structure of the second part of the verse is the same as that of the Adonics of which I have just spoken. Consequently, the entire imitation of structure,

---

Organa cordis   solvimus votis,
Preces servorum   arce polorum,
Christe, precatur,   suscipe pie,
Virgo Odrada.

We also find this strophe, *AH*, 19: no. 277, and *AH*, 52: no. 22, where, however, the imitation of the structure is often only partial.

30. *PLAC*, 4:610.

31. Meyer, *Ges. Abh.*, 1:224.

32. *AH*, 50: no. 224 (see *AH*, 4: no. 319).

which is found in the preceding quoted hymn by Heribert of Eichstätt, as well as in many others,[33] offers us three rhythmic variants for the first hemistich; $\stackrel{\backsim}{} \sim \stackrel{\backsim}{} \sim | \stackrel{\backsim}{} \sim$ and $\sim \stackrel{\backsim}{} \sim | \stackrel{\backsim}{} \sim \sim$ and $\stackrel{\backsim}{} \sim | \sim \stackrel{\backsim}{} \sim \sim$. Of course, some versifiers have a preference for one of these types, and they use it principally. Thus in the hymn *Lucis auctor clemens, lumen immensum*,[34] a Mozarabic poet used mainly the first of these variants. Thomas à Kempis, in contrast, used only the last two of these variants in the hymn *O quam glorificum solum sedere*.[35] It does not seem necessary to stop to discuss each of the different types of partial imitation of structure.[36]

We have already indicated in the preceding chapter that in the Middle Ages, ordinary quantitative Asclepiadean verses most often had trisyllables or polysyllables before the break and at the end. Such is the case, for example, in the following strophe:

> Assunt, o populi, festa celebria,
> Quae felix revehit temporis orbita
> In sese rediens axe volubili;
> Laudem sidereo reddite principi.

6pp + 6pp ▨ These are quantitative verses. A poet imitated them in the following strophe (6pp + 6pp), where we find the same accents and the same structure but where neither the quantity nor the ictus has been taken into account:

> En, pater gloriae,   rutilum gaudium
> Cunctis inclaruit   orbe fidelium,
> Festa celebria   matris altisssimae,
> Quo felix vehitur   regna perennia.[37]

The final cadences before the break and at the end of the verse are always $\stackrel{\backsim}{} \sim \sim$ in the quantitative model as well as in the rhythmic verse.

However, one also encounters in the Middle Ages quantitative Asclepiads

---

33. See, e.g., *AH*, 50: no. 225; 4: nos. 319, 400, 486; 12: no. 183; 43: no. 242; 51: no. 115.

34. *AH*, 27: no. 76.

35. *AH*, 48: no. 475. Thomas borrowed the first verse from the hymn *O quam glorifica luce coruscas*, written in quantitative verse, *AH*, 51: no. 126.

36. See, e.g., *AH*, 12: nos. 115, 233, 345, 360; 23: nos. 68, 436; 27: no. 143; 43: no. 255; 52: nos. 99, 305, 306.

37. See *AH*, 27: nos. 127 and 85.

of the type *Intus tu speculum,* ‖ *tu speculum foris* or *Maiestas, bonitas* ‖ *et pietas tua* where the final word is disyllabic. The structure of these *6pp + 6p* ▨ verses was imitated by the learned poet of Verona who, in the famous rhythmic poem *O admirable Veneris idolum* writes (6pp + 6p):[38]

Archos te protegat   qui stellas et polum
Fecit et maria   condidit et solum;
Furis ingenio   non sentias dolum,
Cloto te diligat   que baiulat colum.

The final paroxytone cadences of these verses result by no means from a lack of skill on the author's part, and they do not violate the rules of rhythmic poetry, as Meyer believed; they show instead that the author was as familiar with the metrics as he was with the mythology of antiquity. It is necessary, in fact, to notice that these final cadences are always formed by disyllables, following the model of the quantitative verse (compare the scheme $\_\_\_\smile\smile\smile$ ‖ $\_\smile\smile\_\smile\smile$ which admits a final paroxytone only if the final word is disyllabic).[39]

If we examine the quantitative scheme of the Asclepiadean verse, we see, moreover, that the entire imitation of the structure was supposed to imply that a word of three syllables at the beginning of the first part of the verse had to be paroxytone, at the beginning of the second part of the verse, proparoxytone. This is also reflected to a certain extent in rhythmic verse. And so in the previously quoted poem from Verona, we find at the beginning of the first hemistich 4 words of 3 syllables, all having the form ~ ́~ ~. At the beginning of the second hemistich we find 5 words of 3 syllables of which 4 have the expected form of ́~ ~ ~ whereas in verses 3 and 5 we have the exception *gaudébit*. Very often in rhythmic Asclepiadean verse, however, a distinction is not drawn, in this respect, between the first and the second part of the verse. The equal number of syllables and similar final cadences have led to a confusion of their structures.[40]

The Asclepiadean strophe that is most often imitated in rhythmic poetry is that which is composed of 3 Asclepiads + a Glyconic. St. Thomas has provided an example for us in the hymn which begins with,

38. Published, e.g., by Strecker, *Carmina Cantabrigiensia*, 48.
39. See, moreover, *AH*, 12: nos. 273, 317; 51: nos. 154, 194.
40. One finds cases of an entire imitation of the structure, with a few exceptions, in *AH*,

Sacris sollemniis   iuncta sint gaudia,
Et ex praecordiis   sonent praeconia,
Recedant vetera,   nova sint omnia,
   Corda, voces et opera.[41]

Sometimes 4 Asclepiadean verses form one strophe, of which we have given an example above, whereas the other forms of strophes are relatively rare.[42]

The quantitative Alcaic, which was not very common in the Middle Ages, ordinarily had the same form as that of the verse *Quis possit amplo* ‖ *famine praepotens*.[43] This verse is imitated, from the point of view of rhythm, in a trope that was sung on Christmas Day, which begins in

Alcaic 5p + 6pp 🔳 this way (Alcaic 5p + 6pp):[44]

Laüdes Deo   dicam per saecula,
Qui me plasmavit   in manu dextera
Et reformavit   cruce purpurea.

The Alcaic rhythmic verse is also, moreover, itself quite rare; and I will limit myself here, therefore, to pointing out that its scheme is ordinarily ⌣ ⌣ ⌣ ⌣́ ⌣ ‖ ⌣ ⌣ ⌣ ⌣́ ⌣ ⌣ , with some possible variants depending on the place of the accent at the beginning of each hemistich (⌣́ ⌣ ⌣ or ⌣ ⌣́ ⌣).

It is instructive to see how people learned to compose

Hexameter 5 to 7 + 8 to 10p 🔳 rhythmic hexameters (hexameter 5 to 7 + 8 to 10p).[45]

23: no. 430; 27: nos. 85, 112; 51: no. 154. Examples of partial imitation are extremely frequent throughout the Middle Ages; one finds cases in almost every volume of *AH*.

41. *AH*, 50: no. 387. See in addition, for example, *AH*, 51: nos. 154, 194; 52: nos. 8, 20, 33, 138, 218, 319.

42. We find some rhythmic Asclepiadean strophes of 4 verses, e.g., *AH*, 12: nos. 273, 448, 449, 450; 27: nos. 85, 120; some strophes of 6 verses in the song from Verona *O admirabile* and in the pilgrims' hymn *O Roma nobilis* (*AH*, 51: no. 189); some strophes of 2 verses *AH*, 51: no. 237; 52: no. 18; *PLAC*, 4:577, where a refrain is added. For the rhythmic strophes of 2 Asclepiads + 1 Pherecratean + 1 Glyconic, see below, p. 119.

43. See, e.g., the hymn *Vox ecce vatum vivida personat*, *AH*, 27: no. 145, where the final word is disyllabic 2 times, but trisyllabic or polysyllabic 78 times.

44. *AH*, 49: no. 383. See also *AH*, 49: no. 410; 27: no. 96, and the two songs of Benzo of Alba *Caput peccati fuit superbia* and *Conditor mundi solus spes omnium* (*MGH, Scriptores*, 11:644 and 651). The versification is very irregular in the song *Angelus Domini Mariae nuntiat* (*PLAC*, 4:474–77) which belongs to the Merovingian period and appears in the poetic version of the *Acta Andreae et Matthiae* published by Blatt.

45. Since the structure of the dactylic hexameter is so variable, it is very difficult to make a distinction here between unsuccessful quantitative verses and rhythmic verses, and even between poetry and prose. Thus Meyer believed that he had discovered rhythmic hexameters

The principle is here the same as we have seen previously: they read the quantitative hexameters while using the ordinary accent of prose, then imitated, without taking account of the quantity, the structure of the verses. They read, for example, the following verses of Virgil:

> Última Cumaéi   vénit iam cárminis aétas;
> Sic fátur lácrimans   classíque immíttit habénas;
> Títyre tu pátulae   récubans sub tégmine fági;
> Árma virúmque cáno,   Tróiae qui prímus ab óris;

they noticed that the break was penthemimeral; then they wrote verses such as these:

> Quur fluctuas anima   merorum quassata procellis?
> Usquequo multimoda   cogitatione turbaris?

---

in some inscriptions of the Lombard period which he tried to analyze in *Ges. Abh.*, 1:230–34. The oldest example is the epitaph of King Cunicpert (d. 700), published by Strecker, *PLAC*, 4:726; this is the text:

> Aureo ex fonte quiescunt in ordine reges,
> Avus, pater, hic filius heiulandus tenetur,
> Cuningpert florentissimus ac robustissimus rex,
> Quem dominum Italia, patrem atque pastorem,
> Inde flebile maritum iam viduata gemet.
> Alia de parte si origine quaeras,
> Rex fuit avus, mater gubernacula tenuit regni,
> Mirandus erat forma, pius, mens, si requiras, miranda.

It is immediately apparent that, if we are truly dealing with hexameters, the prosody and the metrics have been completely neglected. "Diese Verse, an den Hauptstätten der damaligen Schulbildung verfasst, hätten den Toten und den Dichtern nur Spott und Schande eingetragen, wenn sie quantitierende Hexameter sein sollten" [These verses, composed in the chief places of education at that time, would have brought only shame and disgrace to the deceased and the poets, if they had been supposed to be quantitative hexameters], says Meyer, *Ges. Abh.*, 2:11, and thus he concludes that the verses are rhythmic. But from the rhythmic point of view, the verses are as unsuccessful as they are from the metrical point of view. Thus, the final cadences are false in verse 3, *robustíssimus réx*, and in verse 5, *iám viduáta gémet*, since the words, in fact, constitute a fragment of a pentameter. Furthermore the author has flouted the system of breaks although, according to Meyer, the use of fixed breaks was characteristic of rhythmic verse. What is, for example, the break in the line *Cuningpert florentissimus ac robustissimus rex?* The Latin is also very awkward; one hesitates, for example, on the interpretation of lines 4 and 5 (perhaps: *quem Italia dominum, patrem atque pastorem, inde iam viduata maritum flebiliter gemet*). I cannot, therefore, agree with Meyer's thesis; instead, I rather think that we have here prose that includes echoes of funeral poetry. Master Stephen, poet at the court of Cunicpert, could be the author of this epitaph. In any case, one can not cite this inscription as an example of rhythmic poetry.

Mens confusa taediis   itinera devia carpens
Tramites caliginis   subducta luce percurrit.
Non ablatas resculas   mundi fascesque suspires,
Nec casus honoris,   sed ruinas animae plora.[46]

Before the penthemimer a hexameter can have 5 to 7 syllables; after, from 8 to 10 syllables. The poets who write in rhythmic verses, however, set themselves some restrictions. In his *Exhortatio poenitendi*, from which the verses cited above are drawn, Sisebert (7th cent.) uses only verses of 6–7 + 8–9 syllables.[47] Before the break he always has the cadence $\backsim \sim$, if the hemistich has 6 syllables, but $\backsim \sim \sim$ if the hemistich has 7. Therefore he imitates quantitative hemistichs *Última Cumaéi* and *Títyre tu pátulae*, but he avoids structures such as *Sic fátur lácrimans* and *Árma virúmque cáno*. At the end of the verses the cadences are always $\backsim \sim \sim \backsim \sim$ as is the case, most of the time, in the quantitative hexameters.

The author of the *Aenigmata hexasticha*, composed probably in Italy in the course of the eighth century, imposes other restrictions. He writes almost exclusively in verses of 6 + 8 syllables, with the final cadences $\backsim \sim$ and $\backsim \sim \sim \backsim \sim$.

Ego nata duos   patres habere dinoscor.
Prior semper manet   alterque morte finitur.
Tertia me mater   dura mollescere cogit
Et tenera gyro   formam assumo decoram.[48]

The metrical verse imitated here is therefore *Ultima Cumaéi* || *venit iam cárminis aétas*.

The author of the epitaph for Archbishop Thomas of Milan (d. 725) also tries hard to compose verses of 6 + 8 syllables:

Quis mihi tribuat,   ut fletus cessent immensi
Et luctus animae   det locum vera dicenti?

---

46. *PLAC*, 4:762.

47. The only exception is verse 43 with 5 + 9 syllables: *Surge decenter,* || *melius agendo precurre.*

48. *PLAC*, 4:732–59. There are, however, some exceptions: in the first hemistich we find 5 syllables in 19, 3 and 54, 6; in the second hemistich 9 syllables in 19, 3; 25, 3; 38,5; 59, 5; 60, 5, where it is possible to restore the normal number of syllables by reading the verses with synaeresis, and in addition 32, 2; 32, 3; and 43, 5 (see the apparatus criticus).

> Licet in lacrimis   singultus verba erumpant,
> De te certissime   tuus discipulus loquar.[49]

Here the cadence before the break is $\acute{\smile}$ $\smile$ $\smile$, that is to say, the author imitates a hemistich of the type *Sic fátur lácrimans* and avoided *Ultima Cumaéi*. However, at the end of his poem the author no longer has the strength to carry his rigorous scheme to its conclusion, and he writes some verses of 6 + 9 syllables, having at times a different final cadence before the break, like *Tu tribulantium || eras consolatio verax* or *Aspera viárum || ninguidosque montium calles.*

We find the strictest rhythmic rules in the poem *De Petri apostoli liberatione e carcere.* The first hemistich is always composed of 6 syllables, accented like this: $\acute{\smile}$ $\smile$ $\acute{\smile}$ $\smile$ $\acute{\smile}$ $\smile$, and the second hemistich is composed of 8 syllables, with the final cadence $\acute{\smile}$ $\smile$ $\smile$ $\acute{\smile}$ $\smile$. See the following verses:

> Angelus ab arce   descendens poli superno
> Iussu ligaturas   omnes expediit tuas
> Tractum de conclavi   puro te reddidit caelo:
> Solve ergo tuque   nostrorum vincla malorum.[50]

Again a few comments will suffice to show how much, in the quoted poems, the authors followed the structure of the quantitative hexameter. A quantitative hexameter having 8 syllables after the penthemimer has to be constructed in this way: $\_\_\_\_\_\smile\smile\_\smile$. If the second hemistich begins with a trisyllable, this word must—following the laws of Latin accentuation —be paroxytone. This is why in the song quoted, *De Petri apostoli liberatione,* one finds immediately after the break only trisyllabic words of the type *caténis, servátus.* This is also the case, without exception, in *Exhortatio poenitendi* of Sisebert in the hemistichs of 8 syllables.[51] In contrast, the quantitative model with 9 syllables after the penthemimer can be constructed in different ways: $\smile\smile\_\_\_\smile\smile\_\smile$ or $\_\_\smile\smile\_\smile\smile\_\smile$. Here, a trisyllable at the beginning of the hemistich can be either paroxytone or proparoxytone, which the versifiers of rhythmic poems have accurately observed. Sisebert

---

49. *PLAC*, 4:722.

50. *PLAC*, 4:1087. In the first verse, *Carcere vallatus, turba infidelium septus,* one must assume an elision.

51. The word *meretrix*, v. 133, is not an exception; Sisebert, without a doubt, accented *merétrix.*

gives, therefore, to the hemistich of 9 syllables either the form *merórum quassáta procéllis* (about 10 times) or *dóleas exítia cárnis* (more than 40 times).[52]

A quantitative hexameter having 6 syllables before the penthemimer can have the form $\_\cup\cup\_\_\_$ or $\_\_\_\_\cup\cup\_$. If we consider these two forms, we notice that, if the hemistich has to be composed of 2 trisyllables, these must have one or the other of these two systems of accentuation: $\sim\ \sim\ \sim\ |\ \sim\ \sim$ $\sim$ or $\sim\ \sim\ \sim\ |\ \sim\ \sim\ \sim$. This is why in the epitaph of Thomas of Milan, we read *erróre* | *véteri, diffúsa* | *caélitus,* and so on, or *áspera* | *viárum,* but never, for example, *áspera* | *caélitus,* or *erróre* | *viárum.*[53]

In the *Aenigmata hexasticha,* the order of the words after the break is worthy of comment. Thus in the verses,

11, 1   Mortua maiorem;   vivens quam porto laborem;
4, 4   Plures fero libens,   meo dum stabulo versor;
20, 5   Milia me quaerunt,   ales sed invenit una,

instead of *vivens quam,* one would have expected *quam vivens* and the like.[54] But here again, it is evident that, even for a detail such as this, the author was familiar with the structure of the quantitative hexameter and he noticed that the structure *Troiae qui primus ab oris* was more common than *qui Troiae primus ab oris.*[55]

52. The same rules are followed in the epitaph for Thomas and in the *Aenigmata hexasticha.* There are completely normal verses in these, for example verses 1.5 *Nullum dare victum* || *frigénti corpore possum* or 1.6 *Calida sed cunctis* || *salúbres porrigo pastum.* It is only by exception that one finds a trisyllabic proparoxytone after the break in 3 cases: 6.6 *Et amica libens* || *óscula porrigo cunctis,* 28.2 *Qua repleta parva* || *véllera magna produco* and 38.6 *Et aestivo rursus* || *ígnibus trado coquendos.* In verse 19.3 *Dum nascor sponte* || *gladio divellor a ventre,* the second hemistich has 9 syllables, and the use of a proparoxytone word after the break is, therefore, in accordance with the rule. But here it is also possible to read *gladio* with synaeresis. See also verses 25.3, 59.5, and 60. 5.

53. This rule is strictly observed in the song *De Petri apostoli liberatione.* In the *Aenigmata hexasticha,* the two trisyllables of the first hemistich almost always have the structure *Móllibus horrésco,* in conformity with the rule; but there are three exceptions: 7.3, *Implétur invísis,* 16.6, *Acétum erúctant* and 33.3, *Extrémos ad brúmae.* In contrast, the rhythmic hexameters of Sisebert imitate only partially the structure of quantitative verse in this respect. Sisebert allows himself to write not only *Ad régnum proféctó* but also some hemistichs of 7 syllables like *Flagélli impendio,* where the use of the paroxytone trisyllable conflicts with the quantitative model.

54. Meyer noticed this order of the words, *Ges. Abh.,* 2:15, but he did not see the relationship with the quantitative model.

55. See Friedrich Marx, *Molossische und bakcheische Wortformen in der Verskunst der*

We pointed out in a preceding chapter that some new types of hexameters were created in the Middle Ages, types most often resembling those which we have in the verse *Hora novissima, tempora pessima sunt, vigilemus* or *Dextera Christi nos rapuisti de nece tristi*. There are some rhythmic imitations of these kinds of verses; and the result, of course, is completely different from those which we have seen in the cases that we have just studied. An unknown Cistercian monk of the twelfth century composed a poem of which this is the beginning:

Ave Maria,   gratia plena,   Dominus tecum!
Felix et pia,   virgo serena,   quidquid est aequum,
Quidquid est tutum,   quidquid virtutum   et honestatis,
Quidquid est floridum,   nobile, lucidum,   amoenitatis.[56]

The author, who in other poems showed that he was quite familiar with Latin prosody, deliberately neglected it here. In general, the accents are put together in the entire verse in exactly the same manner as in the quantitative models.

The study of quite complicated rhythmic verse forms, which we have dealt with so far, has taught us that these forms were created in the following way: the poet read the quantitative models while noticing, not the quantity or the ictus, but the prose accent and the distribution of the different types of words; and in the new poetry he tried to render these accents and this structure in a more or less exact way without caring about the quantity or the ictus. The achieved result varied considerably depending on the structure of the verse imitated. If the number of syllables was fixed in the quantitative verse, it was similar in the rhythmic verse. If the word accents in the quantitative verse were entirely or partially fixed, it was again the case in the rhythmic verse. But, at the beginning, the fixed number of syllables and the fixed final cadences were not in themselves obligatory, as Meyer thought. They were solely the result of the imitation of structure in most of the cases.

Iambic Dimeter 8pp ▨ We will now take up the study of the rhythmic imitation of iambic verses (iambic dimeter 8pp) and trochaic verses; and, judging from what we have learned in the preceding study, we have every reason to expect some analogous conclusions.

Griechen und Römer, Abhandlungen der philologisch-historischen Klasse des sächsischen Akademie der Wissenschaften 37/1 (Leipzig: B.G. Teubner, 1922): 197–98.
    56. *AH*, 48: no. 288.

About 475, Bishop Auspicius of Toul composed a poem of 41 strophes of 4 verses each. He sent the poem to Arbogast, Count of Trier. Here are the first two strophes:

Praecelso et spectabili	Magnus caelesti Domino
His Arbogasti comiti	Rependo corde gratias,
Auspicius qui diligo	Quod te Tullensi proxime
Salutem dico plurimam.	Magnum in urbe vidimus.[57]

Here, as in the following strophes, the quantity is neglected in such a way that we see that it was not the principle according to which these verses were constructed. Rather, it is clear that the metrical model of Auspicius' poem is the iambic dimeter which, thanks to St. Ambrose, had become common in the hymns. The number of syllables of the verse is, in fact, always 8, and the final word is always a proparoxytone.[58] We have a regular rising rhythm in 42 verses of the type *Salútem | díco | plúrimam*, in 14 verses of the type *Praecélso | ét spectábili* and in 2 verses of the type *Auspícius | qui díligo*. One can assume the same accentuation in 52 verses of the type *Laetìficábas | ánteà, Me èxultáre | gaúdiis*, although here it would not be impossible to assume an accentuation *Laètificábas* and *Mè exultáre*. But we find another system of accentuation in 48 verses introduced by a disyllable and having the structure *Mágnas | caelésti Dóminò*, and also in 4 verses of the type *Cúi | quídquid | tribúeris*, and in 1 of the type *Plús | est | énim | laudábile* (unless it is necessary to read here *plus éstenim*); to that may be added yet another example of the type *Támen nón | generáliter*, which could however also be read *Támen | non gèneráliter*.

These facts concerning the structure of the poem are indisputable. Even so, they have been interpreted in radically different ways by Brandes and Meyer, who engaged in fierce discussions about the bishop's verses.[59] Brandes thought that he had found there a specimen of popular Latin poetry, and he surmised that Auspicius had tried to imitate the binary alternation of iambic verse: ∪_∪_∪_∪_, which had become ~ ~ ~ ~ ~ ~ ~ ~ . Obviously a certain number of verses having the structure *Mágnas | caelésti Dóminò* and *Cúi |*

---

57. *PLAC*, 4:614–17.

58. I spoke in the first chapter about *út-simùl* 34.3 and of the metrical treatment of *désevìt* 22.2.

59. Brandes, *Des Auspicius von Toul rhythmische Epistel an Arbogastes von Trier* and *Die Epistel des Auspicius und die Anfänge der lat. Rhythmik*; Meyer, *Ges. Abh.*, 3:1–41. The opinion of Brandes has, by and large, been supported by Ramorino, *Rivista Storico-Critica delle Scienze teologiche*, 2:374–83, and by Maas, *Byzantinische Zeitschrift*, 17:239 and 587–91.

quídquid | tribúeris do not follow this system of accentuation. But since in the work of Auspicius only the disyllables are not a part of the system, Brandes believed that he could assume an oxytone accentuation of the disyllables. Meyer responded to this that if Auspicius had sought for a regular alternation of unaccented and accented syllables, he should have, in the 48 verses of the type *Mágnas | caelésti | Dóminò*, arranged the words in this way: *Caelésti | mágnas | Dóminò*. Meyer, therefore, explained the structure of the verse in the following way: (1) Poets had derived from the Semitic peoples the principle of forming verses with a fixed number of syllables. (2) The principle of using specific final cadences had come from artistic prose. (3) It is the quantitative iambic dimeter that Auspicius tries to reproduce by forming verses of 8 sylla-bles with final cadences ~ ∸ which had to correspond to the end of the quan-titative verse which is ⌣‒. (4) From the rhythmic point of view, the syllables that are found before the final cadence must be considered as prose. (5) Aus-picius, following a quantitative model, avoids the medial break (only 2 or 3 verses are of the type *Auspicius | qui diligo* and 4 or 5 of the type *Cui quidquid | tribueris*). (6) Moreover, Auspicius avoids absolutely structures like *Hóstium demat spicula* or *Intrat vírginis uterum,* observing the special scholastic rule developed in rhythmic poetry according to which it was necessary to avoid what Meyer called "dactylic word endings" (therefore not ∸ ~ ~ | ∸ ~ | ∸ ~ ∸ for example, but ∸ ~ | ~ ∸ ~ | ∸ ~ ∸). Meyer's explanation is, as we see, far from being simple. In fact, Auspicius had for his model a quantitative iambic dimeter where the final words were trisyllables or polysyllables, and he imitat-ed this structure. The result was a rhythmic verse of 8 syllables with the final cadence ∸ ~ ∸. In his own quantitative model he found all the types of accen-tuation that he uses. In the quantitative hymn of Sedulius we have, for exam-ple, the verses: *A sólis órtus cárdinè, Non pérderèt | quod cóndidìt, Nos àbluéndo sústulìt* (or *Nós abluéndo sústulìt*) and in addition *Chrístum canámus prín-cipèm, Gaúdet chórus | caeléstiùm.* As we saw in the preceding chapter, the me-dial break was sometimes less common in the quantitative iambic dimeter; without any doubt Auspicius had for his model a dimeter of this type. Finally, as for the absence of what Meyer calls "dactylic word-endings," this is still the result of the imitation of structure: no quantitative iambic dimeter can begin with a trisyllabic word of the type ∸ ~ ~, nor can it have the structure ~ ~ | ∸ ~ ~ | ∸ ~ ∸ with a proparoxytone before the last three syllables.[60]

---

60. The theory of Meyer concerning "dactylic word-endings" is very strange. He

The rhythmic iambic dimeter of Auspicius is, therefore, a verse en-
8pp or 8p 🔲 tirely imitating the structure (8pp or 8p); and it would be easy to cite
in the oldest hymnic poetry a large number of analogous cases.[61] I
must, however, point out that the structure of the quantitative model varied
according to the time periods and the authors, and that this variety is, of
course, reflected in the rhythmic imitations. So, in the preceding chapter, we
remarked that using final trisyllabic or polysyllabic words became common
in quantitative iambics only in Sedulius' time, even though St. Ambrose often allows himself some disyllables at the end. It was, in principle, just as correct to imitate St. Augustine as to imitate Sedulius. Again St. Ambrose serves
as a model for the unknown author of the hymn *Bis ternas horas explicans*,
mentioned by Cassiodorus.[62] In this hymn, where the quantity is entirely
neglected, the final word is in fact 24 times polysyllabic, and in that case always proparoxytone; but 8 times it is disyllabic, and since the hymn is not in
quantitative verses, it obviously matters little if it is an iamb or a spondee. We
find 4 times the form *Servándum | praedíxit | nōbis* or *Laudésque | cantántes |
Dĕo*, 3 times the form *Ut sépties | díem | vēre* or *Orántibus | sérvi | Dĕi*, and 1
time the form *Né vox | sóla | Déo | cănat*. The structure of these verses corre-
sponds entirely to the structure of the quantitative verses written by St. Am-
brose *Pontíque | mitéscunt | fréta, Innóxium | sénsum | gérit* and *Tális | décet |
pártus | Déum*, which the author of the hymn read following the accentua-
tion of the prose and which he imitated accordingly. Therefore, even in the
hymn *Bis ternas horas explicans*, we find ourselves in the presence of rhythmic verses imitating entirely the structure of the quantitative verses.[63]

---

explained it, for example, in *Ges. Abh.*, 1:271–72 and 3:105, from which I quote the following:
"Eine Erklärung aus dem thatsächlich empfundenen Rythmus finde ich für meine Person
darin, dass in Zeilen wie *Fortíssĭmŭs sápiens Qui ómnĭă condidit*, die Stimme nach *fortíssĭmŭs*
und *ómnĭă* abschnappt, während sie in den Zeilen *Et fórtĭs ĕt sápiens Omniá qui cóndidit* be-
quem dahingleitet" [Personally, I find one explanation on the basis of the actually experienced rhythm, that in lines like *Fortíssĭmŭs sápiens Qui ómnĭă condidit*, the voice stops short
after *fortíssĭmŭs* and *ómnĭă* while in the lines *Et fórtĭs ĕt sápiens Omniá qui cóndidit* it glides
along easily].

61. Here it will suffice to point out two hymns whose authors are known: the hymn of
Probus in honor of St. Achivus (d. ca. 523), *AH*, 51: no. 213a, and *Versus ad mandatum* of Flav-
ius, bishop of Châlons-sur-Saône (d. 591), ibid., no. 76.

62. *AH*, 51: no. 43.

63. We find the same rhythmic structure, for example, in the hymn *Deus aeterni luminis*,
AH, 51: no. 9. There, the final word is proparoxytone 13 times and paroxytone 15 times. The
paroxytones are always disyllables (*tu es* and *fons es* form a single metrical word), and the disyllables are 9 times iambs and 6 times spondees.

We commented in the preceding chapter that the medial break, avoided more or less rigorously by quite a few authors of antiquity, became common in the Middle Ages in quantitative iambic dimeter. It is the same in

4p + 4pp ▨ the rhythmic imitation of this verse (4p + 4pp). Thus, in the Carolingian period, the poet Dicuil wrote verses (11 times out of 24) of the type *Quísquis vídens | volúerit* (4p + 4pp),[64] a type which appears in the work of Auspicius only 4 (or 5) times in 164 verses. The medial break is particularly common in Irish and Anglo-Saxon poetry. Let us, however, observe that poets usually avoid the structure *Non túmidaè | superbiae* (4pp +

4pp + 4pp ▨ 4pp) that Dicuil, for example, uses only once.

The partial imitation of the structure most often implies, for the verse form that we are discussing here, that the author dealt more or less freely with proparoxytone words before the final cadence. In the hymn *Cónditor | alme síderum*,[65] we find a trisyllabic proparoxytone at the beginning of the verse in the verse just quoted and even in 3, 4 *Vírginis | matris clausula*. However, the initial trisyllabic words still have, 8 times in this hymn, the expected form ⁓ ⁓ ⁓ . One cannot, therefore, say that the author remains indifferent in his treatment of them. Likewise, in *Mediae noctis tempus est* we find 2 times a proparoxytone trisyllable but about 15 times a paroxytone trisyllable at the beginning of the verse.[66] In the hymn *Lucis largitor splendide*,[67] we have 1 time the structure *Diris páteant | fraudibus*, while 9 times we have a paroxytone trisyllable in the same place in the verse as the word *pateant* in the verse quoted. Other authors, however, allow themselves complete freedom in this respect. In the hymn *Illuminavit hunc diem*, which seems to belong to the Carolingian period,[68] the initial trisyllabic words are 10 times proparoxytone and just as often paroxytone. The structure of the verse, therefore, on this point, does not matter to the author who, even so, always observes the final cadence ⁓ ⁓ ⁓ (*húnc-dièm* in the first verse is a single metrical word).

There are some other essential points regarding the rhythmic iambic

---

The use of disyllables at the end of an Ambrosian rhythmic verse does not correspond to the theory of Meyer, who said that he found no rhythmic rule in the hymn *Bis terna horas explicans, Ges. Abh.*, 3:103. Obviously, he should have submitted his theory to a critical revision.

64. In the rhythmic song published by Strecker, *PLAC*, 4:659. We have left aside the doxology, since doxologies often do not belong to the original song.

65. *AH*, 51: no. 47. 66. *AH*, 51: no. 1.

67. *AH*, 51: no. 6 (5.4).

68. *AH*, 14: no. 45. Proper nouns are not included in the figures given above.

dimeter; we will return to them a little later in this chapter and in the following chapter.

As for the rhythmic imitation of the catalectic iambic dimeter, I will be rather brief. The imitation of the structure is entire in, for example, the Mozarabic hymn *Quieti tempus adest, Quo fessa membra quies,* which reproduces the Mozarabic quantitative hymn *Assunt tenebrae primae.*[69] The final cadence is obviously always ´~ ~ in the rhythmic form, whether the final word is disyllabic or polysyllabic; there are 7 syllables in a verse. We have a partial imitation of the structure in, for example, the hymn *O genetrix aeterni* of St. Peter Damian (d. 1072). The final cadence is always ´~ ~ , but one finds 7 times at the beginning of the verse proparoxytone trisyllables, for example *Óscula grata fige,* a practice which does not agree with the structure of the quantitative model.[70]

Catalectic Iambic Dimeter ▦

Braulio of Saragossa (d. 651) provides us an example of a quantitative iambic trimeter of the typical form for the Middle Ages when he writes,

> Ut conditoris haec patent miracula,
> Sic claudicantes mentis aegritudine
> Serpens repulsus deserat nequissimus
> Sic nigra corda nubilo socordiae
> Fulgore sudo praemicent clarisima.[71]

The break is always penthemimeral; the ends of verses are always formed from polysyllabic words which, of course, are proparoxytone. The rhythmic imitation of this verse (iambic trimeter 5p + 7pp) must therefore have the form ~ ~ ~ ´~ ~ || ~ ~ ~ ~ ´~ ~ ´~ (= 5p + 7pp) with fixed accents at the end while the beginning of the hemistichs offers different possibilities of accentuation that one finds if one does not scan the verses of Braulio but reads them while observing the ordinary accent of the words *(Sérpens repúlsus* or *Fulgóre súdo; haec pátent miráculà* or *déseràt nequissimùs).* From the period in which Braulio lived, we have rhythmic imitations composed in the different countries where Latin

Iambic Trimeter 5p + 7pp ▦

69. *AH,* 27: nos. 73 and 72.

70. *AH,* 48: no. 54. In addition *AH,* 23: no. 31; 51: nos. 219 (4) and 247; *PLAC,* 4:651 and 659–60; 3:215–16; *Carmina Latina Epigraphica,* ed. Bücheler, 1622; Meyer, *Preces,* 88 and 89; du Méril, *Poésies populaires* (1847), 255.

71. *AH,* 27: no. 87 (14).

was the written language. In the middle of the seventh century, Theofrid of Corbie wrote his poems, whose form we have analyzed in another work.[72] At the end of the same century, Master Stephen wrote at Pavia; and from Ireland we are familiar with, among others, the hymns *Precamur patrem, Sancti venite,* and *Celebra Iuda.*[73] These rhythmic imitations follow, on the whole, the system of accentuation that I have pointed out above. This is a strophe of Theofrid:

Aspice, Deus,   de supernis sedibus
Quos Theodofridus   condedit versiculos
De sex aetates   et mundi principio
A protoplausto   usque in novissimo.
Deus, qui iustus   semper es, laudabilis.

An entire imitation of the structure implies, of course, that some trisyllabic words of the type ´ ~ ~ must not be placed at the beginning of the verse. Nor does this case ever occur in the hymn *Sancti venite,* in which the initial trisyllabic words are always paroxytone, as in this strophe:

Caeléstem panem   dat esurientibus
De fónte vivo   praebet sitientibus.[74]

However, quite a few writers allow themselves exceptions in this respect. Thus in the old Irish hymn *Precamur patrem,* the author uses, more than 20 times, some initial trisyllabic words of the normal type ~ ´ ~; but, 4 times, he has some of the type ´ ~ ~. Likewise, Beatus of Liébana has 20 normal cases and 2 exceptions; Paulinus of Aquileia, in the 7 hymns that are attributed to him that have strophes of 5 verses, has more than 100 normal cases and close to 25 exceptions.[75] Some other poets, like Theofrid of Corbie and Master Stephen, are indifferent on this point and write as often *Áspice Deus* ‖ *de supernis sedibus* as *Laudátur Ioseph* ‖ *propter continentiam.* In the second hemistich, one can also find some imitations of the entire structure, but sometimes also partial imitations. However, I will speak about this hemistich in relation to the trochaic septenarius, the subject we will examine next.

72. *La poésie latine rythmique,* 41–53.
73. See *PLAC,* 4:728–31; *AH,* 51: nos. 215, 228, 234.
74. See also, e.g., *AH,* 27: no. 199; *PLAC,* 3:706; 4:657; Meyer, *Preces,* 82.
75. *AH,* 27: no. 130; 50: nos. 100–106.

The oldest example of the trochaic rhythmic

Trochaic Septenarius 8p + 7pp ▨   septenarius (trochaic septenarius 8p + 7pp) that we have is in the abecedarian hymn *Audite omnes amantes,* which is said to have been written by St. Secundinus or Sechnall (d. 447).[76] We see in the very first strophe that this hymn is rhythmic and not quantitative:

> Audite, omnes amantes   Deum, sancta merita
> Viri in Christo beati,   Patrici episcopi,
> Quomodo bonum ob actum   similatur angelis
> Perfectamque propter vitam   aequatur apostolis.

For most of the verses used by Secundinus, we can easily find structural models in the quantitative septenarius. The hemistichs *Víri | in Chrísto | beáti* and *Quómodo | bónum | ob áctum* correspond, for example, to the verses of Prudentius *Écce | quem vátes | vetústis* and *Córporis | fórmam | cadúci.* However, it is noteworthy that Secundinus 9 times begins with a paroxytone trisyllable, for example, in the first verse *Audíte | omnes amantes.* Either he had here as a model a quantitative poem of the archaic type of which we have given some examples above from the Middle Ages, or else we have here only a partial imitation of the structure, which seems more plausible.[77] It is interesting to note that Secundinus uses iambic or pyrrhic disyllables several times at the ends of verses, for example, 6, 2 *Apostolicum exemplum || formamque praebet bonis.*[78] His quantitative model had to have adopted in this case a practice analogous to what we find in the work of Prudentius, for example. About a century after Secundinus, the grammarian Fulgentius wrote a small poem of 11 rhythmic septenarii, *Thespiades Hippocrene || quas*

---

76. *AH,* 51: no. 252. Grosjean has questioned the authenticity of this hymn, *Analecta Bollandiana* 63 (1945): 110–11, but Bieler says in *The Life and Legend of Saint Patrick* (Dublin, 1949), 38, "There is no valid reason for doubting the authorship of Secundinus." See also Bieler, *The Works of St. Patrick, St. Secundinus' Hymn on St. Patrick* (Westminster, Maryland, 1953), 58. In any case, this hymn belongs to the oldest Latin songs composed in Ireland, as does the hymn *Audite bonum exemplum, AH,* 51: no. 243, the versification of which is entirely similar.

77. The imitation is only partial in the hemistichs *Suámque páscere plébem,* 15.3 (no quantitative septenarius can have the structure ⏑ ⏑̆ ⏑ | ⏑̆ ⏑ ⏑ | ⏑̆ ⏑), and *Innúmeros de zábuli,* 21.4 (where even the final cadence before the break is free).

78. See, besides, the verses 6.3, 6.4, 7.4, 12.2, 18.4, and 22.1; the words *in cruce,* 8.4, form a single metrical word. The versifier has missed the break once. It is in the hemistich *nuptiali indútus,* 17.2: the quantitative model can never finish with a paroxytone trisyllable.

spumanti vertice, in which the ends of the verses are always composed of proparoxytone polysyllables.[79] This changing of technique corresponds to what we found in the preceding chapter in the quantitative trochaic septenarius at the end of antiquity.

The well-known rhythmic poem beginning with the strophe

4p + 4p + 7pp ▨   (4p + 4p + 7pp)

> Apparebit   repentina   dies magna Domini
> Fur obscura   velut nocte   improvisos occupans

must also have been written at the end of antiquity.[80] These verses can be clearly distinguished, by their structure, from the strophe of Secundinus that I quoted above. Indeed, by means of a secondary break the author has regularly divided the first part of the septenarius into 4 + 4 syllables. He has, therefore, imitated the quantitative trochaic septenarius of which St. Hilary of Poitiers had provided an example in his hymn *Adae carnis* ‖ *gloriosae* ‖ *et caduci corporis.* Provided that one avoids a monosyllable at the end, the accentuation of the 4 syllables ‿◡‿◡ must always be ´ ~ ´ ~ : the possible structures are *hóstis | fállax, húnc | audíte,* and *glòriósae.* Because of the secondary break, the alternation of the accents has, therefore, become absolutely regular in the first hemistich of the trochaic septenarius, in its quantitative form as well as in its rhythmic imitation.[81] We have here a feat worth remembering and one that we will mention again soon.

There are, therefore, several types of rhythmic imitation of the trochaic

79. Fulgentius, *Mythologiae,* 1:11; see Nicolau, "Les deux sources de la versification latine accentuelle," 86. In this poem, the verses begin with a paroxytone trisyllable two times: *Inrórat loquacis nimbi* and *Verbórum canistra plenis.* In this respect, the structure of Fulgentius' poem is therefore the same as that of the hymn of St. Secundinus. The imitation is only partial in the verse *Quod cécinit pastorali Maro silva Mantuae,* unless one should change the order of the words into *Cécinit quod pastorali* and so on.

80. *PLAC,* 4:507–70. The same versification is found in the poem *Alma fulget in caelesti perpes regno civitas, PLAC,* 4:512–14, a poem probably composed by the same versifier, as Strecker has shown.

81. See Meyer, *Ges. Abh.,* 3:166–67. In *Apparebit repentina,* the secondary break is lacking only in verse 4, 2 *Claris angelorum choris;* in *Alma fulget in caelesti,* in verse 9, 1 *Illic et apostolorum.*

Some other songs with the same structure are *Deus a quo facta fuit,* composed in Ireland about the year 647 (*PLAC,* 4:695–97), and *Alexander urbis Romae* and *Hymnum novum decantemus* (*PLAC,* 2:135–36, and *AH,* 11: no. 222), both of the Carolingian period. The examples from more recent periods are very numerous; see Meyer, *Ges. Abh.,* 3:178–79.

septenarius. With regard to the first hemistich, we can distinguish between the following types:

a. A secondary break divides the hemistich into 4 + 4 syllables, which produces an invariable system of accentuation ~́ ~ ~́ ~ ‖ ~́ ~ ~́ ~ : *Apparebit ‖ repentina, Magnus illis ‖ dicet iudex, Fur obscura ‖ velut nocte,* and so on.

b. No secondary break, but regular alternation of accents ~́ ~ ~́ ~ ~́ ~ ~́ ~ : *Mílies fecúnda mílle, In his ómnibùs advérsis, Lònganìmitáte vígens, Pròse-quéntibùs hortátur, Ídeò evìgilávit, Ét in sànctimòniále,* and so on.

c. No secondary break and irregular alternation of accents, but following the models of quantitative verse. These cases are divided into three different types:

1. ~́ ~ ~ ~́ ~ | ~ ~́ ~ : *Iúvenis quídem etáte, Féssa quiétem quaerébam, Dóno quem máter supérno* (see also Prudentius: *Córporis fórmam cadúci, Écce quem vátes vetústis*).

2. ~ ~́ ~ | ~́ ~ ~ | ~ ~́ ~ : *Graváta rúrsus sopóre:* (see also the quantitative verse of the archaic type: *In caélo súmmi trophéum*).

3. ~ ~́ ~ | ~ ~́ ~ | ~́ ~ : *Donári gradátim sácris, Nec ábsque tortóre saévo* (see the quantitative verse of the archaic type: *Torméntis signísque térret*).

d. No secondary break, alternation of irregular accents, only partial imitation of the structure.

1. ~ ~́ ~ ~ | ~́ ~ ~ ~ : *Annálibus rèserátis, Aspícient máli bónos,* cases in which the third syllable of the verse is the penultimate of a proparoxytone word, which can never happen in the quantitative trochaic septenarius (_∪_∪ |_ ∪_∪ can never become ~ ~́ ~ ~ | ~́ ~ ~ ~).

2. ~́ ~ ~ ~ ~́ ~ ~ | ~́ ~ : *Ómnium hóminum fácta,* or ~ ~́ ~ | ~́ ~ ~ ~ | ~́ ~ : *Suspénde paúlulum íram,* cases in which the fifth syllable of the verse is the penultimate of a proparoxytone, where, in the same way, the imitation is only partial (_∪_∪_∪ | _∪ cannot become ~ ~ ~ ~́ ~ ~ ~ | ~́ ~).

Rhythmic poems which imitate the structure of St. Hilary's trochaic septenarii, that is to say, *Apparebit repentina* and all the poems of this genre of which I have given examples above, contain only verses of type a. In the Middle Ages there are, moreover, several rhythmic poems which we will discuss a little later where we find only some verses of types a and b. As for the poems which imitate the classic septenarius, they contain some verses of types a, b, and c1. An example is *Epitaphium Himiltrudis*,[82] where we find 9 verses of type a, 6 verses of type b, and 3 verses of type c1. The poems which imitate the archaic septenarius contain verses of types a, b, c1, c2, and c3. We choose as an example *Hymnus beati Ursmari* of Heriger of Lobbes (dating from about the year 1000)[83] where we have 18 verses of type a, 18 verses of type b, 12 verses of type c1, 11 verses of type c2, and 10 verses of type c3. Finally, poems that only partially imitate the structure of the quantitative model contain some verses of types a–d. One such poem is, for example, *Lamentum poenitentiae* of Sisebert,[84] where we have counted 118 verses of type a, 97 of type b, 92 of types c1, c2, and c3, and 32 of type d.[85]

As far as the second hemistich of the rhythmic septenarius is concerned, if, as is normal in the Middle Ages, the final word is a proparoxytone, there are only two possible variants in the accentuation $\acute{\smile} \sim \acute{\smile} \sim \acute{\smile} \sim \acute{\smile}$ or $\sim \acute{\smile} \sim \acute{\smile}$ $\acute{\smile} \sim \acute{\smile}$. Only the first type can be found in the poem by the grammarian Fulgentius and in the hymn *Apparebit repentina*.[86] However, in the rhythmic septenarius of the Carolingian period and later, the second type becomes more or less the standard.[87] In the previously studied hymn of Heriger of Lobbes, the type *ánte cúncta saéculà* is presented 51 times (including two cases of the type *quís-fuit alíquando* and one case of the type *fúsa préce gréxtuùs)*; the type *eléctis Ierúsalèm* appears 18 times (including two cases of the

82. *PLAC*, 2:93.

83. *PLAC*, 5:208–10.

84. *PLAC*, 4:770–83.

85. In verses of type d, *Annálibus réserátis*, and so on, and in verses of type c1 which have the form *Iúvenis quídem aetáte*, Meyer believed he had found what he called "dactylic word endings," of which he says, *Ges. Abh.*, 3:177: "Daktylischer Wortschluss wird zu allen Zeiten der rythmischen Dichtung von anständigen Dichtern gemieden" [Dactylic word ending is avoided in all periods of rhythmic poetry by respectable poets]. In reality, versifiers generally avoid verses of type d because these verses do not strictly imitate the structure of the quantitative model. But versifiers never avoided verses of the type *Iúvenis quídem aetáte*, a type which corresponds exactly to the quantitative verse of Prudentius' *Corporis formam caduci*. We find, for example, this type of verse 5 times in the work of Heriger of Lobbes in his *Hymnus beati Ursmari*, 7 times in the poem *O mi custos* by Gottschalk of Orbais, *PLAC*, 6:89–97, and 3 times in *Salutatio s. Mariae* by St. Anselm, *AH*, 48: no. 102. It would be easy to cite even more examples which show that Meyer's rule concerning the "dactylic word endings" is not corrrect because he did not understand that authors of rhythmic poems imitate the structure of quantitative poems.

86. Another example is *Epitaphium Himiltrudis, PLAC*, 2:93, whose author imitated the classical form of the trochaic septenarius.

87. See also Meyer, *Ges. Abh.*, 3:182.

type *o máter ecclésià*). Throughout the Middle Ages, poets preserved this practice of alternating these two options for accentuation. We see that a poet like Adam of St. Victor, who attaches great importance to the regularity of accentuation, often allows himself strophes such as,

O quam felix, quam festiva
Dies, in qua primitiva
Fundátur ecclesia,[88]

where the two verses of eight syllables have a regular alternation of accents, but not the final verse of seven syllables. The evolution of rhythmic poetry reflects, in this case, as in most of the others, the evolution of quantitative poetry. At the end of antiquity, it was rare that the second hemistich of the trochaic septenarius began with words of the type ＿＿＿ or ＿ | ＿＿, as we pointed out in the preceding chapter.[89] But in the Carolingian period and later, it became common in quantitative poetry to form this hemistich following the type *dēvōti persolvimus* (or *quōs mīsīt coelestibus*).

A partial imitation of the structure in the second hemistich of the rhythmic trochaic septenarius means that some structures are found like *terríbilis | ímpiis* or *mors ántequam | rápiàt,* that is to say, where the third syllable counted from the break is the penultimate of a proparoxytone (＿◡＿◡ | ＿◡＿ cannot become ~ ´~ ~ ~ | ´~ ~ ~).[90]

The second hemistich of the rhythmic trochaic septenarius has exactly the same structure as the corresponding part of the rhythmic iambic trimeter. It will not, therefore, be necessary for us to deal with the latter separately. I can also indicate very briefly that some rhythmic poems are constructed entirely in seven-syllable verses of this type. One of them is this song by

7pp ▨   Gottschalk of Orbais (7pp):[91]

Inest quibus caritas,
Ipsis placet veritas.

---

88. *AH,* 54: no. 154 (7).

89. See above p. 70 and my article "L' origine de la versification rythmique," 86–87.

90. I took the examples quoted above from Sisebert, whose poem *Lamentum paenitentiae* presents 10 cases of it. Most versifiers avoid this verse structure.

91. *PLAC,* 6:106. See also Meyer, *Preces,* 11; *AH,* 23: no. 129, and the song *Ante saecula et tempora, PLAC,* 4:524, which depends on Theofrid of Corbie, as I have shown in *La poésie latine rythmique,* 50–57. After the Carolingian period, verses of this type become common.

Hortor ergo fervidas,
Immo flammantissimas
Quin et frequentissimas
Agant Deo gratias.

There are also verses which are identical to the rhythmic trochaic
4p + 7pp ▨ septenarius from the secondary break of the first hemistich (4p +
7pp). See, for example, the beginning of the poem *Oratio pro itineris et
navigii prosperitate,* composed by Gildas and dating from the sixth century:[92]

Dei patris   festinare maximum
Mihi cito   peto adiutorium.
Iesu Christi   imploro suffragia,
Qui natus est   ex virgine Maria.
Sancti quoque   spiritus presidio
Fungar semper   hic vel in exilio.

These verses, which are joined together in couplets by the rhyme and by the
sense, are composed of 4 + 7 syllables; and what I have said above about the
septenarius is valid for the structure of these verses.

Finally, there are rhythmic poems written in verses of 8 syllables
8p ▨ (8pp) which are constructed in exactly the same way as the first
hemistich of the rhythmic trochaic septenarius. Thus in a song from
the Merovingian or Carolingian period we find strophes of 4 verses of this
type with a refrain:[93]

Qui signati estis Christo
Mementote repromisso,
Quod daturum se in caelo
Vobis dixit in futuro,
Abicite vana loqui.

---

92. *PLAC,* 4:618–19. The imitation of the structure is only partial in verse 4, *Qui nátus est
|| ex vírgine Maria,* and in some cases where the final cadence is paroxytone. The same rhyth-
mic verse is found in *Lorica s. Gyldae Sapientis, AH,* 51: no. 262 (see also ibid., nos. 235 and
231.9); in the parodic song *Andecavis abbas esse dicitur, PLAC,* 4:591; in a paraphrase of
Sedulius published by Meyer in *Nachrichten der Gesellschaft der Wissenschaften zu Göttingen,*
Philol.-hist. Klasse (1917), 594–96; and in the song that is well-known to experts in the Ro-
mance languages, *Phoebi claro || nondum orto iubare, PLAC,* 3:703.
93. *PLAC,* 4:612.

The song contains 64 verses of which 27 belong to type a, 15 to type b, 10 to type c1, 4 to type c2, 4 to type c3, 2 to type d1, and 2 to type d2; the refrain belongs to type d1. To type a, with the obligatory break, belong all the verses of an Irish hymn *Sancte sator* ‖ *suffragator, legum lator* ‖ *largus dator,* in which the words before the break rhyme with those at the end of the verse.[94]

REGULAR ALTERNATION OF ACCENTS
(IMITATION OF THE ICTUS)

We were able to see that the imitation of the quantitative trochaic septenarius brought about completely different results according to the type of model. The difference between verses like *Audíte ómnes amántes Déum sáncta mérità* and *Apparébit rèpentína díes mágna Dómini* is striking. It is quite easy to understand that many people found the regularity of the accentuation of the second verse attractive and that they then attempted more

8p + 7pp ▓ and more often to obtain the same effect (8p + 7pp). In poems in rhythmic septenarii from the beginning of the eighth century, therefore, we can note that the poets prefer verses of types a and b (see above p. 109) while they avoid the two types c and d. In this way St. Cú Chuimne of Ireland, about the year 700, according to tradition, wrote the song *Cantemus in omni die,* consisting of a total of 26 verses.[95] If we limit ourselves to the first hemistich, 18 of these verses belong to type a with a secondary break, *Conclamantes* ‖ *Deo dignum;* 5 belong to type b, *Gábrièl advéxit vérbum;* and only 3 to type c, *Cantémus in ómni díe.* The hymn *Urbs beata Hierusalem* is almost contemporary with the preceding one; its oldest form has been preserved for us in a liturgical book from Poitiers dating from the beginning of the ninth century.[96] Apart from the doxology, the hymn has 18 verses. Among these, 9 are of type a, 7 of type b, 1 of type c, and 1 of type d. The first poem that can be dated with certitude in which verses of types c and d are completely avoided is the song in honor of the town of Milan, composed about

94. *AH,* 51: no. 229. See also ibid., nos. 230 and 231; Meyer, *Preces,* 139; and the song *Phoebus surgit caelum scandit* quoted by Virgil the Grammarian (Meyer, *Ges. Abh.,* 1:202). The structure is freer in the songs *AH,* 14: no. 17; *PLAC,* 4:489, 521, 573, 587, 646, and 5:560–61; Meyer, *Preces,* 40, 142, and 175, the last strophe of which is borrowed from the *abecedarius* entitled *Versum de castitate* (incipit "Ama, puper, castitatem"), *PLAC,* 4:573, *rhythmus* 48.4.

95. *AH,* 51: no. 233.

96. *AH,* 51: no. 102.

739, *Alta urbs et spaciosa manet in Italia*.[97] Besides the doxology, the poem consists of 69 verses, of which 40 are of type a and 29 of type b. Types c and d do not appear at all. As far as I know, a quantitative poem of this structure does not exist which could serve as the model.[98] This means, therefore, that for the first hemistich of the septenarius the author is no longer imitating the structure of quantitative verse but that he is trying to render _∪_∪_∪_∪ by the rhythmic system ´~ ~ ´~ ~ ~ ´~ ~, or rather that he finds the absolutely regular alternation of accents pleasant and worthy of being pursued. We find ourselves here in the presence of a new principle for the composition of rhythmic verse, a principle which afterwards will play a role of great importance. This new principle was adopted by poets of the Carolingian period who had received their training in Italy: Paul the Deacon, Peter of Pisa, Paulinus of Aquileia, Pacificus of Verona, and all of whom accept in their trochaic septenarii only verses of types a and b. Therefore, the alternation of accents became entirely regular in the first hemistich. It is noteworthy that for the 7 syllables after the medial break poets often kept the form imitating the structure, and consequently allowed either ´~ ~ ´~ ~ ´~ ~ ´~ or ~ ´~ ~ ~ ´~ ~ ´~. The anonymous author of *Laudes Mediolanensis civitatis* has, for example, 61 times the type *mánet ín Itálià* and 8 times the type *ornáta perspícuà*. In this poem the first and second hemistichs of the verses have therefore been handled in accordance with two different principles. This is what also appears in the fact that it is possible to have an anacrusis only in the first hemistich, as we are going to show in the next chapter. Paul the Deacon establishes the same distinction in his treatment of the two hemistichs. Peter of Pisa, Paulinus of Aquileia, and Pacificus of Verona do the same. [99]

---

97. See Traube, *Karolingische Dichtungen*, 119–22.

98. But, in a more recent time period, this structure was used several times in quantitative poems. For example, Smaragdus of St. Mihiel used it in his song *De superna Ierusalem*, *PLAC*, 1:619. If we analyze the structure of this poem, written in archaic trochaic septenarii, we find there 19 verses of type a, 18 of type b, and only 2 of type c. I note in passing that Smaragdus accented *hós beàs* and *sínt dìì* at the end of the verse and likewise in some other places in the verse *ést ubì, ét fibràs, tú decùs, quí sitìt, quós piàs*.

99. For the rhythmic technique of Paul the Deacon, Peter of Pisa, and Paulinus of Aquileia, see Meyer, *Ges. Abh.*, 3:182–84. Pacificus of Verona has to be the author of the poems *Spera caeli quater denis* and *Spera caeli duodenis*, *PLAC*, 4:692 and 693–95 (see *La poésie latine rythmique*, 111). The first hemistich of these two verses is 13 + 42 times of type a and 8 + 21 times of type b; types c–d are missing. In the second hemistich we find 18 + 52 times the type *hóris dúm revólvitùr* and 3 + 11 times the type *appáret vicínior*. Other poems composed in Italy in the Carolingian period have the same structure; see, for example, *Respice de caelo Deus* and *Gastrimargia est primum*, *PLAC*, 4:582–84 and 662–63.

The next phase in the development of rhythmic composition was the formation of the second hemistich of the septenarius with a regular alternation of accents. This happened in a poem which was written by an unknown poet on the occasion of Pepin's victory over the Avars in 796, *Omnes gentes qui fecisti* ǁ *tu Christe Dei sobules.*[100] The first hemistich of this poem, which always has the system of accentuation $\acute{\sim} \sim \acute{\sim} \sim \acute{\sim} \sim \acute{\sim} \sim$, is 34 times of type a and 11 times of type b.[101] The second hemistich always follows the system of accentuation $\acute{\sim} \sim \acute{\sim} \sim \acute{\sim} \sim \acute{\sim}$.[102] Because the two hemistichs begin with accented syllables, one can add an anacrusis before the second as well as before the first. The same verse construction appears again in the Carolingian period in the two poems *Queri solet a quibusdam* and *Aurem flecte pietatis,* which were also written in Italy.[103]

The different forms of rhythmic trochaic septenarius with a regular alternation of accents that arose in the Carolingian period were frequently used during the following centuries. The type having an invariable system of accentuation for the first hemistich and a freer accentuation for the second is therefore very common. In his song *Stella maris, stilla mellis,*[104] Alexander Neckham has 25 + 3 verses of 8 syllables of types a + b, but in the 10 verses of 7 syllables of the type *cédrum fécit hýsopùm* he has mixed into them 4 of the type *serénat perpétuà (plus stíllis dulcífluà).* In St. Bonaventure's *Laudismus de sancta Cruce* we find 123 + 33 verses of 8 syllables of types a + b, but in the verses of 7 syllables the alternation of accents is regular 69 times and irregular 9 times.[105] In contrast, Udalschalk of Augsburg (d. 1149) has in his hymn *Udalrici gloriosi pangat natalicia* an invariable system of accentuation in verses of 8 syllables as well in those of 7 syllables.[106]

The preference for verses of 8 syllables of type a, that is to say with a medial break, which we can notice in the work of Neckham, St. Bonaventure, and Udalschalk, and in other poets of the last centuries of the Middle Ages, is re-

---

100. *PLAC,* 1:116–17.

101. I read 5, 1 *Dei* and 6, 3 *mulieri* with synaeresis.

102. I read 13, 1 *Deo agamus gratiam* with synaeresis and 3, 3 *süadente demone* with diaeresis, and I accent *cúm Tarcán primátibùs* 10, 2 and *ét procréet fílios* 14, 2 (see *tradáta* 3, 3). For the elisions in verses 12, 1 and 15, 2, see above, p. 29.

103. *PLAC,* 4:664–65, and *AH,* 23: no. 41. Notice in the first poem the accentuation *díebus* 1, 3, *láüs* 3, 3, *candélabra* 8, 2, *Adám* 13, 2, in the second *cònsüéta* 4.2, *dùodécim* 7.2, *pró dolòr* 8.2, *níl erìt* 14.1, *sí patèr* 16.1, *sít honòr* 18.1. In these poems, there is no anacrusis.

104. *AH,* 48: no. 280.

105. *AH,* 50: no. 383.

106. *AH,* 4: no. 468. The 8-syllable verses are type a 21 times and type b 3 times.

lated in general to the fact that the rhyming technique that we see in this strophe of Reginald of Canterbury becomes common:

Pater Deus, factor meus, regum rex et Domine,
Te cum nato increato, te cum sancto flamine
Supplex oro et adoro, licet pressus crimine.[107]

This verse structure, known in antiquity and common in the work of Adam of St. Victor and among others, is in fact exactly the one used by St. Hilary of Poitiers in the hymn *Adae carnis* ‖ *gloriosae* ‖ *et caduci corporis,* as well as by the anonymous author of the rhythmic imitation *Apparebit* ‖ *repentina* ‖ *dies magna Domini.* It is impossible for us to determine if Reginald of Canterbury, Adam of St. Victor, and other poets of their time attached more importance to the system of breaks or to the regularity of the system of accentuation.

What I have just said about the construction of the rhythmic trochaic septenarius following a system of regular accentuation is, of course, also valid for the other rhythmic trochaic verses. Wido of Ivrea (11th cent.) wrote, for example, strophes composed of verses of 8 syllables of types a and b
8p ▨ (8p), as we see in the following strophe:

Sanctus Tegulus nos tegat
Et regente Christo regat,
Ut sub caritatis alis
Protegamur pulsis malis.[108]

But Hildebert of Lavardin, who used the same verse in his famous poem *Alpha et O, magne Deus, Heli, Heli, Deus meus,*[109] prefers type a, and seems, therefore, to attribute at least as much importance to the system of breaks as to the regularity of accents.

Compared to the difference of forms which we have just studied and which are imitations of trochaic verses, rhythmic poems that imitate iambic verses are only rarely written according to an invariable system of accentuation. However, some authors like the regular alternation of accents even when the rhythm is rising. With respect to, for example, the Ambrosian strophe, there are examples of a tendency to avoid all structures except those that

---

107. *AH,* 50: no. 294.
108. *AH,* 48: no. 98; see also *AH,* 48: nos. 86, 87, 88, 91, 97.
109. *AH,* 50: no. 318.

8pp ▨ give the system of accentuation ⁓ ⁀ ⁓ ⁀ ⁓ ⁀ ⁓ ⁀ (8pp) . This tendency is already apparent in poems of the Carolingian period, so in
the hymn *Te trina, Deus, unitas,*[110] 27 verses correspond to this system of accentuation while only 5 do not. And the alternation of accents is regular
throughout a small poem which begins in this way:

> Placare supplicantibus
> Salvator unigenite
> Nostrique favens precibus
> Propicius inlabere.[111]

This poem dates from the Carolingian period. To the thirteenth century belongs the hymn by John Pecham which begins,

> In maiestatis solio
> Tres sedent in triclinio.
> Nam non est consolatio
> Perfecta solitario.[112]

Here also the regularity of accents is noteworthy, as well as in some poems
written in a rising rhythm by Johannes Franco (14th cent.), of which
3 x 8pp, 7p ▨ we will provide the following strophe as an example (3 x 8pp, 7p) :

> Illius assit gratia,
> Qui stricta cinctus fascia
> Caelorum ambit spatia
>   Et manet ante solem
> Et moritur pro gregibus
> Et dat salutem regibus,
> Ut suis subdat legibus
>   Totius orbis molem.[113]

There is no longer any quantitative model for the formation of this strophe. The principle of writing following an invariable system of accentuation
was in fact often applied from the twelfth century on, even in rhythmic poetry entirely liberated from ancient verse, poetry which we will return to in the
following chapters.

---

110. *AH,* 23: no. 1.   111. Meyer, *Preces,* 107.
112. *AH,* 50: no. 391.   113. *AH,* 29:185.

We want to emphasize, however, that poets never tried to write, for example, Sapphic verses following the system of ictus: ´ ~ ´ ~ ´ ~ ~ ´ ~ ´ ~.

IMITATION OF THE NUMBER OF SYLLABLES

There are also other ways of imitating ancient verse than those we have
examined so far. A hymn from the end of the Middle Ages, written in honor
of St. Rumold (also known as Rombaut), begins with the follow-
3 x (5 + 6), 5 🔲 ing strophes (3 x [5 + 6], 5):

> Aulae coelestis   laudemus consulem,
> Dilectum Christi   Rumoldum praesulem,
> Quem Dei nutu   felix Machlinia
>   Fovit exsulem.
>
> In qua defunctum   orans suscitavit,
> Quam operibus   sanctis decoravit,
> Et eam fuso   sanguine proprio
>   Sanctificavit.[114]

We see immediately that this is an imitation of a Sapphic strophe. But we
also see very clearly that the anonymous author totally neglected not only
the quantity but also the structure and that he did his best to compose only
strophes of four verses, 3 each having 5 + 6 syllables, and 1 having 5 syllables.
        The only thing borrowed from ancient verse is therefore the break
3 x (6 + 5) 🔲 and the number of syllables. Behind the verses, (3 x [6 + 5]),

> Alma lux siderum,   robur martyrum,
> Te decent omnia   laudum carmina,
> Te sancti, Domine,   laudant hodie,
>
> Quia sanctissimum   Dionysium
> Ariopagitam   iam caelicolam
> Illis sociasti   sede perenni;[115]

one likewise recognizes the 6 + 5 syllables so much in favor in the Middle
Ages, of which the verse *Squalent arva soli* || *pulvere multo* is composed.

114. *AH*, 12: no. 413. See, for example, also *AH*, 11: no. 262, and Thomas à Kempis, *AH*, 48:
no. 481.
115. *AH*, 51: no. 153. See, moreover, *AH*, 23: no. 512; 4: no. 120.

The number of syllables in the well-known Asclepiadean stro-
2 x (6 + 6), 7, 8 ▦   phe of Horace is found in the following verses (2 x [6 + 6], 7, 8):

> Gaude visceribus,   mater muneribus
> Ioachim referta,   solvens vota certa,
>   Expurget piae mentis
>   Corde natus ex parentis.[116]

3 x (6 + 6), 8 ▦   Here is another Asclepiadean strophe (3 x [6 + 6], 8):

> Pangat Lirinensis   chori laetitia
> Laudibus immensis   martyrum praemia,
> Qui fulti laetantur   coelica gloria,
>   Fideles qua praemiantur.

> Prece prae nimia,   virtutibus ratis,
> Pro salutis via   moribus probatis,
> Aggregatur gregi   Mumoli abbatis
>   Atque verae Christi legi.[117]

Most of these examples are drawn from the later Middle Ages. But the principle of counting only the number of syllables without regard for the structure or for the system of accentuation goes back much farther. Already in old
Irish hymns we find some very clear tendencies in this direction. In the seventh century a monk of Bangor composed the hymn *Audite, πάντες, τὰ
ἔργα* in honor of St. Comgall in verses which he believed without any doubt
were rhythmic Ambrosians.[118] Of the 196 verses no fewer than 21 have a final
paroxytone cadence of the type *Aedificare plantáre, Quis ascendit ad supérna,
Humilis, sanctus, benígnus;* and in these verses there remains nothing else of
quantitative verse than the number of syllables. The Anglo-Saxons learned
their versification from the Irish, and thus in their rhythmic iambic dimeters

116. *AH,* 23: no. 342 (Asclepiadean strophe B in the work of Nougaret, 109). See also *AH,*
14: no. 30
117. *AH,* 11: no. 102 (1 and 4) (Asclepiadean strophe A, see Nougaret, 109). See also *AH,* 11:
no. 82; 19: no. 32. The 6 + 6 syllables of the Asclepiadean verse were also imitated by Hugh of
Orléans in his poem number 16: *Nunc demum rumpere* ‖ *cogor silencium.* The first hemistich
ends with a Latin proparoxytone 55 times, with a paroxytone 56 times; the second hemistich
with a proparoxytone 114 times, with a paroxtyone 32 times; see Meyer, *Die Oxforder Gedichte
des Primas,* 89–93.
118. *AH,* 51: no. 244.

also there are polysyllabic paroxytones at the ends of the verses, often mixed together with the proparoxytones that one would expect.[119] When the Anglo-Saxon Æthelwald wants to describe these verses, he speaks only of the number of syllables: *non pedum mensura elucubratos sed octonis syllabis in uno quolibet versu compositis . . . cursim calamo perarante caraxatos*[120] [not composed with great labor by measuring feet but hastily written with a scratching pen by using eight syllables in any one verse]. However, neither the Irish nor the Anglo-Saxons were, in general, completely indifferent to the structure of the rhythmic Ambrosian. Yet the monk Clemens of Landevenec is indifferent; in the middle of the ninth century, he composed an abecedarian hymn in honor of St. Winwallus (also known as Guénolé), in which we find among others strophes such as these:[121]

Alme dignanter supplicum	Britigena mirabilis
Precibus munda delictum,	Luminibus expers solis
Winwaloe, coelestium	Nostrae lucifer patriae
Coenobita sublimium.	Missus es regum rectore.

This hymn contains 92 verses, of which 46 end with a proparoxytone and the same number with a paroxytone (of which 30 are polysyllabic, 15 disyllabic with a long penult, and 1 disyllabic with a short penult). Judging from the structure, one cannot determine whether the model of these verses of 8 syllables is an iambic dimeter or a trochaic dimeter. Let us note that it is not through ignorance that Clemens wrote his verses in this manner, since he knew how to compose regular quantitative distichs, but it is because he started from the principle that the number of syllables was the only basis to be used for constructing rhythmic verses.

The same goes for the monk of Metz who, toward the year 1000, composed a poem in hexameters about St. Clement, a poem into which he inserted two rhythmic songs, the first of which begins with the following

8 + 8 🔳 strophes (8 + 8):[122]

---

119. See Meyer, *Ges. Abh.*, 3:330–36.

120. *MGH, Epist.*, 3:239.

121. *AH*, 23: no. 530.

122. *PLAC*, 5:116–17 and 121–23. Strecker says in his edition that it is a matter of "steigende Achtsilber" [an eight-syllable line with rising rhythm]; in reality, one cannot determine if the rhythm is falling or rising.

Unus et ineffabilis, immensus Deus, perhennis,
Pantacrator altitonans, secula cuncta gubernans.

Omnipotens summe bonus, perfecta trinitas Deus,
Personis discretis trinus, usia individuus.

In the two poems, the number of paroxytones and of proparoxytones at the ends of the verses is also high, but the poet is quite careful to write eight-syllable verses. It is also this principle of an exact number of syllables that Wipo adopts. Some decades later, he concluded his work *Gesta Chuonradi* with a song whose strophes are presented in the following way:

Qui habet vocem serenam, hanc proferat cantilenam
De anno lamentabili et damno ineffabili,
Pro quo dolet omnis homo forinsecus et in domo.
Suspirat populus domnum vigilando et per somnum:
    "Rex deus, vivos tuere et defunctis miserere."

Each strophe is composed of 4 verses having 8 + 8 syllables to which is added a refrain constructed in the same way. There is no trace of a regular structure.[123] As examples of poets who wrote poems of this type during the following centuries, I will mention Geoffrey of Vendôme (d. 1132), William of Deguilleville (d. after 1358), Arnold Heimerich (d. 1491), and Jean Tisserand (d. 1494).[124]

With regard to the catalectic iambic dimeter (7), we can make some analogous observations. The structure of the quantitative model is, on the whole, preserved in the old Irish song which in the Bangor antiphonary is called *Versiculi familiae Benchuir*,[125] and where the normal verses have the form

---

123. *Carmina Cantabrigiensia*, 33. Strecker thinks (see the edition, p. 86), as did Meyer (*Ges. Abh.*, 3:265), that the versification of Wipo is that of Old High German and that one should, for example, scan *Qui hábet vócem serénàm*. That is a completely arbitrary hypothesis and one which does not take account of the fact that the number of syllables of the verses is always the same.

124. See *AH*, 50:405–7 (nos. 314–17); 48:321–409 (nos. 346–61); 50:646–47 (no. 424), 650–57 (nos. 427–28). Some other examples of this versification are found in *AH*, 12: nos. 53–56, 58–60; 43: no. 260; Migne, *PL*, 158:1038.

125. *AH*, 51: no. 260. We find the same versification in the hymn *Pro peccatis amare*, *AH*, 51: no. 258, where the final cadences are paroxytones 42 times and proparoxytones 6 times.

In the catalectic iambic dimeter, the use of a medial break became ordinary in the Middle Ages in the same way as the acatalectic iambic dimeter. I emphasized above, p. 104, that one finds often, especially in Irish and Anglo-Saxon rhythmic poetry, verses such as *Rècordémur*

Recta atque divína, Caritate perfécta, Spe salutis ornáta, and so forth (7p).
Only a few verses do not respect the structure: on the one hand, 4 of the type
Certe cívitas | firma, with a proparoxytone in the middle; on the other hand, 3
which end with a proparoxytone: *Benchuir bona régula, Stricta, sancta, sédu-
la,* and *Supra montem pósita.* But when we come to a poem attributed to St.
Columbanus *Mundus iste transibit,* only the number of syllables remains
from the original verse structure.[126] Of its 120 verses, in fact, 57 end with a
paroxytone and 63 with a proparoxytone. We find in the same song some
verses which correspond through their structure to catalectic iambic dimeters, for example,

> Mundus iste transibit   cottidie decrescit,
> Nemo vivens manebit,   nullus vivus remansit,

but also some verses which correspond to catalectic trochaic dimeters, for
example,

> Pulchritudo hominum   senescens delabitur,
> Omnis decor pristinus   cum dolore raditur.

5 + 7 🞖   We note the same evolution for the rhythmic iambic trimeter (5 + 7).
There still exist some traces of the original structure in the hymn transcribed in the Bangor antiphonary.[127] The hymn begins in this way:

> Precamur patrem   regem omnipotentem
> Et Iesum Christum,   sanctum quoque spiritum.

The ends of the verses are 66 times proparoxytones, as one would expect, and
18 times paroxytones; but, in the work of the Spanish monk Vigila of San

---

|| *iustítiaè, Bónam vítam* || *iustitiàm.* Likewise, a medial break divides the catalectic verses:
Càritáte || *perfécta, Récta átque* || *divína.* Hence the frequency of the system of accentuation
$\sim \sim \; \sim \; \sim \; \sim \sim \; \sim$ in the verses of 7 syllables that we are discussing which are derived from the
catalectic iambic dimeter. But since this system of accentuation recalls the system of ictuses
of Pherecratean verses, Meyer was led to believe, wrongly, that these are Pherecratean verses
(*Ges. Abh.,* 1:222).

126. *AH,* 51: no. 259. See, in addition, the verses of Cruindmáel *In nomine Domini Tempus
certa croaxare, PLAC,* 2:681, of which 3 have a paroxytone ending and 9 have proparoxytone
ending; those of Dicuil *Ceu tesserae in pirgis Mutantur ludificis, PLAC,* 4:660, of which 3 have
a paroxytone ending, 5 a proparoxytone ending; and those of Waldrammus *Sancte pater iuva
nos, AH,* 50: no. 187, of which 21 have a paroxytone ending and 55 a proparoxytone ending.

127. *AH,* 51: no. 215.

Martin of Albelda (10th cent.) or in the hymn in honor of St. Gregory from which the strophe below has been drawn, only the number of syllables remains:[128]

> Celebs mónachus   fit abbas largifluus,
> Strenuus rector   pauperumque diléctor
> Dat ut naúfrago   argenteam angelo
> Scutellam marcis   ceteris erogátis.

What the author tends toward here is writing verses of 5 + 7 syllables without taking into account any structure at all (12). Jerome of Werdea (d. 1475) wrote some strophes of this type:

12 ▨

> Eia, eia ergo, advocata nostra,
> Tuae nos pietatis advocatio
> Commendet ei, qui nostram advocatam
> Te statuit, uti caelestem patriam
> Donare velit nobis post exsilium,[129]

where the break itself is abandoned and where the only principle followed is that each verse contains 12 syllables.

Even when it came to the rhythmic trochaic septenarius, the number of syllables was, in the eyes of the Irish, more important than the structure. In the hymn *Archangelum mirum magnum*,[130] written in a manuscript of the eighth century, we find proparoxytones at the end 35 times, a fact which corresponds to the structure, but paroxytones 11 times. Clemens of Landevenec, of whom we have already spoken, entirely abandoned the original structure in one hymn, of which the strophes are composed of 2 times 8 + 8 + 7 syllables (2 x [8 + 8 + 7]):[131]

2 x (8 + 8 + 7) ▨

> Aurea gemma, floridis
> Candescens mire coronis
>   Miris cum comitibus
> Undenis stipatus viris
> Mundum calcans hunc cruentum,
>   Winvaloe, praepulchris.

---

128. *AH*, 27: no. 56; 19: no. 250.
130. *AH*, 51: no. 249.

129. *AH*, 48: no. 451 (9).
131. *AH*, 23: no. 529.

In the 6 strophes that the hymn contains, there are 24 verses of 8 syllables ending 10 times with a proparoxytone and 14 times with a paroxytone; there are also 12 verses of 7 syllables ending 3 times with a proparoxytone and 9 times with a paroxytone which can be disyllabic or polysyllabic. We have already mentioned the Spanish monk Vigila, who also composed a poem in *metrum trocaycum decapenta sillaba* of 29 strophes of 3 verses

3 x (8 + 7) ▨   each.[132] Here is the first of the strophes (3 x [8 + 7]):

Montano Dei electo,   Christi namque famulo,
Vigila licet infimus   functus sacerdotio
Felicitatem, salutem   in Domino eterno.

We see that Vigila counts only the syllables, since 42 times the final cadences are proparoxytones, as one would expect, but 45 times paroxytones (of which 13 are disyllables and 32 polysyllables).[133] Likewise Wipo took account only of the number of syllables (8 + 7) in the poem which begins in this

2 x (8 + 7) ▨   way (2 x [8 + 7]):[134]

Romana superstitio   indiget iuditio,
Romanum adulterium   destruet imperium.

Papa sedet super papam   et contra legem sacram,
Nupta est tribus maritis   unica Sunamitis.

An interesting versification of the tenth century is that which we

10 syllables ▨   have in the strophe (10 syllables)

132. De Bruyne published the poem in *Revue Bénédictine* 36 (1924): 16–18. Vigila composed his song in the year 980, and he provided it with not only the acrostic *Membrana missa a Vigilane Montano*, but with still another remarkable device: the last letters of each strophe are always the same; see the final words of strophe 6 *oportent, scilicet, exprimunt*, or those of strophe 8 *pariter, similiter, obserbentur*.

133. Verses 10, 42, and 88 lack a break; in verse 43 the text is corrupt. In the other 83 verses, the cadence before the break is proparoxytone 26 times and paroxytone 57 times. We find the same versification in the hymn *Fons Deus aeternae pacis, AH,* 27: no. 119, which must belong to the same time period.

134. See Grauert, *Historisches Jahrbuch,* 19 (1898): 254, and Karl Hauck, the article "Mittellateinische Literatur," in Stammler, *Deutsche Philologie im Aufriss,* 1881.

One can also compare the song *Gaudet polus, ridet tellus, iocundantur omnia, Carmina Cantabrigiensia,* 41, where the final cadence of the verse is paroxytone 10 times and proparoxytone 11 times. Since versification of this type does not agree with the theory of Meyer, he tried to explain the irregularity of the final cadences of this song by supposing that it had been composed by a lady of the court who was ignorant of rhythmic rules.

Psallere quod docuit cytara
Egregia manus Davidica,
Psallere condiscat ecclesia,
A Christo de Libano vocata,
Sanguine cuius exstat redempta.[135]

Here, in five strophes that have continuous rhyme in -*a*, an anonymous author imitated the number of syllables of the catalectic dactylic tetrameter: *Germine nobilis Eulalia*. The final words are proparoxytones 12 times and paroxytones 13 times in spite of the fact that they are most often polysyllables. The versifier was not, therefore, concerned about the structure of his model. Dating back to about the same time period is an often-quoted song; its first strophe is,

Iam, dulcis amica, venito,
Quam sicut cor meum diligo;
Intra in cubiculum meum
Ornamentis cunctis ornatum.[136]

In this song the verses have, most of the time, 9 syllables; but it is noteworthy that they are composed 2 times of 8 syllables and 4 times of 10 syllables. The only quantitative model which shows the same variation is the catalectic anapestic dimeter. In the quantitative poem of Berno of Reichenau *Omnis chorus ecclesiarum*[137] the verses therefore have 9 syllables 22 times, 8 syllables 1 time, and 10 syllables 4 times. But the anonymous author of *Iam dulcis amica venito* has not imitated the structure of his model: he often admits some final proparoxytone words.

IMITATION OF THE NUMBER OF WORDS

In chapter 4, I called the reader's attention to the fact that at the end of antiquity poets sometimes amused themselves by composing poems in regular hexameters in which the number of words was fixed at 5 or at 6 for each verse, and I gave some examples originating from the kingdom of the Van-

---

135. *AH*, 2: no. 139; see the corrections and additions of Spanke, *Beziehungen zwischen romanischer und mittellateinischer Lyrik: mit besonderer Berücksichtigung der Metrik und Musik, 78.*
136. *Carmina Cantabrigiensia*, 27.
137. *AH*, 23: no. 23.

dals in North Africa. It is possible to imitate a verse of this type from the rhythmic point of view by counting the number of words or the main accents of the model—and no longer by counting the number of syllables—and by forming in this way verses whose characteristic is that they are composed of, for example, 5 or 6 words. This may very well be the origin of the curious rhythmic verses that we find for the first time in an inscription composed in Spain near Córdoba in 642 (3 + 3 words):[138]

3 + 3 words ▩

Haec cava saxa   Oppilani continet membra,
Glorioso ortu natalium,   gestu abituque conspicuum.
Opibus quippe pollens   et artuum viribus cluens
Iacula vehi precipitur   predoque Bacceis destinatur.
In procinctum belli necatur   opitulatione sodalium desolatus.
Naviter cede perculsum   clintes rapiunt peremtum,
Exanimis domu reducitur,   suis a vernulis humatur.
Lugit coniux cum liberis,   fletibus familia prestrepit.
Decies ut ternos ad quater   quaternos vixit per annos,
Pridie Septembium idus   morte a Vasconibus multatus.
Era sescentensima et octagensima   id gestum memento.
Sepultus sub die quiescit   VI id. Octubres.

To all appearances quantity plays no role in this poem, any more than does the number of syllables (the number of syllables varies from 5 to 13 in the first hemistichs and from 6 to 15 in the second hemistichs). However, each verse is regularly composed of 3 + 3 words. We do not mean "composed of words" in the graphic sense of the term, but of metrical words, which means that the monosyllabic prepositions and the conjunctions *et* and *ut* (verses 3, 11, and 9) are proclitics.

A few years later, it seems, the prologue of the antiphonary of Leo was written, composed of verses of 2 + 2 metrical words :

2 + 2 words ▩

Traditio Toletana   institutioque sancta
Melodie cantus   mirifice promserunt.

138. Bücheler, *Carmina Latina Epigraphica*, 721. I discussed this inscription in *L'origine de la versification latine rythmique*, 89–90. In each verse, the final words of hemistichs are linked together by rhyme or assonance: *saxa—membra, natalium—conspicuum,* and the like, but the assonance is lacking in verses 9, 11, and 12 because of the technical expressions.

This text was published and analyzed by Meyer,[139] who very rightly pointed out that the curious grammarian called Virgil the Grammarian, who wrote during the same century, shortly after Isidore,[140] was familiar with the principle of composing rhythmic verses with a fixed number of words. It also emerged from the explanation of Virgil that this usage was new and 3 words   ▨   rare.[141] As an example of verses of 3 words, Virgil quotes,

> Archadius rex terrificus
> Laudabilis laude dignissimus,

4 words   ▨   and as an example of verses of 4 words:

> Sol maximus mundi lucifer
> Omnia aera inlustrat pariter.

But in spite of the popularity enjoyed by Virgil during the following century, poetry that took account of the number of words (or if one prefers, that counted the main accents) did not play an important role.[142]

IMITATION OF QUANTITY

It is not surprising that versifiers who composed rhythmic verses while using quantitative poetry as their model succeeded at times in making regular quantitative verses. In his work *De arte metrica,* the Venerable Bede had already observed this phenomenon, as we see from what he says about rhythmic poetry: *Plerumque tamen casu quodam invenies etiam rationem in rhyth-*

---

139. *Ges. Abh.,* 3:204–13. According to Meyer, the principle of counting the words came from formal prose-rhythm.

140. Concerning the time period in which Virgil the Grammarian lived, see the literature quoted in *Clavis Patrum Latinorum,* 1559.

141. See Virgil the Grammarian, ed. Huemer, 15: *sunt qui adiciunt trifonos et quadrifonos versus* (= verses of three or four words) . . . *Auctoritate . . . nulla suffulti permissum magis sequi quam exemplum voluerunt.*

142. One finds, for example, some verses of 3 + 3 words in the song that Pope Hadrian I sent to Charlemagne about the year 774 and in the poetic life of St. Eloi, as Meyer showed, *Ges. Abh.* 3:234–42. Another specimen of this versification is the song in honor of St. Yrieix that I published and analysed in *La poésie latine rythmique,* 66–70. But when Meyer believes he has found the same versification in the work of Dhuoda and in certain *Preces* of the Mozarabic liturgy, *Ges. Abh.,* 3:242–46, and *Die Preces der mozarabischen Liturgie,* passim, his interpretation is incorrect or uncertain.

mo, non artifici moderatione servata, sed sono et ipsa modulatione ducente[143] [Yet very often you will find by chance even in rhythmic poetry a system, not because control has been exercised by the craftsman but because the sound and the rhythmical measure itself provide guidance]. There existed, however, some forms in which rhythm and quantity were mixed and in which one took quantity into account more or less systematically. Thus, Meyer has shown that, in the hymns written in strophes of 5 iambic trimeters, traditionally attributed to Paulinus of Aquileia, Paulinus to a certain extent took quantity into account.[144] In the hymn in praise of St. Mark *Iam nunc per omne lux refulget saeculum,*[145] composed without a doubt at Aquileia during the Carolingian period, Meyer found that, in the 50 verses of which it was composed, the third syllable is short 49 times and long only once. As for the fourth syllable, according to the laws of Latin accentuation, it was always supposed to be long if it was in a polysyllable. However, if the word before the break was disyllabic, rhythmic poetry as a rule did not establish a distinction between those words in which the first syllable is long and those in which it is short. One is, therefore, struck by the fact that all 25 disyllables which are found before the break in the hymn of St. Mark have a long first syllable. In other words, the author of this hymn composed his verses following a system which mixes metrics and rhythm and which we can reproduce with this formula: ~ ~⌣— ~ ‖ ~ ~ ~ ~ ~ ~̆ ~ ~̆ .

There also exist rhythmic poems in which we detect some quantitative elements but in such an irregular way that we sometimes wonder into what category we should put them. Let me give an example. Paulinus of Aquileia created a strophe which enjoyed a certain popularity; it is composed of three rhythmic iambic trimeters + one rhythmic Adonic.[146] In the middle of the ninth century, an unknown poet from the South of France wrote, following this type of verse, a *Planctus Hugonis abbatis,*[147] which one is tempted at first glance to classify as rhythmic poetry, because it contains strophes such as,

---

143. *Grammatici Latini,* 7:258.

144. Meyer, *Ges. Abh.,* 2:356–65. Meyer draws from it the conclusion that these hymns are not composed by Paulinus, but here his argument is untenable.

145. *AH,* 50: no. 104.

146. See below, 148–49.

147. *PLAC,* 2:139.

Sed non ob hoc tu   perforandus lanceis,
Nec membra tŭa   lănianda fŭerant,
Cum plus prodesse   quam nocere cŭique
        Semper amares.

As far as quantity, the second verse has the form: $\_\_\_\cup\cup\cup \| \cup\cup\_\cup\cup\cup\_$, which seems to confirm the point of view of Meyer, who placed this poem in his list of rhythmic poems.[148] But if one makes a list of the quantities in the 24 senarii which the poem contains, the result is different.

First syllable: long 22 times, short 2 times (*tălenta* 5, 2 and *ĕt* 6, 3).

Second syllable: long 23 times, short 1 time (*ŭbi* 6, 3).

Third syllable: short 18 times, long 6 times (*prōdesse* 3, 3; 7, 3; 8, 3, *vīdisset* 4, 2; 5, 2, *immō* 5, 1).

Fourth syllable: long 23 times, short 1 time (*tŭa* 3, 2).

Fifth syllable: short 14 times, long 10 times.

Sixth syllable: long 23 times, short 1 time (*lănianda* 3, 2).

Seventh syllable: short 23 times, long 1 time (*ūllis* 4, 2).

Eighth syllable: long 22 times, short 2 times (*turpitĕr* 4, 3; *extitĭt* 6, 2).

Ninth syllable: long 16 times, short 8 times.

Tenth syllable: long 20 times, short 4 times (*fŭerant* 3, 2, *tŭmulo* 6, 1, *mŏnachus* 6, 2, *spĕciem* 7, 1).

Eleventh syllable: short 24 times.

From this list it emerges that the poet tried to write quantitative verses of the following form: $\_\_\cup\_\underline{\cup} \| \_\cup\_\underline{\cup}\_\underline{\cup}\underline{\cup}$. In contrast, the treatment of the first syllables of words like *ubi, tua, fuerant,* clashes with this scheme; and we can hardly presuppose, if we think about the time period and the milieu in which he lived, that the poet was ignorant of the exact prosody of these words. Therefore we must suppose that we are witnessing concessions made by the poet to the rhythmic poetry, which provided him with his model for strophic form. In other words, this poem is at the same time rhythmic—and, as such, imitating entirely the structure—and quantitative.

We hope to have shown sufficiently by these examples that the boundaries between rhythmic and quantitative poetry are sometimes quite vague.

---

148. *Ges. Abh.,* 1:212.

SEVEN ■ RHYTHMIC VERSIFICATION AND MUSIC

Rhythmic poetry was, in general, intended to be sung and not to be read. We have, therefore, good reason to examine the relationship between the melody and the text. Obviously, given the nature of the documents that we possess, this examination will have a hypothetical result in quite a few cases; yet in others it will be more certain; and we are, in any case, compelled to state the problem.

At first, we must take note that there is a distinction to be made between syllabic melodies and non-syllabic melodies.[1] In the first, one syllable of the text corresponds to each tone; in the second, by contrast, one syllable of the text can correspond to several tones. In the latter case, the musical embellishments can be more or less rich or more or less simple. They were particularly rich when the song was performed with virtuosity by a soloist and when the text was beautiful prose. But, in this chapter, we are only going to deal with melodies that are relatively simple, that is to say, with melodies that could be sung by those assembled or a choir that was not trained for technical brilliance; these melodies accompanied a poem in strophes.

In a poem intended to be sung, the words may have been written first and the music composed afterwards to accompany the text. The contrary may also have happened, and the structure of the melody then determined the words. If one composes strophes following the syllabic principle for an already-existing melody, one that has a rhythm that is hardly noticeable, the result has to yield verses where it is the number of syllables that matters. In the preceding chapter I proved the existence of poems of this type, of which the earliest, so far as we know, are old Irish hymns; and I showed the relations of this poetic form to ancient quantitative forms. We can perhaps sup-

1. See, for example, P. Wagner, *Einführung*, 1:171–72.

pose that this poetry was created in the following manner: to accompany an already existing melody someone wrote a text, following the syllabic principle and without taking care for the structure of the quantitative poetic form which was in fact at the root of the hymn and for which the melody had perhaps at one time been composed.

One scholar has even supposed that melody could have played an important role in the creation of the oldest rhythmic Latin poem with which we are familiar, that is, the *Psalmus contra partem Donati* of St. Augustine[2]

8p + 8p ▨ (8p + 8p). It is an abecedarian poem composed of 393 verses. It consists of a prologue of 6 verses and an epilogue of 30 verses framing 20 intermediary strophes that begin with the letters of the alphabet from A to V. Each strophe has 12 verses + a refrain. Each verse is made of 8 + 8 syllables; there is always a paroxytone before the break and at the end of the verse, which is always in -*e*.[3] This could indicate that St. Augustine imitated a trochaic octonarius, but without caring about the quantity. But this supposition runs into some difficulties.

It is, for example, noteworthy that the structure of the verse before the final cadence is entirely free. We can see this from the first three lines of the first strophe:

Abundantia peccatorum   solet fratres conturbare.
Propter hoc Dominus noster   voluit nos praemonere,
Comparans regnum caelorum   reticulo misso in mare.

The words *Dóminus* and *retículo* are put in some places of the verse where proparoxytones are impossible in trochaic quantitative verses. Of course, this is not inconceivable in the rhythmic poetry. We found quite a few examples in the preceding chapter, where I called this phenomenon partial imitation of the structure. But in the oldest rhythmic poetry this phenomenon is relatively rare. Thus we are then very surprised to find this use of proparoxytones in the work of St. Augustine, 47 times in 276 verses. St. Fulgentius of Ruspe who, about a century later, imitated the verses of St. Augustine in an

2. See Tréhorel, 322. The poem was published by Lambot, *Revue bénédictine* 47 (1935): 318–28.

3. The only exception is v. 31 *ut spem ponant in hómine.* One ought to correct *accipere* v. 2 to *acceptare* and follow the text of the new manuscript that Lambot has discovered for verses 221–22: *Legite quomodo adulter puniatur in sancta lege; Non enim dicere potest quia peccavit a timore.*

abecedarian poem against the Arians,[4] provides us about 113 cases of partial imitation in 301 verses. In the work of an author such as St. Augustine, who takes great care, among other things, to avoid a detail like a hiatus,[5] it cannot be a question of negligence or of failure to do something. If he directly imitates a quantitative trochaic octonarius, the partial imitation has certainly been a conscious principle in his work. ·

The *Psalmus* of St. Augustine is distinguished still more from the oldest rhythmic poetry by the high frequency of synaereses and elisions. Again, these are not unknown phenomena. But Irish poetry, which went the furthest in the use of synaeresis, provides only a few cases in each poem, whereas in St. Augustine's *Psalmus* I counted more than 90.[6]

But let me emphasize especially that the trochaic octonarius that St. Augustine would have imitated is known to us only from the *cantica* of Roman tragedies and comedies. Even if, by some unlikely chance, people had been singing them in the theater at the time of St. Augustine, he would never have had the idea of taking such texts as metrical models. It is not even likely that he borrowed the melody from one of these profane songs.[7] We know, on the contrary, that he had for models the psalms composed by the Donatist bishops who wished in that way to propagate their heresy among the people. It is therefore in the propaganda songs of the heretics of North Africa that we must search for the source of his metrics. Unfortunately, none of these songs has been preserved, and all speculation as to their form would not lead us very far. The only thing that we know about this poetry is that it was addressed to uneducated people and that the melody played an essential role in it.[8]

It seems therefore that St. Augustine's *Psalmus contra partem Donati* puts us in front of an insoluble problem. We do not know anything about the models for his versification. The only imitation made afterwards is that of St. Fulgentius, and one cannot prove any direct link with the rest of rhythmic poetry. It is possible that there is a relationship between music and the origin

4. Published by Lambot, *Revue bénédictine* 48 (1936): 221–34.
5. I treated this detail in "Ad sancti Augustini Psalmum abecedarium adnotationes."
6. In the work of St. Fulgentius I found only about 30 cases.
7. See Gerold, 143.
8. On hymns in the works of the heretics, see Leclercq in *Dictionnaire d'archéologie chrétienne et de liturgie*, 6:2859–68; the psalms of the Donatists are examined on p. 2866. It is quite possible that the Donatists followed the models given by Bardesanes of Edessa and by the other eastern heresiarchs.

of rhythmic Latin poetry; that is an appealing hypothesis, but one that is impossible to verify.[9]

What is more certain is the relationship between the melody and certain strophic forms in Ambrosian hymns (8pp, 8pp, 8 + 8pp).

8pp, 8pp, 8 + 8pp ▨ Among the oldest of the hymns we note *Ad cenam agni providi* and *Aurora lucis rutilat*,[10] rightly celebrated for their poetic beauty. These two hymns are rhythmic and their verses imitate the structure of the quantitative iambic dimeter.[11] It is, however, noteworthy that in the following verses the final words clash with the structure of the model: 83, 5, 3 *Redempta plebs captiváta*, 84, 5, 3 *Quem poena mortis crudéli*. These two cases are in the third verses of the strophe. This third verse is also the only verse in which the rhyme is sometimes omitted. The rhymes are, in fact, arranged following the system aaaa for most of the strophes but aaba in the following strophes: 83.4; 84.2, 9, 10, and 11.[12] The irregularity of the final cadence and the absence of rhythm in the third verse seem to show that, while the first and the second verse each form an independent metrical member, the third verse is dependent and forms with the fourth a single metrical member. We could emphasize this fact by giving the following formula of the construction of the strophes: a + a + ba. It is in the music, and not in the classical dimeter that provided the underlying structure, that we will find the explanation for this particular position of the third verse in the strophe. Indeed, the melodies of Ambrosian hymns are sometimes constructed following the scheme AABA. This melodic structure, whose existence one can already prove in Syrian madrasahs, must have been known in the West since the time when the first hymns were composed.[13] Consequently, if the author of the two hymns of which we speak—and which were in all likelihood composed

9. For the rhythmic form of St. Augustine's psalm see the detailed explanation by Tréhorel.

10. *AH*, 51: nos. 83 and 84.

11. In the verses *Osculant pedes Domini, Reddita vitae praemia, Quaesumus auctor omnium*, and *Caelum laudibus intonat*, the imitation is only partial. The Latin of these hymns is not classical. One finds in it, for example, a prosthetic vowel 83, 1, 2 *Estolis albis candidi* and 84, 4, 4 *Esplendens clamat angelus*, and a nominative (or accusative) absolute 84, 10 *Ostensa sibi vulnera in Christi carne fulgida* and 83, 2 *Cuius sacrum corpusculum in ara crucis torridum*.

12. In the hymn of Sedulius *A solis ortus cardine, AH*, 50: no. 53, the rhyme is similarly lacking in the third verse of strophes 2, 5, 19, and 20.

13. See Besseler, 52; P. Wagner, *Einführung*, 3:473; Gennrich, *Grundriss*, 232–33; Ebel, 74. According to Sessini (*Poesia e musica*, 76, 84), in the melodies on which St. Ambrose's hymns

by one and the same person—wrote the words to an already existing melody having this structure, that is to say, if we are in the presence of a case where the music is primary and the text secondary, we can understand this particular metrical trait.

The same can be said for the strophic forms ab + ab (or ab + cb) (8 + 8pp, 8 + 8pp), which also appear in the texts and in the melodies of Ambrosian hymns.[14] But of these we possess a greater number of texts. We have a typical example in the hymn *Christe caeli Domine*,[15] comprising 12 rhythmic Ambrosian strophes. Verses 2 and 4 of the strophes always end with a proparoxytone (9.2 *á patrè* is a single metrical word; 9.4 all the manuscripts have *Domine*, which the editors have wrongly corrected to *Deus)*. In contrast, the words at the ends of verses 1 and 3 take all possible forms. There are proparoxytones 7 times and paroxytones 15 times (to that may be added the names *Seraphin* 7.1 and *David* 9.1, the accentuations of which are uncertain). The paroxytone words are polysyllabic 11 times (for example, 3.1 *Tu verbum patris aeterni*), disyllabic with a long penult 3 times (for example, 6.3 *Odoramentis plenas gestans*), disyllabic with a short penult 1 time (9.3 *Qui in nomine Dei*, which the editors have unnecessarily changed). This fact indicates that the metrical boundaries between verses 1 and 2 and between verses 3 and 4 have been effaced, that is to say, that the strophe is really composed of 2 verses of 16 syllables. It is necessary also to observe that there is some variation as to the number of syllables in verses 1 and 3 of the strophes.[16] Verse 8.1 has only 6 syllables *Sanctus, sanctus, sanctus;* 1.1 *Christe caeli Domine* and 1.3 *Qui nos crucis munere* have, for example, 7 syllables; and 6.1 *Te multitudo seniorum* and 6.3 *Odoramentis plenas gestans* have, for example, 9 syllables. This variation in the number of syllables, to which we will shortly return, indicates also that the form of the strophe is ab + ab.

The same structure also appears more or less clearly in other hymns, for example, in *Sacri triumphale tui*,[17] where we find, at the end of the verses,

(margin note: *8 + 8pp, 8 + 8pp*)

Aeterne rerum conditor and Iam lucis orto sidere were sung, the cadences of the musical phrases that correspond to verses 1, 2, and 4 are the same whereas verse 3 ends differently.

14. Some melodies having the structure AB + AB have been indicated by P. Wagner, *Einführung*, 3:472, and Ebel, 74. Maas discovered that some texts exist presenting this structure; see *Philologus* 68 (1909): 157–60.

15. *AH*, 51: no. 10.

16. See, however, verses 9.2, 9.4, and 10.2, which in the manuscripts have 7, 10, and 7 syllables.

17. *AH*, 51: no. 182. Very curious is the versification of the hymn *Christe redemptor omni-*

paroxytone polysyllables in 8, 1 and 8, 3, and disyllables with short penulti-
mates in 1.1, 1.3, 2.1, 2.3, 3.1, 4.3, 7.3. The hymn *Mediae noctis tempus est*[18] has
paroxytone polysyllables at the end in 12.3 and 13.3 and, moreover, 9 syllables
in place of 8 in verses 10.1 and 11.1. In the hymn *Rex aeterne Domine,*[19] we find
paroxytone final cadences 2 times: 9.1 *Tu hostis antiqui vires,* and 10.1 *Tu illum a nobis semper.* We also find there 7 syllables instead of 8 in verses 1.1 and
1.3; 5.3, 6.1, 14.1, 15.3. Moreover, numerous hymns have 7 syllables in place of 8
exclusively in odd-numbered verses.[20]

We also find the structure ab + ab in other verse forms. In the rhythmic
imitation of a catalectic iambic dimeter (7p) composed by Jonas of Bobbio
in the first part of the seventh century, the strophes have 4 verses or, more
precisely, 2 double verses:[21]

Clare sacerdos clues,   almo fultus decore,
Tuis, Columba, decus,   qui redoles in orbe.

7 + 7p ▦   In this song, composed of 58 double verses (7 + 7p), the second part of
the double verse always has a paroxytone word at the end, and it always

---

um, AH, 51: no. 50, where we find final paroxytone words in the following verses: 6.2 *Redempti sanguine sumus,* where *sumus* is perhaps enclitic; 3.1, where the penult is long, and 2.1,
2.3, 4.1, 4.3, 5.1, 5.3, 6.1, 6.3, where the penult is short. In all these cases, the final word is disyllabic. I have shown above, p. 103, that the use of a disyllable at the end of the rhythmic Ambrosian verse can perhaps be allowed, even in the case where the imitation of the structure is
entire. But what is curious here is that the author has restricted the use of disyllables to verses having odd numbers.

18. *AH,* 51: no. 1. I am accenting, according to the rule given above in chapter 1, *út Deò* 1.3,
hóc habèt 3.1, *nón eràt* 4.3, *ét malùm* 6.3; one can even defend the accentuation *út Iesù* 10.3; finally, *sumus* is enclitic in the verse *Nos vero Israél sumùs* 6.1. However, it is only in verses 1 and
3 that the author allowed himself these rhythmic liberties with the exception of verse 12.2 *Te
laudamus Christe Deus.* In verses 9.1–2, we read with one of the best manuscripts *Estultae
vero remanent Quia stinctas habent lampadas;* see our article "Contributions à l'étude du latin vulgaire."

19. *AH,* 51: no. 2. The two final paroxytone words of this hymn are disyllabic, which in itself is not abnormal.

20. See, for example, *AH,* 51: nos. 12 (2.3), 138 (4.3), 5 (4), 7 (1), 9 (3), 10 (1), 139 (5.1; see the
final paroxytone cadence 3.3 and 5.3); *AH,* 4: nos. 358 (1.1), 1 (3), 3 (1), 4 (1); *AH,* 12: nos. 74
(1.1), 87 (4.3); *AH,* 14: nos. 49 (1.3), 105 (1.3), 6 (3), 130 (1.3); *AH,* 22: nos. 150 (3.3; paroxytone
final cadence 2.1 and 4.3), 153 (2.1), 4 (1), 8 (1; paroxytone final cadence 2.3 and 6.1), 164 (5.1),
9 (3), 14 (3), 15 (1), 173 (5.3), 8 (3), 429 (4.1), 5 (3), 10 (1; paroxytone final cadence 2.1, 2.3, 3.3,
4.1, 4.3, 5.3, 6.1, 6.3, 8.3, 9.1, 9.3, 10.1); Meyer, *Preces,* 47, 2, 1; 4, 1.

21. *Ionae Vitae sanctorum Columbani, Vedastis, Iohannis,* ed. B. Krusch (Hanover and
Leipzig, 1905): 224–27.

has 7 syllables.[22] In contrast, the first part has 4 times a proparoxytone at the end, and it has 21 times 6 syllables (of which there are 3 cases where one can suppose a prosthesis.)[23] The song of Hibernicus Exul in honor of Charlemagne presents another kind of rhythmic verse:

> Carta, Christo comite,   per telluris spatium
> Ad Caesaris splendidum   nunc perge palatium.[24]

We have here an imitation of the second hemistich of the trochaic septenarius (7pp). There are 12 strophes, and each consists of two double verses. While the second part of each double verse regularly imitates the structure, the first part presents, on the one hand, 4 cases of paroxytone ending (for example, *Felices ac victóres* ‖ *genitoris moribus*), and, on the other hand, 1 case of 8 syllables instead of 7 *(Det, ut illis promiserat,* ‖ *in futuro gloriam).*

The variation in the number of syllables in rhythmic verses is a phenomenon that we must treat separately. This phenomenon appears not only in the cases we just discussed, but in a certain number of others also. Here again, it is a question of a phenomenon that can be explained only if one sees its relation to music.

Let us first look at the cases where one unaccented syllable is added or removed at the beginning of a verse, cases which are linked to the anacrusis that one has in music. Indeed, one sees quite frequently in rhythmic poetry

22. We read in verse 4: *Te sofum proceres,* [te] *vatem dixere reges;* see 27 *Tu lenitate polles,* ‖ *benignitate clares.* [The brackets around *te* are those of Norberg.]

23. Some strophes of two times 7p + 7p are also found in the song *Audite omnes gentes* ‖ *et discite prudentes, PLAC,* 4:501–3. In it there are 6 syllables in place of 7 in verses 4, 1; 7, 1; 10, 3; 11, 1; 13, 1; 17, 1; 19, 1; 20, 3; 22, 1 (in verses 7, 2; 10, 2; and 12, 2 one must, as Strecker has pointed out, read with prosthesis *estirpes, espinea,* and *espongia;* verse 15, 2 must be corrrected to *Dominus et salvator).* Seven verses have 8 or 9 syllables (2, 3; 4, 3; 8, 3; 16, 4; 20, 4, and 4, 4; 12, 3), but in all of them, one can obtain the normal number of syllables by reading with elision or synaeresis. The final cadence is always paroxytone (8, 3 *Arreptum suum gládium* with synaeresis, 9, 4 *tradédit,* 14, 2 *nescíunt* with reconstruction). Some other songs that are composed of hemistichs of 7 syllables but with a free cadence are *Deus amet puellam* ‖ *claram et benivolam, PLAC,* 5:553–54; *Carta dirige gressum* ‖ *per maris et navium,* Gaselee, *The Oxford Book of Medieval Latin Verse,* 61; the strophe *Hinc fluit gramma prima,* ‖ *hinc poetica ydra, Carmina Cantabrigiensia,* 37; perhaps also the song *Ubi resplendent semper* ‖ *angelorum milia, Nachrichten der Gesellschaft der Wissenschaften zu Göttingen,* Philol.-hist. Klasse (1917): 600–602, where the text is often uncertain. In these songs, the number of syllables of the first hemistich varies from 6 to 8 syllables. One can therefore describe the double verses of these songs by the formula: 6–8 + 7.

24. *PLAC,* 1:399–400.

that one initial unaccented syllable can be suppressed or indeed that occasionally one unaccented syllable can be added before an initial accented syllable. Thus the rhythmic iambic dimeter often had, both when recited and when sung, the form ~ ´ ~ ´ ~ ´ ~ ´ . When one suppressed the initial unaccented syllable, that form then was replaced by a verse of seven syllables ´ ~ ´ ~ ´ ~ ´ . To a verse like *Merídiè orándum èst* (the beginning of a celebrated hymn[25]) corresponds verse 2 of the same strophe, *Chrístus dèprecándus èst,* with the suppression of the anacrusis. The variations we have just discussed in the number of syllables in the Ambrosian strophe have, therefore, in general, yielded verses of 7 syllables in place of 8. In the catalectic iambic dimeter, a verse of 7 syllables such as *Audíte vócem hýmni* and one of 6 such as *Kàndidáti éstis* are both possible.[26] If, however, we examine the rhythmic imitation of the trochaic septenarius, we notice a different state of affairs. The eight syllables before the break have most often the form ´ ~ ´ ~ ´ ~ ´ ~. In such a system, it is impossible to remove a syllable. In contrast, one can add a syllable before the initial accented syllable. To the verse of 8 syllables *Álta úrbs et spàtiósa,* in the poem in praise of Milan, dating from about 739, corresponds the verse of 9 syllables *Que áb antíquitùs vocátur.* The characteristic of this poem is—we have emphasized it above, p. 114—that the 8 syllables before the break are always divided up according to an invariable system of accentuation, whereas the 7 syllables after the break can have a variable accentuation and begin either with ´ ~ ´ or with ~ ´ ~ . When it is a matter of knowing if one has to employ an anacrusis or not, it is important to note that, in this poem, there is an anacrusis no fewer than 12 times in the hemistichs of 8 syllables, but never in the second hemistichs of 7 syllables. [27] On the other hand, in the poem *De Pippini victoria Avarica,* dating from 796,[28] there is a system of regular accentuation in the second hemistichs of 7

25. *AH,* 51: no. 64. See, besides, Meyer, *Preces,* 2 and 55. I have treated this phenomenon in a more detailed way in *La poésie latine rythmique,* 28–29.

26. *AH,* 23: no. 31 (1.1 and 5.1), where the editor, who has not understood the versification, adds *iam* before *estis* contrary to the manuscript.

27. One must read *Mediolanum* 1, 3 and 14, 1 and *fidei* 20, 3 with synaeresis (see *Vexillum fidei ferimus, AH,* 51: no. 2 [9.4]). In verse 20, 1 *Viribus robusti cives adstantium certamine* the editors have made a mistake. I inspected the text of the manuscript and noticed that the reading of the manuscript is *Viribus rubusti cives adstant in certamine.* Another song of this structure is *Avarus cupiditatem, PLAC,* 4:541–42. It was probably composed in the same time period and in the same milieu.

28. See above, p. 29 and p. 115.

syllables just as there is in the first hemistichs of 8 syllables. The anacrusis appears there before the second hemistich as well as before the first; and therefore we can express in the following way the rhythmic system of the poem: $(\smile)\; \acute{\smile} \smile \acute{\smile} \smile \acute{\smile} \smile \acute{\smile} \smile \parallel (\smile)\; \acute{\smile} \smile \acute{\smile} \smile \acute{\smile} \smile \grave{\smile}$. The first hemistich of this poem can, therefore, have the form *Ómnes géntes quí fecísti* or *Ut víam éius còmitáret,* and the second hemistich can have the form *últimìs tempóribùs* or *de ára sàcratíssimà.*[29]

In the other verse forms an unaccented syllable can also be added or suppressed following the same principles, but I have given enough examples of these elsewhere.[30]

One extra syllable can, however, be inserted into the verse in places other than the beginning. There, again, the explanation requires turning to the melody. Weinmann has shown[31] that in the monastery of Pairis in Alsace in the Middle Ages they sang to the same melody the normal Ambrosian *Veni redemptor gentium* of 8 syllables and the verse of 9 syllables *Intende qui regis Israel.* Likewise the musical phrase for singing normal verses of 8 syllables could be used for verses like *Appare Ephrem coram excita Potentiam tuam et veni,* which they sang without elision so that the verses had 10 syllables in one case and 9 syllables in the other. This melody was, therefore, to a certain extent, plastic and capable of being adapted to verses of different lengths. This is why we can find rhythmic poems dating from the early Middle Ages in which the number of syllables exceeds the normal count, even when it is not a question of anacrusis. Thus, in Gaul, in the Merovingian period, a poem was sung on the Last Judgement which, by the power of its poetic inspiration, can bear comparison with the *Dies irae.*[32]

> Diem magnum formidate,
> Quando mundum iudicare
> Christus, imperator caeli,
> Venit, fulgens in virtute
> Et in magna claritate,
> Regnum sanctis preparare,

29. One syllable is added before the first hemistich in 4, 3; 13, 2; 15, 2; before the second in 1, 1; 2, 3; 3, 1; 3, 2; 8, 2; 9, 2; 11, 3; 14, 3. The songs *Arve, poli conditorem, Graciam excelso regi,* and *Felicis patriae Pictonum, PLAC,* 4:542, 592, and 654, provide other examples of rhythmic trochaic septenarii where anacruses have been added.

30. See the cases that I have analyzed in *La poésie latine rythmique,* 27–28 and 106–7.

31. Weinmann, *Hymnarium Parisiense,* 38. See also ibid., 27–28.

32. *PLAC,* 4:521–23.

this is the second strophe, each verse of which has 8 syllables and has reproduced regularly the structure of a trochaic dimeter. But this poem also contains some verses like *Ét archángeli fòrmidábunt, Pró homínibus crùcifíxum,*
where the number of syllables goes up to 9. The first verse even has 10 syllables according to the tradition of two manuscripts: *Quíque de mórte éstis
redémpti.* In other words, the unknown poet seems, without taking account
of the metrical demands, to have profited from liberties that the melody allowed to him. It is very likely that he had for a model in this case the musical
performance of hymns like *Intende qui regis Israel,* which we just discussed.[33]

If one wrote the words to an already existing melody, without following
strictly the syllabic principle, one would be led to introduce certain variations in the number of syllables. Quite a few writers of the Middle Ages
found in this activity the possibility of a freer versification since they could
write verses of variable length and could increase or decrease the number of
syllables.[34]

It is, therefore, the rhythmic form of the ordinary Ambrosian verse that
constitutes the framework of the hymn *Te Christe patris filium.*[35] Of the 123
complete verses that make up this hymn, 75 are, in fact, of 8 syllables with a
proparoxytone final cadence, in keeping with the first verse, and 22 are of 8
syllables with paroxytone final cadence (for example, *Sibi credo coaetér-
num*). But there are, in addition (6 to 9), 14 verses of 7 syllables of the
type *Credo et confíteor* and 8 of the type *Heü decipit práva* or *Multorum
torquens poéna,* 3 of 6 syllables *(Pellens paradiso, Unde est eiectus* and
Caelosque ascendo) and finally 1 verse of 9 syllables *(Offendi te en paenitet
me).* Side by side with entirely regular, rhythmic Ambrosian strophes we see
strophes as irregular as these:

6 to 9 ▨

> Personis qui cum sit trinus,
> Deitate sed est unus,
> Pater verbo omnia
> Creans, vivificans cuncta,

33. Songs of this type were often composed in the Merovingian period; see the edition of
Strecker, *PLAC,* 4:457–58, and Meyer, *Ges. Abh.,* 1:208–9, 213–15.

34. The composition of free verses in which the number of syllables varied can be an
artistic principle but can also come from an inability to follow the rules of rhythmic poetry. I
have treated a few examples of this latter case in *La poésie latine rythmique,* 26–27, 32, and
52–53.

35. Published by Mone, 1:34–36, based on a Reichenau manuscript of the eleventh century. The melody is, according to Mone, noted in neumes above the verses.

which must have been sung to the same melody as the others. The hymn *Te Christe Deum Dominum* is by the same author.[36] In it I have counted 40 verses with the form 8pp and 13 with the form 8p. The form 7pp is found 3 times, 7p 8 times, 6p 4 times, 9pp 3 times, 9p 1 time. I could cite a large number of poems of this type, in which most of the verses are octosyllables but where many syllables also diverge from the norm.[37]

The poem *Hanc quicumque devoti,* written at Reichenau at the end of the eighth century,[38] offers us a majority of rhythmic 7-syllable verses having their origin in the catalectic iambic dimeter. In it I count 14 7-syllable verses of the type *Hanc quicumque devóti,* 2 of the type *Cernite conspícuum,* 4 6-syllable verses of the type *Lamina niténti,* and 4 8-syllable verses of varied structures (6 to 8). As an example of the style that the strophes of this poem can have, let us refer to this one:

6 to 8

Titulo qui tali
Ornavit virginis templum
Aetherea fruatur
Sede felix in aevum.[39]

---

36. Mone, 1:37. I read verses 67–68 as *Fac mecum diebus / Manere haec et noctibus.*

37. The oldest of these poems is *Beatus quidem opifex, PLAC,* 4:637–38, which is found in a manuscript from the beginning of the eighth century. The acrostic of the poem is *Basinus,* and Strecker thinks that the anonymous author dedicated this song to Basinus, bishop of Trier, about the year 704 when he gave him the precious manuscript where the song is inscribed. In this case, one would have to find the dative *Basino.* It should also be noted that there are many copying errors in the poem, which show that our manuscript is not the archetype. It is just as possible that a certain Basinus, of whom we know nothing, is the author of this song.

See, moreover, the songs *Oves ovilis Christi, PLAC,* 4:640; *Audi me Deus piissime, PLAC,* 4:484–86 (analyzed by Meyer, *Ges. Abh.,* 3:60); *Altus auctor omnium, Adiutor in te sperantium* and *Arrius et Sabellius, PLAC,* 4:903–10; *Audi preces supplicum,* Meyer, *Preces,* 143; *Confitebor tibi pater, Nachrichten der Gesellschaft der Wissenschaften zu Göttingen* (1917): 605; *Quae est ista veniens,* Migne, *PL,* 164:1285.

38. *PLAC,* 4:639; see *La poésie latine rythmique,* 23–24. Meyer believes he has found in this poem Old High German versification, *Ges. Abh.,* 3:261, and scans, for example, *Hánc quicúmque devóti.* Obviously he does not see the relationship with songs such as *Clare sacerdos cluis, Deus amet puellam,* or *Carta dirige gressum,* which I mentioned above in this chapter.

39. Other songs written in verses which have, for the most part, 7 syllables but whose length may vary are *Miserator Domine,* Meyer, *Preces,* 168, and the Irish song *Adelphus adelpha meter,* published by F. J. H. Jenkinson in *The Hisperica Famina* (Cambridge, 1908).

In the song celebrating the coronation of Emperor Henry III in 1028,[40] we find 5-syllable verses, that is to say, rhythmic Adonics with variants 4 to 7 ▦ (4 to 7). Here is the beginning of this song:

O rex regum   qui solus in evum
Regnas in celis,   Heinricum nobis
Serva in terris   ab inimicis.

Each verse is composed normally of 2 rhythmic hemistichs of 5 syllables; 49 times they end with a paroxytone, 2 times with a proparoxytone. In addition to those, we have 5 4-syllable verses of the type *Ó rex régum,* 12 6-syllable verses of the type *Qui sólus in évum* or *Tíbi bènedíci* and 7 of the type *Clérus et pópulus,* and 3 7-syllable verses of the type *Síbi dèvotíssimo.* Certain strophes can, therefore, have forms as varied as the last strophe, of which this is the text:

Laus creatori,   angelorum regi
Cuius imperium   manet in evum
Per infinita   seculorum secula.[41]

In the cases to which I have referred, of poems written in 8-, 7-, and 5-syllable verses with variation, one still clearly notices the relationship with Classical Latin verse. I believe that, in all of these cases, we are in the presence of poems composed on already existing melodies, without the versifiers strictly following the syllabic principle. Since the Merovingian period there have existed in the different countries Latin poems with verses that could in this way be varied in length; and therefore, it is hardly likely that a foreign influence explains the practice. One cannot, however, deny that, on a good many points, the varying 8-syllable verses recall Old High German verses. In certain special cases, it is permissible to admit its influence. Hence this influence can be admitted in the translation into Latin of the song in honor of St.

40. *Carmina Cantabrigiensia,* 16.

41. One finds the same variable verses, which most of the time are composed of 5 syllables, in *Preces* of the Mozarabic liturgy: Meyer, 5, *Amara nobis est vita nostra,* and 8, *Alleva iugum colla prementem* (see the rhythmic Adonics that imitate the structure of the quantitative model, ibid., 9, 57, 137, 152), and, moreover, in the poetry of Dhuoda and of her precursors who seem to have borrowed this form from liturgical *Preces, PLAC,* 4:703–17 (Meyer gives another interpretation of this versification, *Ges. Abh.,* 3:72–82). See also the didactic poem *De ratione temporum, PLAC,* 6:188–203.

Gall composed in Old High German by Ratpert.[42] Here is the first strophe of the translation:

> Nunc incipiendum   est mihi magnum gaudium,
> Sanctiorem nullum   quam sanctum umquam Gallum
> Misit filium Hibernia,   recepit patrem Suevia.
> Exultemus omnes,   laudemus Christum pariles
> Sanctos advocantem   et glorificantem.

Meyer wanted, probably justly so, to recognize in these verses Old High German verse accented on four syllables: *Núnc incìpiéndùm est míhi mágnum gaúdiùm, Sànctiórem núllùm quam sánctum úmquam Gállùm,* and so on. The same may be said for the poem in two languages:

> Nunc almus thero evvigero   assis thiernum filius
> Benignus fautor mihi,   thaz ig iz cosan muozi
> De quodam duce,   themo heron Heinriche,
> Qui cum dignitate   thero Beiaro riche bevvarode,[43]

where the influence of Old High German verse on the Latin verse is visible. Meyer also believed he had found, in quite a few *Carmina Burana,* that the Latin verse there is constructed following the principles of German verse.[44]

But music not only changed already existing verse, it also created new forms of it. This is what appears quite clearly when one examines the prosaically formed refrains and their influence.

The abecedarian poem, *Audax es vir, iuvenis,* in rhythmic Ambrosians, [45] dates from the Merovingian period. To the strophes, a refrain of two verses is added, constructed in a manner entirely different from that of the rest of the poem (9pp). Here is the refrain after the first strophe:

> Adtende homo quod pulvis es
> Et in pulverem reverteris.

42. PLAC, 5:536–40. Meyer analyzed the verses and the strophes, *Ges. Abh.,* 3:65–72.

43. *Carmina Cantabrigiensia,* 19.

44. *Ges. Abh.,* 3:87–93. Meyer also succeeded in showing that the author of the Irish hymn *Sacratissimi martyres summi Dei, AH,* 51: no. 236, imitated the versification of a Byzantine model, *Ges. Abh.,* 3:310–15.

45. PLAC, 4:495–507. A few verses have only 7 syllables because the initial unaccented syllable that corresponds to the anacrusis of the melody has been omitted; see *La poésie latine rythmique,* 29.

These words are borrowed from a liturgical formula *Memento homo quod pulvis es et in pulverem reverteris,* a formula which, in turn, goes back to Genesis 3.19.[46] The words of the refrain are then, from the ancient point of view, to be considered as prose. But they were intended to be sung, and one can assume that the melody was syllabic and rhythmic. From the rhythmic point of view, the two new verses of 9 syllables sound fine. They were *2 x 9pp* ▦ also used quite early in rhythmic poems to form strophes (2 x 9pp), as we read in the poem below.

Remitte omnia crimina
Nosque placatus iustifica.

Intende benignus supplices,
Gemitus omnium suscipe,

these lines are from a Spanish liturgical poem whose author—although Meyer, the editor, did not see it—names himself in an acrostic: Suintharic; and he must be identical to the bishop of Valencia who had the same name and who flourished about 675.[47] A novel form of strophe was also created by adding to a rhythmic Sapphic verse two verses of 9 syllables (5p *5p + 6p, 2 x 9pp* ▦ + 6p, 2 x 9pp):

Ne derelinquas   plebem supplicantem.
Exaudi precem et respice,
Quae postulamus adtribue.[48]

In the Carolingian period, a poet from the North of Italy also used these 9-syllable verses in a secular poem, composed of strophes of 5 verses.[49]

Another case of the same kind is the following. The very old Merovingian *Angelus venit de caelo,* written in rhythmic trochaic septenarii, has a free re-

46. See Thalhofer-Eisenhofer, *Handbuch der katholischen Liturgik,* 1:605; 2:473. For the responsorial song in the liturgy, see, for example, Jungmann, *Missarum Sollemnia,* 2:89–103, 188–211.

47. Meyer, *Preces,* 43. Verses 1, 1; 2, 1; and 3, 1 contain only 8 syllables because the anacrusis is suppressed. The same verse is found in the *Preces* 1, 60 and 75. We know that Suintaric of Valencia participated in the Council of Toledo in 675; see *España Sacra,* 8 (Madrid, 1769): 171.

48. Meyer, *Preces,* 32. See also ibid., 53 and 78.

49. It is the song *Audite versus parabole, PLAC,* 4:572–73, which I have treated in *La poésie latine rythmique,* 98–103.

frain: *Venite et audite, quanta fecit Dominus,* which also has a liturgical origin.[50] The rhythm and the melody of the refrain pleased the author of the song *A superna caeli parte* so much that he made an analogous refrain composed also of 2 verses of 7 syllables with different final cadences (7p + 7pp): *Venite et gaudete ‖ nato Christo Domino.*[51] This new verse was used in the composition of poems from the Merovingian period onwards. It appears in the poem,

7p + 7pp ▨

> A patre missus veni   perditos requirere
> Et hoste captivatos   sanguine redimere.[52]

It is not rare to find among the refrains some verses of 6 syllables of the type (6p), *Miserere nobis.*[53] The refrain *Deus miserere, ‖ Deus miserere ‖ in peccatis eius,* in a Mozarabic poem, comprises 3 verses of this type, which can also be regarded as a single line of 6 + 6 + 6 syllables. From this refrain the verses of the poem to which the refrain belongs derived their form (6p + 6p + 6p):

6p ▨

6p + 6p + 6p ▨

> Ecce nunc advenit   dirae mortis dies   et hora extrema.[54]

In another Mozarabic poem, the refrain is formed from 4 verses of 6 syllables: *Deus miserere, ‖ Deus miserere ‖ miserere nobis ‖ pro peccatis nostris.*[55] Hence, the following strophe in the same poem:

> Audi nos clamantes,
> Christe Ihesu bone,
> Adtende misertus
> Nostra exoratus.

50. *PLAC,* 4:564–65. For the refrain, see the offertory of the fourth Sunday after Easter: *Venite et audite et narrabo vobis omnes qui timetis Deum, quanta fecit Dominus animae meae;* see Psalm 65.16.

51. *PLAC,* 4:477–80.

52. Meyer, *Preces,* 147. The same author probably composed song 148, ibid., of which this is the first strophe:

> Portatus sum ut agnus   innocens ad victimam,
> Captus ab inimicis   ut avis in muscipulam.

Here the first verse is composed of 7p + 7pp; but the second verse, of 7p + 8pp (that is to say, an anacrusis is added before the last hemistich). These two poems are found in a manuscript of the eighth century (see E. A. Lowe, *Codices Latini Antiquiores,* 5:653).

53. Meyer, *Preces,* 62, 129, and 179.   54. Meyer, *Preces,* 138.

55. Meyer, *Preces,* 165.

We have here the same strophe as in the celebrated hymn *Ave maris stella,* dating probably from the Carolingian period and very often imitated in the Middle Ages.[56] It is not necessary, therefore, to search for a quantitative model for that strophe.

The refrain added by Marius Victorinus to the first of his hymns in the middle of the fourth century is analogous in nature.[57] The text itself of the hymn, which begins with *Miserere Domine, quia credidi in te, miserere Domine, quia misericordia tua cognovi te* is, by its form, literary prose; and its refrain, *Miserere Domine, miserere Christe,* is also composed as if it were prose. But this refrain has a marked rhythm, 7pp + 6p, which certainly made itself felt in the melody and seems to have produced a certain impression. In fact, we find the same rhythm in other refrains of analogous

7pp + 6p 🔲 content. Thus, in one of the Mozarabic *Preces* we have this (7pp + 6p): *Supplicanti populo* ‖ *Christe miserere,* and in a song of Merovingian Gaul, we have this: *Christe resuveniad te* ‖ *de mi peccatore.*[58] It seems that the Mozarabic song *Miserere Domine,* ‖ *miserere nobis* was based on a melody of the same type, although the number of syllables in the verses varies.[59] Abelard used this rhythm in a few verses of his *Planctus Iacob super filios suos:*

> Pueriles nenie   super cantus omnes
> Orbati miserie   senis erant dulces;
> Informes in facie   teneri sermones
> Omnem eloquentie   favum transcendentes.[60]

Goliardic Verse 🔲   When the same rhythm reappears, it is in a secular song of Hugh of Orléans (Goliardic Verse) :

56. *AH,* 51: no. 123. Abelard and Thomas à Kempis, among others, imitated this strophe, *AH,* 48: nos. 187–190, ibid., no. 463; some anonymous imitations are found in almost all the hymnaries. The poet counted only the number of syllables in the hymn *Genitrix intacta, AH,* 12: no. 57; the number of syllables can vary in the hymn *Salve plaga sancta,* composed by Pope John XXII, *AH,* 31: no. 66.

57. Migne, *PL,* 8:1142.

58. Meyer, *Preces,* 51; *PLAC,* 4:651. One can also compare the refrain added to a poem by Gottschalk of Orbais *Ó Déus, míserì* ‖ *mìserére sérvi, PLAC,* 3:729–31.

59. Meyer, *Preces,* 131.

60. Abelard, *Planctus,* ed. Vecchi , 46.

Filii burgensium,   filii crumene,
Quos a scholis revocat   cantus philomene.[61]

We have here the well-known verse, called Goliardic, which was so wide-spread toward the end of the Middle Ages, especially in the secular poetry. We do not know why this verse became so popular in the twelfth century. But as I have shown above, it is probably in religious poetry that one must search for its origin.

It is also interesting to study more closely a few verses of ten sylla-
4p + 6p ▨ bles (4p + 6p) that one finds in different refrains. Number 110 of the
Mozarabic *Preces* has for a refrain these two verses: *Miserere* ‖ *finis nos-ter adest. Succurre Christe.* The first of these verses is composed of 4 + 6 syllables with falling rhythm; and the strophes of the song are constructed on this model:

Bone pastor   moriens pro grege,
Oves tuas   a malo defende.

This is a form of verse used from time to time, even at the end of the Middle Ages.[62]

More important were verses of ten syllables (4 + 6pp) of the type
4p + 6pp ▨ *In tremendo* ‖ *die iudicii,* words which make up the refrain of the
song *Apparebit repentina,* probably belonging to antiquity. This verse was imitated by other writers in an entire series of refrains, such as *Immi-nente* ‖ *die iudicii, In pavendo* ‖ *die iudicii, Poenitenti* ‖ *Christe da veniam, Miserere* ‖ *mei piissime, Ab inferno* ‖ *Christe nos libera.*[63] The form was even imitated in the poem *Andecavis abbas esse dicitur,* which is a parody, and its refrain has this for its second verse: *Eia laudes* ‖ *dicamus Libero.*[64] St. Jubinus, who in 1082 became archbishop of Lyon, uses the same sort of verse in a poem whose strophes have the following appearance:

61. See Strecker, *Die zweite Beichte des Erzpoeten,* 244–52.
62. See, for example, the hymn *Deo demus grates, hymnos, laudes, AH,* 11: no. 313. John of Jenstein uses the same verse but without a fixed break in the hymn *Mittitur archangelus fi-delis, AH,* 48: no. 422. See also *AH,* 29: nos. 291 and 302; *AH,* 31: no. 73.
63. See *PLAC,* 4:491–95, 507, 602–4. Another form, 4p + 5p, presents the refrain *In perennis die sabbati,* ibid., 512, probably composed according to the model of *In tremendo die iudicii* by someone who pronounced the word *iudicii* with synaeresis. This way of reading was stan-dard in the British Isles, and the refrain *In perennis die sabbati* is preserved only in an English manuscript. We can presume that it does not belong to the authentic song.
64. *PLAC,* 4:591.

In te loca   pulcra <sunt> omnia,
Nullus turbo,   procul sunt nubila,
Clari dies,   serena tempora.[65]

This rhythmic verse of ten syllables was extremely popular in the twelfth century and later. It is composed of 4 + 6 syllables; the cadence before the break is free but the final cadence is always proparoxytone. It was thought that it had its origin in the quantitative catalectic dactylic tetrameter, *Germine nobilis Eulalia,* in which breaks occasionally appear after the fourth syllable, of the type *Úrbe pótens* ‖ *pópulis lócuples* or *Infrémuit* ‖ *sácer Euláliae.* Such an origin is not impossible, but neither is it necessary. In a direct imitation of the catalectic dactylic tetrameter we would have expected rhythmic verses, certainly, but without a fixed break—as in the following strophe *10pp* ▓ of Benzo of Alba (11th cent.) (10pp) :

In sanctis narratur aecclesiis
Quod homo sit kyrrios bestiis,
Utens est quippe rationibus,
Quod denegatum est peccoribus.[66]

Still another example which shows in an instructive way how new forms of verse were created is found in number 133 of the Mozarabic *Preces.* Before a verse of type 6p, *Ave maris stella,* which we have just examined, the author has placed the vocative *Domine* (3 + 6p):

3 + 6p ▓

Domine,   audi lacrimantes,
Domine,   veniam petentes.

65. See Wattenbach, "Lateinische Gedichte aus Frankreich im elften Jahrhundert." It is not at all by chance that the same verse appears in Old French, in the same time period and in the same region, in the poem which begins,

Quant li solleiz   converset en leon
en icel tens   qu'est ortus pliadon,
          per unt matin
Une pulcellet   odit molt gent plorer
et son ami   dolcement regreter. . . .

See, for example, Vossler, *Die Dichtungsformen der Romanen,* 172 (this song is not, as Vossler claims, a sequence).
66. *MGH, Scriptores,* 11:645–46. It is, however, possible that Benzo wrote this text to an already existing melody. Characteristic of his versification is that he often allowed 11 syllables instead of 10 in the third verse.

This has prompted the writer to form new verses of 3 + 6 syllables, such as *Subveni* || *misertus et clemens, Succurre* || *et iam miserere.*

What I have said about the creation of new verses probably suffices to allow us to say that it was by basing his verses on a melody rather than by working from theoretical speculations on quantitative forms and their combinations that Paulinus of Aquileia, for example, created his *8p + 4p* 🔲 songs (8p + 4p) *Congregavit nos in unum* || *Christi amor,* and *Hic est dies in quo Christi* || *pretioso,* having verses of 12 syllables with a break after the eighth.[67] At approximately the same time that Paulinus was writing and in almost the same part of *7–8p + 6pp* 🔲 Italy, the poem (7–8p + 6pp) *Placidas fuit dictus* || *magister militum* was created, whose particular rhythm, (~) ~ ~ ~́ ~ ~ ~ ~́ ~ || ~ ~ ~ ~ ~́ ~ ~ , has been analyzed in detail by Meyer.[68]

A few words remain to be said about the strophic form of rhythmic poems during the early Middle Ages. At the beginning, rhythmic strophes were entirely dependent on models furnished by quantitative poetry, as we have seen already on several occasions when we have observed strophes of Horace and Prudentius reappearing in rhythmic form. But more and more poets freed themselves from the classical model, and even in this development, the refrain played an important role: often it was an appendage independent of the strophe that could quite easily be incorporated into the strophe. In another work, I have shown how Paulinus of Aquileia created a new rhythmic strophe by incorporating a refrain.[69] He had read in the work of Eugenius of Toledo a song written in quantitative iambic trimeters where each strophe was composed of 3 verses followed by the refrain *Parce redemptor.* This inspired him to create a new strophe formed of 3 rhythmic vers-
3 x (5p + 7pp), 5p 🔲 es of 12 syllables + a rhythmic verse of 5 syllables (3 x [5p + 7pp], 5p) for the abecedarian song that begins in this way:

67. *PLAC,* 4:526–29 and 580–82. For the author of these songs, see *La poésie latine rythmique,* 87–97.

Another verse of 12 syllables is that which we find in the poem *Laxis fibris resonante plectro linguae,* written in memory of William Longsword in 942; see *Zeitschrift für französische Sprache und Literatur* 63 (1940): 190–97. In this song, the verse is composed of 4 + 4 + 4 syllables with proparoxytone cadences.

68. *PLAC,* 4:593–99; see Meyer, *Ges. Abh.,* 3:277–84.

69. *La poésie latine rythmique,* 96–97.

Ad caeli clara   non sum dignus sidera
Levare meos   infelices oculos,
Gravi depressus   peccatorum pondere,
　　Parce redemptor.

Bonum neglexi   facere quod debui,
Probrosa gessi   sine fine crimina,
Scelus patravi   nullo clausum termino,
　　Subveni Christe.[70]

Naturally, the formation of this strophe was made easier for Paulinus in this case since the Sapphic strophe provided a certain model. In this way we can explain quite a few other new forms of strophes. We find, for example, three rhythmic Ambrosian verses + one Adonic in the song

3 x 8pp, 5p 🔲   (3 x 8pp, 5p)

Creator mundi Domine
Qui aequitatem iudicas,
Tu nos a malo libera
　　Dextera tua,

and also four rhythmic trochaic dimeters + one Adonic, in

4 x 8p, 5p 🔲   the song (4 x 8p, 5p)

Quid interrogare qualis
Attinet, cum non sit talis,
Cui Pater est aequalis
Et Spiritus principalis,
　　Deus et homo.[71]

2 x (5p + 6pp), 7pp 🔲   In one strophe like this (2 x [5p + 6pp], 7pp),

---

70. *AH*, 50: no. 107. It may happen that a Sapphic strophe breaks down into 3 Sapphic verses and a refrain; this is the case in song 79 of the Mozarabic *Preces*, formed from 5 rhythmic Sapphic strophes where the Adonic is always the refrain *Et miserere*, sung by those assembled.

71. Meyer, *Preces*, 86 (see ibid., 107, where an Ambrosian strophe is followed by the refrain *Et miserere*), and Migne, *PL*, 164:1269. There are even some new rhythmic verses which are composed of a trochaic dimeter + an Adonic (see Meyer, *Preces*, 141) or of an iambic dimeter + an Adonic (see ibid., 33, where, for example, verse 1 *Pie precantes supplices* || *exaudi Christe*, shows that the Adonic is an incorporated refrain).

> Audi clamantes   Pater altissime,
> Et quae precamur,   clemens attribue;
>   Exaudi nos Domine,[72]

the third verse still has a form and a meaning that show that it is an incorporated refrain; the first two verses are rhythmic Alcaics. Morever,
2 x (4 + 8p), 5p ▓ let us compare the strophe (2 x [4 + 8p], 5p),

> Seniores   iuvenes atque lactantes
> Dira morte   perimuntur in dolore,
>   Redemptor parce,[73]

where, after two verses of 12 syllables, comes a rhythmic Adonic of the same
kind as that which Eugenius of Toledo was already using as a refrain.
        The following long refrain has a new and interesting form of
2 x (8p + 6p) ▓ strophe (2 x [8p + 6p]):

> Miserere, miserere   Deus miserere.
> Veniam ei concede   et peccata dele.[74]

This strophe is composed of two verses, each having 8 + 6 syllables with
some paroxytone cadences, and it was used throughout a few poems.
Thus, in the Mozarabic *Preces* we find it in number 130 which begins in this
way:

> Per quem te semper in celis   credimus regnantem,
> Ita careamus malis   te auxiliante,

and Gottschalk of Orbais must have borrowed, from the same liturgical
source or from another analogous one, the form of his well-known poem:[75]

>   O Deus, miseri   miserere servi.
> Ex quo enim me iussisti   hunc in mundum nasci,

---

72. Meyer, *Preces*, 54; the same strophe is again found, ibid., 68. In this strophe the third
verse always has (with the exception of 68, 4) the rhythm ~ ´ ~ ~ ´ ~ ~ . We find this same
rhythm in the refrain *Et ésto propítius*, ibid., 33, and in the 7-syllable verse of which song 49 is
composed: *Excélse perpétue Quae póscimus tríbue. Audítum piíssimum Inclína orántibus.* The
editor has rightly put forward the opinion that the melody to which singers sang these verses had a definite rhythm on which the versification depended.

73. Meyer, *Preces*, 36.   74. Meyer, *Preces*, 141.
75. *PLAC*, 3:729–31.

Prae cunctis ego amavi   vanitate pasci.
    Heu quid evenit mihi.

Here the first and the last verses are a refrain that returns in all of the strophes, but each of the two intermediate verses has the same construction of 8
+ 6 syllables as the songs that I have just mentioned.

Number 3 of the Mozarabic *Preces* can illustrate another way of forming
new verses and new strophes. This song begins with this prayer in prosaic
form: *Averte Domine* ‖ *iram furoris tui,* to which those assembled respond:
Et miseratus parce ‖ *populo tuo.* The first of these verses is made of 6 + 7
syllables with a proparoxytone before the break and a paroxytone at the end;
the second, of 7 + 5 syllables with some final paroxytone cadences. Following
the same rhythm and the same melody, the author formed

6pp + 7p, 7p + 5p ▓   the strophes of the song whose first strophe is this (6pp + 7p,
7p + 5p):

Omnium precibus   pium auditum praebe
Et quae rogamus, Sancte,   cito concede.

In the same way, in number 29, the introduction *Verbum patris altissimi*
(8pp) + the refrain *Redemptor peccantibus* ‖ *miserere* (7pp +

8pp, 7pp ▓   4p) have given birth to the strophe (8pp, 7pp):

Ad te levamus oculos
    Exaudi propitius.[76]

In the eleventh century an abecedarian poem was composed at Metz having
the same strophe; the poem begins in this way:

Adtende rex piissime
    Planctus hos ecclesie,

and a little while later, Leo of Vercelli composed two poems into which enter
the same elements and which are joined to strophes in the fol-

3 x (8pp + 7pp) ▓   lowing way (3 x [8pp + 7pp]:

---

76. See also Meyer, *Preces,* 61.

Christe, preces intellege,   Romam tuam respice,
Romanos pie renova,   vires Romae excita;
Surgat Roma imperio   sub Ottone tertio.[77]

The Mozarabic *Preces* will show us again an example of the way in which the forms of complicated strophes were created. Here is the introduction of number 153: *"Indulgentia!"* || *dicamus omnes, Domine,* || *tu dona ei veniam.*

The strophes of the same poem clearly derived their form
5pp, 7pp, 8pp ▨   from this prosaic introduction (5pp, 7pp, 8pp):

Rex altissime
Et perennis Domine,
Tu dona ei veniam.

The form of the strophes of number 50 is almost entirely sim-
5pp, 2 x 7pp ▨   ilar (5pp, 2 x 7pp):

Patris dextera,
Virtus, sapientia
Placatus da veniam,

the only difference is that by the absence of an anacrusis the last verse has 7 syllables instead of 8.[78] We find in number 4 an expansion of this strophe; by the verbal resemblance we also see its direct dependence on
5pp, 2 x 7pp, 3pp ▨   number 153 (5pp, 2 x 7pp, 3pp):

Rex altissime
Et perennis Domine,
Precem quam effundimus
Accipe.

A 3-syllable verse was added here, at the end. In number 38, in contrast, the expansion of the strophe has been achieved by the addition of
8pp, 5pp, 2 x 7pp ▨   a verse of 8 syllables at the beginning of the strophe (8pp, 5pp, 2 x 7pp):

---

77. *PLAC,* 5:494–95 and 477–80. This strophe is found again in the work of St. Peter Damian, *AH,* 48: nos. 55–57, 70.
78. In songs 35 and 81 of the *Preces,* the poets imitated the form of song 50.

Omnipotens ingenite,
    Unigeniti
Genitor sanctissime
Precem nostram suscipe.[79]

The melodies obviously must have had, in all of these cases, a common structure.

    We see then that the poets of the early Middle Ages created several strophes that were new in structure and more or less varied by incorporating refrains or by following given melodies, yet these strophes are still, on the whole, rather simple. Thus, in the fragment of a secular poem of the Merovingian period, we find this simple beginning (2 x 7p, 9p):

2 x 7p, 9p

Dum myhy ambolare
Et bene (= veni?) cogetare,
Audivi avem adcladtire,

2 x 6, 8   or in the pilgrim song (2 x 6, 8):

Audi nos rex Christe,
Audi nos Domine,
Et viam nostram dirige.[80]

However, after the year 1000, we can also find more complicated forms. In an exegetical work on the Song of Songs attributed to St. Bruno of Segni we read, for example, this strophe:

Diximus ecclesiam
Sponsam regis regiam,
Cuius estis oculi,
    Vos prophetae,
Vos dentes fortissimi,
    Paule, Petre,
Qui eam reficitis
    Assuete,

---

79. See song 87, composed of strophes whose form is similar.
80. *PLAC*, 4:652, and Boucherie, "Mélanges latins et bas-latins," *Revue des langues romanes* 7 (1875): 33.

whose form, 2 x 7pp, 3 x (7pp + 4p), recalls what we find in a contemporaneous hymn in honor of St. Peter and of St. Paul, 7pp, 2 x (7pp + 4):

> Passio pontificum
> Petri, Pauli rutilat
> Orbem totum,
> Annua quam colimus
> Per tempora.[81]

Very curious is the abecedarian poem on the Last Judgement of which this is the first strophe:[82]

> Audi tellus, audi magni maris limbus,
> Audi homo, audi, omne quod vivit sub sole.
> Veniet prope est   dies irae supremae,
> Dies invisa,
> Dies amara,
> Qua caelum fugiet,
> Sol erubescet,
> Luna mutabitur,   dies nigrescet,
> Sidera super terram cadent.
> Heu, miseri,
> Heu, miseri,
> Quid homo ineptam
> Sequeris laetitiam.

In this poem, the verses of the different strophes have a varying number of syllables. The first verse has 9–13 syllables, the second 7–14, the third, in contrast, is composed always of 6 + 7 syllables, while in the following verses, there are again some variations. The words *Heu miseri*, and so on, form the refrain. It is in keeping with the various demands of the melody that the poet has composed the different verses which constitute the strophes.[83] The choir

---

81. Migne, *PL*, 164:1262, and *AH*, 22: no. 372; see the song *Ave caeli ianua*, *AH*, 2: no. 72, whose strophes have, for the most part, the form 3 x 7pp, 4p + 7pp. In the work attributed to St. Bruno, several songs have a new form. Thus the famous *Quis est hic qui pulsat ad ostium*, Migne, *PL*, 164:1266, where the form of the strophes is 3 + 7pp, 7pp, 3 x (4 + 7pp). See, in addition, for example, Gottschalk of Orbais, *PLAC*, 3:731–32, *Ut quid iubes pusiole*: 2 x 8pp, 2 x 8p, 4p; and *Carmina Cantabrigiensia*, 17, *Lamentemur nostra, socii, peccata*, etc.: 2 x (6p + 6p, 8p + 5p).

82. *AH*, 49:369–76 (no. 778); Meyer, *Ges. Abh.*, 1:237–38.

83. Blume reproduced the melody, *AH*, 49:376–77.

sang the largest part of the first and second verse on the same tone, the *tenor* or the *tuba* [the "held" recitation tone, the main recitation note], to which is added a cadence:

Au - di tel - lus au - di mag - ni ma - ris lim - bus, Au - di ho - mo

au - di om - ne quod vi - vit sub so - le

Here, it was easy to adapt the melody to verses of different lengths. But the melody of the third verse has another character:

Ve - ni - et pro - pe est di - es i - rae su - pre - mae

This melodic structure forced the poet to compose verses according to the syllabic principle.

It is, therefore, obvious that the melody played a fundamental role for the author of this poem. The form of the strophes is so artistically constructed that only experienced singers could have performed it. These complicated forms, however, are already dependent on the development of a liturgical poetry of a more artistic character, a development to which we will devote the next chapter.

EIGHT ▦ SEQUENCES, TROPES, MOTETS, RONDEAUX

The oldest Christian religious service was not at all lacking in songs or poems. Well before St. Ambrose introduced in the West the poetic hymn that assumed the form of ancient versification, singers had been singing, in the East as well as in the West, hymns and songs, either borrowed from the Bible or composed after models offered by biblical poetry. In the Bible, it was mainly the Psalter that supplied the material for these songs. But singers also sang other hymns from Holy Scriptures, for example, the canticles of Moses (Exodus 15 and Deuteronomy 32), the canticle of the three boys (Daniel 3.52–90), and the *Magnificat, Benedictus,* and *Nunc dimittis* (Luke 1–2).[1] Following the models supplied by biblical poetry, poets also composed new poems, as we see by numerous pieces of evidence in the patristic literature and by some hymns that have been preserved for us.[2] The best known among these, belonging to the first centuries of Christianity, is the *Te Deum,* which by the parallelism between its words and its ideas, gives us a representative image of this form of poetry:

> Te Deum laudamus,
> Te Dominum confitemur,
> Te aeternum patrem omnis terra veneratur.
> Tibi omnes angeli,
> Tibi caeli et universae potestates,
> Tibi cherubim et seraphim incessabili voce proclamant:
> Sanctus, sanctus, sanctus Dominus Deus Sabaoth.

1. See P. Wagner, *Einführung,* 1:7.
2. See, for example, the article "Hymnes" in *Dictionnaire d'archéologie chrétienne et de liturgie;* Simonetti, *Studi sull'innologia populare cristiana dei primi secoli;* Kroll, "Die Hymnendichtung des frühen Christentums," *Die Antike* 2 (1926): 258–81; von den Steinen, *Notker der Dichter* (Bern: A. Francke, 1948), 1 [Darstellungsband]: 90–105.

This poetry in prose had nothing in common with Greco-Latin versification. It is not possible to confine the structure of the verse within any particular form, nor is it possible, as regards its composition, to indicate the precise boundaries between this poetry and artistic prose.

But this poetry was written to be sung. The melodic character could be simple and syllabic, but after the period of Constantine it often became quite rich and embellished with melismas, that is to say, with melodic figures sung on a single vowel. The psalmody was originally responsorial: a soloist sang first and the community responded with a refrain. When the melodies were more and more embellished with melismas, the responses were often given by a professionally trained choir. A new way of singing the psalms and the canticles was introduced at the time of St. Ambrose, who had the texts sung by two alternating choirs: such a song is called antiphonal.

In the preceding chapter, we examined several forms of responsorial poetry, for example, the hymn of Marius Victorinus:

> Miserere Domine
> Quia credidi in te,
> Miserere Domine
> Quia misericordia tua cognovi te. . . .

to which one responded with the refrain: *Miserere Domine, miserere Christe.* We also saw in the preceding chapter how it was especially the refrains, because of their well-defined and simple rhythm, that gave birth to new forms of verse. Since these refrains had their origin in poetry in prose and in melody, they were entirely independent of ancient [Greek and Roman] meter.

Poetry in liturgical prose continued thoroughout the Middle Ages. As a typical example, I quote the antiphon *Salve regina misericordiae,* which was for a long time attributed to Hermannus Contractus (d. 1054): [3]

> Salve, regina misericordiae,
> Vita, dulcedo et spes nostra, salve!
> Ad te clamamus exsules filii Evae,
> Ad te suspiramus gementes et flentes
> in hac lacrimarum valle.

3. *AH,* 50: no. 245. Scholars have argued a great deal about who was the author of this chant: see the article "Salve regina" in *Dictionnaire d'archéologie chrétienne et de liturgie.*

> Eia ergo, advocata nostra,
> Illos tuos misericordes oculos ad nos converte
> Et Iesum, benedictum fructum ventris tui,
>> nobis post hoc exilium ostende,
>> O clemens, o pia,
>> O dulcis Maria.

Related to this free-form poetry are a certain number of new poetic forms, often having quite complicated rhythms, which we are going to study in this chapter.

We begin with the sequence, which was linked to a precise moment of the Mass. From the most remote times on, two intercalary songs have been placed between the reading of the Epistle and the Gospel: the Gradual and the Alleluia (or, during times of penitence, the Tract). It is especially the Alleluia that was the object of a rich musical ornamentation (the Hebrew word *Alleluia* means "praised be the Lord"). The Alleluia was a responsorial song, and, already at the beginning of the Middle Ages, it was being presented in this way: a soloist first sang *Alleluia;* the choir repeated it but added a long final vocalization (the *Jubilus*); after that, the soloist sang a *Versus Alleluiaticus,* ordinarily borrowed from the Psalter (on Christmas Day, for example, this Alleluia verse is *Dies sanctificatus illuxit nobis, venite, gentes, et adorate Dominum, quia hodie descendit lux magna super terram*); and the choir then responded again with *Alleluia + Jubilus.*[4]

The melismatic song on the last syllable of *Alleluia* varied each Sunday and had a more or less rich form, as Cassiodorus tells us: *Hoc ecclesiis Dei votivum, hoc sanctis festivitatibus decenter accommodum. Hinc ornatur lingua cantorum; istud aula Domini laeta respondet et tamquam insatiabile bonum tropis semper variantibus innovatur* [This is a prayer offered for the churches of God, this is properly suited to sacred festivities. By it the language of the singers is embellished; the court of God answers it with joy; and, as if an insatiable good, it is renewed with ever-changing tropes].[5] The song itself is called a sequence, as Amalarius of Metz, among others, explains it to us at the beginning of the ninth century: *Haec iubilatio quam cantores sequentiam vocant illum statum ad mentem nostram ducit, quando non erit necessaria locutio verborum sed sola cogitatione mens menti monstrabit quod retinet in se*

---

4. See Jungmann, *Missarum sollemnia,* vol. 2 (Paris, 1952), 197–98.
5. *In Psalm. 104,* Migne, *PL,* 70:742.

[This rejoicing, which singers call a sequence, brings to our mind that state when the speaking of words will not be necessary but by thought alone the mind will show to the mind what it holds in itself].[6]

Amalarius does not indicate if it is possible to add words to the vocalizations which follow the *Alleluia*. We know, however, that about 851 this possibility was put into practice at the abbey of Jumièges. The abbey was plundered about that time by the Norsemen, and one of their monks fled to St. Gall, carrying the Jumièges antiphonary, in which were some poems composed on the melodies of the *Jubilus*. It is Notker Balbulus (d. 912) who tells about this episode in the foreword of his book of sequences.[7] He had had difficulty remembering some of the long melodies and was inspired by the antiphonary of Jumièges to compose some liturgical poems on these melodies. Each syllable of the text had to correspond to a tone of the melody. This new poetic form was called *versus ad sequentiam, sequentia cum prosa*, or more briefly, *prosa*, which was the most common term in France. The poem was also called *sequentia*, a term taken from the domain of music and transferred to that of literature.[8]

From succinct pieces of information provided by Notker we can draw out some characteristic features of the sequence. The melody was, according to Notker, the essential feature, the text being only secondary. Moreover, Notker's teacher, Iso, had taught him this: *Singulae motus cantilenae singulas syllabas debent habere* [Every movement of the music ought to have a single syllable]. The melody, therefore, had to be sung syllabically. It follows from what I have just said that the oldest sequences are to be compared, with regard to their form, with the liturgical poems in prose of which we spoke a short while ago. There is not a trace of classical versification in the oldest se-

6. Amalarius, *Liber officialis*, 3:16.3 (*Studi e testi*, 139, p. 304). See Gautier, *Histoire de la poésie liturgique*, 13, n. 1.

7. See the interpretation of the words of Notker in the work of von den Steinen, *Notker der Dichter*, 1 [Darstellungsband]:154–63 and 504–8.

8. Scholars have speculated a great deal about the origin of sequences. P. Wagner, *Einführung*, 1:256–69, searched for the primitive type in Byzantine liturgical poetry; see also Wellesz, *Eastern Elements*, 154; Handschin considered the influence of Irish music, "Über Estampie und Sequenz," 2:117; according to Gennrich, *Grundriss*, 96–140, it is the melodies of Alleluia verses that played a great role; other scholars, for example, Bartsch, *Die lateinische Sequenzen des Mittelalters*, and Blume, *AH*, 53:xxi–xxiii, think that the long melismas on the last syllable of the word *Alleluia* were sung by two alternating choirs and that this antiphonal chant explains the parallelism of the structure of the sequence. See now von den Steinen, "Die Anfänge der Sequenzendichtung."

quences nor of the rhythmic verse that came from it; all the attempts that one could make to establish a relationship to these two forms are irremediably doomed to failure.[9]

Each strophe of the poem corresponds to a musical period; each verse of the strophe, to a phrase of the period. Since the melodies are, so to speak, plastic, it is often difficult to set exactly the limits of the different verses of the strophe. But, as a rule, the text is constructed following the model provided by the melody, and thus the melodies are often the only key that we have for understanding the text's form.[10] This is a point that has not always been observed by text editors. In the sequence *Eia fratres cari,* written at St. Gall in the tenth century in honor of St. Otmar, the last editor[11] presented in the following way the first two strophes that follow the words of introduction *Eia fratres cari, festivitatem sancti:*

Otmari patris	Cuius gratiam
Agamus exultantes	Per eius meritum nos
Gaudio sancti spiritus,	Consequi posse credimus.

But here the melody indicates to us another division: it is neatly divided into two phrases having the same final cadence. If we follow the melody, the double strophe must be presented in the following way:

Otmari patris agamus	Cuius gratiam per eius
Exultantes gaudio sancti spiritus	Meritum nos consequi posse credimus.

The final rhymes in -*us* which now appear show us also that this division of the verse is the valid one. This sequence was, in fact, written at a time when the pursuit of end rhyme made itself felt at St. Gall.

With regard to rhyme one can, in the oldest sequences, distinguish between a French type and a German type. In the French type, each verse often ends with an -*a*. The melody of the *Jubilus* was sung on the vowel -*a*, the final vowel of the word *Alleluia,* and composers therefore made the sequence

9. One cannot accept the theories of Kunz, "Rhythmik und formaler Aufbau," and "Die Textgestalt der Sequenz 'Congaudet angelorum chori.'"

10. Reichert has shown, in "Strukturprobleme der älteren Sequenz," that the literary interpretation of the sequence must often start from the structure of the melody.

11. Von den Steinen, *Notker der Dichter,* 2 [Editionsband]:129. The same author, following Schubiger, reproduced the melody in *Beilage* 2.

verse end with the same vowel. One sequence composed in France before the time period of Notker begins in this way:[12]

Beata tu virgo Maria,

Mater Christi gloriosa   Deique plena gratia,

Nimium credula
Gabrielis verba,
O alma Maria,   O beata Maria.

Notker freed himself from this obligation to rhyme in -*a*, and, following his example, the oldest German sequences generally lack rhyme. Following the melody of the song which we have just quoted, *Beata tu virgo Maria,* Notker wrote a sequence which begins in this way:[13]

Gaude Maria, virgo Dei genitrix,

Quae promissis Gabrihelis   Spe devota credidisti.
Numine tu sancti
Spiritus repleta
Gignis clausa filium,   Qui mundi regit machinam.

Each melody was given a title so that it could be recognized among the different melodies. These titles are often the first word of the sequence or else an allusion to its content (*Planctus cygni* [The Swan's Lament], *Virgo plorans* [Weeping Virgin], *Mater* [Mother], and so on). Sometimes the title contains a judgment on the melody (*Amoena* [Pleasant], *Aurea* [Golden]) or a geographic designation (*Graeca* [Greek], *Romana* [Roman], *Metensis* [of or from Metz]). As a result of the close relationship between the melody of the Alleluia verse and the sequence, the melody of the sequence often had a name drawn from one or some words of the verse. Thus the melody for the sequence of Christmas Day composed by Notker is called *Dies sanctificatus* after the first words of the Alleluia verse that I have quoted above. For the feasts of several saints, the biblical verse *Iustus ut palma florebit, sicut cedrus quae in Libano est multiplicabitur* (Ps. 91, 13) was sung. The resulting sequence melody that had longer and shorter forms had the titles *Iustus ut pal-*

12. Von den Steinen, *Notker der Dichter,* 1:571.
13. Von den Steinen, *Notker der Dichter,* 2:20.

ma maior and *Iustus ut palma minor* respectively. These are just some of the ways of giving titles to melodies.[14]

Some melodies were used many times for the composition of sequences. Thus, approximately 50 texts were written to the melody *Mater*.[15] German scholars have grown accustomed to calling the oldest sequence of an established melody "Stammsequenz" [the root sequence]. From the perspective of music history, as from that of philology, it is often very interesting to compare the oldest sequence and its imitations. Here our knowledge runs into problems whose solution is still only roughly outlined.

The most characteristic feature of the construction of the ordinary sequence, with regard to the text as well as the melody, is progressive repetition: each strophe is followed by an antistrophe sung to the same melody; at the same time, these pairs of strophes differ from one another. Two choirs performed the sequences: the tenors sang the strophe and the sopranos the antistrophe, as we read in the text of one sequence:[16]

Nunc vos, o socii,	Et vos, pueruli,
Cantate laetantes	Respondete semper
Alleluia,	Alleluia.

On the printed page, the strophe and the antistrophe are most often presented in this way, facing one another. The two choirs customarily sang the final strophe together, in which case there was no repetition. Likewise, the introduction to the sequence was often sung by the two choirs together. In the oldest sequences, this introduction was the word *Alleluia,* that is to say, it was only for the vocalizations performed on the last vowel of the word that one provided a text. In France, this tradition persisted for a long time. In contrast, in the German type of sequence, the word *Alleluia* was replaced with a specially written strophe of introduction. Thus, in a French sequence, the introduction and the first strophe are as follows:[17]

---

14. In *Zeitschrift für schweizerische Kirchengeschichte* 40 (1946): 210–12, von den Steinen has given a general survey of the titles of melodies.

15. Von den Steinen, *Notker der Dichter,* 1:567.

16. *AH,* 53: no. 34 (18).

17. See Blume, *AH,* 53:xviii.

Alleluia

Qui regis sceptra
   Forti dextra
   Solus cuncta. . . .

In contrast, a sequence of Notker, composed for the same melody, begins in this way:

Angelorum ordo sacer

   Dei sereno
   Vultu semper
   Iocundate. . . .

In these two cases the word *Alleluia* as well as the words *Angelorum ordo sacer* are sung to the same melody, in the first case with certain melismas, in the second case syllabically; but in France the sequence could also begin with a special introductory strophe, sung by both choirs at the same time.

The metrical and musical structure of the normal sequence can therefore be rendered by the following scheme: A BB CC DD EE . . . Z. However, the final cadences of the melody of different strophes are often similar or limited to a small number of types. We will take as an example the melody *Trinitas*,[18] for which Notker composed the sequence *Festa Christi omnis Christianitas celebret*.[19] In this melody, the last three tones of the introductory strophe and of the six double strophes are the same; but only the final strophe has a different clausula which is particular to it. It is this, no doubt, that explains the fact that the text presents the same final cadence $\smile \sim \sim$ in all the strophes, except the last. Everywhere we find a final word of three syllables of the type *célebret, pópulis, géntium, lúcida, glóriam,* and the like, except in the final strophe, which ends with the word *praeceptóri*.

The sequence *Alleluia, Concelebremus sacram huius diei euprepiam,* the text and the melody of which have been published by Gennrich,[20] has an interesting structure. The first six double strophes of this sequence all have the same musical clausula. From the eighth strophe, the text is as follows:

18. Published by von den Steinen, *Notker der Dichter, Beilage* 5, following Schubiger.
19. Von den Steinen, *Notker der Dichter,* 2:22.
20. Gennrich, *Grundriss,* 97–100.

| *8a* | Eia igitur egregia | *b* | Regia tollens in excelsa, |

9 Almas dic odas.

| *10a* | Quo exstat basileus | *b* | Cosmum salvans omnique |
| | Hicce tibi primas | | Pressura liberans |

11 Ut nobilis pars apostolica.

| *12a* | Unde rogamus temet, | *b* | Adeptam quo nobis tu |
| | Nostri patriarcham, | | Deferas veniam, |

13 Iungas eterna tecum doxa.

The final cadence, which is characteristic of the sequence melody, is absent from the eighth strophe. In its place, a strophe without repetition has been added, *Almas dic odas,* whose melody is that of the absent cadences. Likewise, the final cadence is missing in the melody of the double strophe *Quo exstat* and *Cosmum salvans.* The following strophe, without repetition, *Ut nobilis pars apostolica,* is, however, sung on a prolonged cadence form. The particular structure of the melody in this case then gave birth to some strophes that are without repetition. In contrast, the author of this sequence did not attempt to make the fixed clausula of the melody correspond to an established rhythm in the text.

The art of constructing the strophes and the antistrophes varies from author to author, and the comparisons are instructive. One well-known sequence, written before the time of Notker,[21] begins in the following manner:

1 Nostra tuba

2a	Regatur fortissima	*b*	Aure placatissima
	Dei dextra		Et serena.
	Et preces audiat		Ita enim nostra

3a	Laus erit accepta,	*b*	Et ut haec possimus,
	Voce si quod canimus, canat		Omnes divina nobis semper
	Pariter et pura conscientia.		Flagitemus adesse auxilia.

We can ascertain immediately that the author in no way achieved a balance between the strophe and the antistrophe. The phrases boldly run on from

---

21. Von den Steinen, *Notker der Dichter,* 2:107.

the strophe to the antistrophe and again to the following strophe. The rhythmic structure of corresponding verses is most often different: *regátur fortissima* thus corresponds to *aúre plàcatíssima,* but the rhythm and distribution of words differ. Let us compare to this the following passage drawn from the sequence of Notker, *Psallat ecclesia:* [22]

Hic novàm prolem	Angeli cives
Gratia parturit	Visitant híc suòs
Fecunda spiritu sancto:	Et corpus sumitur Iesu.
Fugiunt universa	Pereunt peccatricis
Corpori nocua:	Animae crimina.
Hic vox laetitiae persónat:	Hic pax et gaudia redundant.

Here the parallelism between the strophe and the antistrophe is striking, in both the words and in the thought. When the choir of tenors sings, for example, that the maladies of the body fly away, the choir of sopranos responds that the sins of the soul disappear. Each strophe corresponds, from the syntactic point of view, to the antistrophe; and the correspondence is occasionally emphasized by an anaphora *(hic—hic);* there is no enjambment. From the rhythmic point of view, the agreement is total, if we observe the same rules of accentuation here as those which we studied in the first chapter above. Thus Notker has, by reconstruction, accented *persónat* which corresponds to *redúndant.* He has, furthermore, accented *híc novàm* and *híc suòs* following the rule that I also indicated in the first chapter.[23] The boundaries of the words themselves coincide in the strophe and the antistrophe as one sees very easily by the following arrangement:

22. Von den Steinen, *Notker der Dichter,* 2:74.

23. The sequences of Notker are especially interesting for the study of the accentuation of Latin words at St. Gall. We find there, for example, *ín crucè,* von den Steinen, vol. 2 [Editionsband], p. 16, v. 7.1; *ád deùm,* p. 18, v. 5.2; *apúd cleméntem,* p. 20, v. 15.3; *siné dolò,* p. 38, v. 6.2; *vóx pià,* p. 22, v. 11, 2; *tú meùs,* p. 22, v. 12.1; *natúm tuùm,* p. 58, v. 4.1, p. 106, v. 11.3; *membrá suà,* p. 84, v. 6, III; *corpús suùm,* p. 105, v. 3.1; *oré suò,* p. 108, v. 11, II; *morté suà,* p. 110, v. 11, II. See von den Steinen, *Notker der Dichter,* 1 [Darstellungsband]:489–92.

The rhythmic correspondence between the strophe and the antistrophe is greater in the German sequences than in the French, probably because the Germans pronounced the Latin words with a stronger stress accent.

Hic-novam	prolem	gratia	parturit	fecunda	spiritu	sancto.
Angeli	cives	visitant	hic-suos	et-corpus	sumitur	Iesu.

In contrast, Notker and a few poets occasionally allow themselves a certain variety between the strophe of the tenors and that of the sopranos. We have an example of this variety in the melody *Duo tres,* for which Notker composed the sequence *Tubam bellicosam.*[24] The second pair of strophes of this sequence is the following:

Tuba mutemus   Et quos virtutum
Consonae vocis, socii,   Meritis socordes nequimus
                            Imitari, pangamus melo.

The first verse of the strophe of the sopranos was sung according to the same melody as the first verse of the strophe of the tenors, but the melody of *Consonae vocis socii* is repeated in the strophe of the sopranos with two different variants, which is reflected also in the different form of the text and in the number of verses. In other cases, we can find an asymmetry between the strophe and the antistrophe because the order of musical phrases has been reversed, so that, for example, ABC of the strophe of the tenors corresponds to BAC of the strophe of the sopranos.

Besides the ordinary sequence, whose structure I have tried to explain, there are also sequences for a single choir, in which, consequently, the principle of repetition is not used. These sequences are not distinguished in their rhythmic construction from antiphons of the type *Salve regina misericordiae,* about which we spoke above. In addition, a small group exists where the schema of the sequence is repeated: A BB CC DD EE . . . Z + A BB CC DD EE . . . Z. This type ("Dacaposequenzen" [da capo sequences]) appeared as early as the ninth century, but it had a very limited local use. Nevertheless, it continues to be of interest both because of its age and because it contains the sequence that provided the rhythmic model for the famous prose of St. Eulalia, the oldest song in Old French.[25]

24. Von den Steinen, *Notker der Dichter,* 2 [Editionsband]:84. The melody is published in *Beilage* 6.

25. The sequence with a pattern that is repeated has been discussed by von Winterfeld, "Die lateinische Eulaliensequenz und ihre Sippe"; Handschin, "Über Estampie und Sequenz"; Spanke, "Rhythmen- und Sequenzen-studien," and "Aus der Vorgeschichte und Frühgeschichte der Sequenz." But, above all, we should consult the critical account of von den Steinen in *Zeitschrift für schweizerische Kirchengeschichte,* 40 (1946): 241–68.

The sequence is the most independent and the most original literary creation in Medieval Latin. This new poetic form freed poets from the influence of ancient models and brought them entirely new possibilities of expression. Following its introduction, verses and strophes could be constructed freely, in accordance with a melody, and with a wealth of variants, in contrast to the small number of forms that ancient poetry allowed. The finesse of the play between the tenors' and sopranos' strophes brought at the same time stability to the form and new possibilities of nuances. One famous sequence of Notker will serve as an example to show the heights a master was able to attain with the new poetic form:[26]

1   Quid tu, virgo

2a	Mater, ploras	*b*	Cuius vultus
	Rachel formosa,		Iacob delectat?
3a	Ceu sororis aniculae	*b*	Lippitudo eum iuvet?
4a	Terge, mater,	*b*	Quam te decent
	Fluentes oculos!		Genarum rimulae?—
5a	Heu, heu, heu,	*b*	Cum sim orbata
	Quid me incusatis fletus		Nato, paupertatem meam
	Incassum fudisse?		Qui solus curaret,
6a	Qui non hostibus cederet	*b*	Quique stolidis fratribus,
	Angustos terminos		Quos multos, pró dolòr,
	Quós mihi		Extuli,
	Iacob adquisivit,		Esset profuturus.—

7   Numquid flendus est iste,
Qui regnum possedit caeleste,
Quique prece frequenti
Miseris fratribus
Apud Deum auxiliatur?

Throughout the Middle Ages, poets wrote sequences of this type, which was called the archaic style. However, as early as the year 1000, a new type developed which implied a rapprochement with the hymn. The Easter

26. Von den Steinen, *Notker der Dichter,* 2 [Editionsband]:86.

sequence of Wipo (d. 1048) offers us an example of progress in this direction:[27]

1   Victimae paschali laudes
Immolent christiani.

2a	Agnus redemit oves,	b	Mors et vita duello
	Christus innocens patri		Conflixere mirando,
	Reconciliavit		Dux vitae mortuus
	Peccatores.		Regnat vivus.
3a	Dic nobis, Maria,	b	Angelicos testes,
	Quid vidisti in via?		Sudarium et vestes.
	Sepulcrum Christi viventis		Surrexit Christus, spes mea,
	Et gloriam vidi resurgentis,		Praecedet suos in Galilaea.
4a	Credendum est magis soli	b	Scimus Christum surrexisse
	Mariae veraci		Ex mortuis vere.
	Quam Iudeorum		Tu nobis, victor
	Turbae fallaci.		Rex, miserere.

The rhythmic structure of the verses is limited here to a certain number of types. Thus verses of 7 syllables of the type *Immolent christiani* reappear in strophes 2 and 3; verses of 6 syllables of the type *Reconciliavit* return in strophes 3 and 4. The final cadences are always paroxytone. One notices also an effort toward rhyme, although the poet has not introduced it systematically.

The poets, however, went even further than that. As early as the middle of the eleventh century there appeared among the *Carmina Cantabrigiensia* a song composed of regular rhythmic verses that were of a type that had been used for a very long time before then, in hymns and other genres (8p + 7pp).[28] This is the first strophe of it:

Aurea persónet lira   clara modulamina,
Simplex corda sit extensa   voce quindenaria,
Primum sonum mese reddat   lege hypodorica.

---

27. *AH,* 54: no. 7.

28. Song 10 of *Carmina Cantabrigiensia,* attributed by tradition to Fulbert of Chartres (d. 1028). The musical form of this song is discussed by Ludwig, "Musik des Mittelalters," 162, and Spanke, "Ein lateinisches Liederbuch des 11. Jahrhunderts," 138.

All 16 strophes have the same form; and if we examine the text only, we cannot see that it is a sequence. However, the music shows us the typical repetition; the musical system is AA BB CC AB AA BB CC AB. Thus it is only through the melody that the sequence form appears. It is the same with a great number of liturgical sequences of the new style. All 20 strophes of *Stabat mater*, for example, have the same form:

Stabat mater dolorosa
Iuxta crucem lacrimosa,
    Dum pendebat filius.

This strophic form, 8p + 8p + 7pp, whose relationship with the verse of 8p + 7pp is obvious, was the most frequently used in the sequences. The most respected poet of the new style, Adam of St. Victor (d. 1192), most often uses this same strophic form.[29] This form is also the basis of the famous sequence of St. Thomas of Aquinas *Lauda Sion salvatorem*, which contains, however, a variant of the strophic form.[30]

The rhythm of the verses, which is strictly regulated and which reappears more or less in the same form, strophe after strophe, as does the full two-syllable rhyme, gives to the sequences of the second style an entirely new character. The verse has more resonance and is, in certain respects, closer to us. Several sequences of this style can be considered the most perfect works of the Latin poetry of the Middle Ages. However, it would be difficult to deny that the ancient style of sequences where the form of the verse was free had some advantages that were lost in the new style where the rhythm was more strict.[31]

The growing popularity of the sequence form caused it to be used more and more, often even independently of the liturgy. Already among the *Carmina Cantabrigiensia* we find some songs with the sequence form whose content is completely secular, for example, the song of Lantfrid and Cobbo

---

29. The latest editions of Adam of St. Victor's sequences are those of Blume and of Bannister, *AH*, 54, and Franz Wellner, *Adam von Sankt Viktor, Sämtliche Sequenzen*. See also Spanke, "Die Kompositionskunst der Sequenzen Adams von St. Victor," *Studi Medievali* 14 (1941): 1–29, reprinted in *Studien zu Sequenz, Lai und Leich*, ed. Ursula Aarburg (Darmstadt: Wissenschaftliche Buchgesellschaft, 1977), pp. 203–31.

30. *AH*, 50: no. 385.

31. It is very rare that sequences were written in classical verses; see von den Steinen, *Zeitschrift für schweizerische Kirchengeschichte* 40 (1946): 251–52.

or that of the Swabian liar and his foolhardy wife.[32] Individual singers performed these kinds of songs with musical accompaniment. The principle of repetition had then lost the meaning that it had originally had when there was a performance with two choirs. Even so, repetition itself remained a poetic and musical form.

Hence one often finds, in the different collections of Latin poetry which have been preserved for us, secular poems that present a more or less regular form of the sequence. The structural variation between the different pairs of strophes can be important: it is explained by the fact that the musical form was always fundamental, allowing for a free composition of the verses and of the strophic forms, even if the rhythm of each verse was composed from a regular alternation between accented and unaccented syllables. I will quote a single example on this point: in the excellent selection of Latin poems of the Middle Ages published by Gaselee, we find the most complicated strophic form in the poem *Hiemale tempus vale,* which the editor has printed as if it were composed of 5 lyric strophes. In fact, we can understand such a strophic form only if we assume the following sequence structure:

1a	Hyemale Tempus vale, Estas redit cum leticia,	*b*	Cum calore, Cum decore, Que estatis sunt indicia.
2a	Terra floret Sicut solet, Revirescunt lilia,	*b*	Rose flores Dant odores, Canunt alitilia.
3a	De terre gremio Rerum pregnatio Progreditur Et in partum solvitur Vivifico calore.	*b*	Nata recentius Lenis Favonius Sic recreat, Ne flos novus pereat Treicio rigore.

c Herbis adhuc teneris
Eblanditur eteris
Temperies,
Ridet terre facies
Multiplici colore.

---

32. *Carmina Cantabrigiensia* 6 and 14. A secular sequence of the tenth century is *O muse Cicilides;* see Spanke, *Beziehungen zwischen romanischer und mittellateinischer Lyrik,* 79–80.

4a	Herba florem,	*b*	Sementiva
	Flos humorem,		Reddunt viva,
	Humor floris,		Reddunt culta
	Flos humoris		Fruge multa
	Generat materiam.		Et promittunt copiam.

5a	Fronde sub arborea	*b*	Mens effertur letior,
	Filomena Terea		Oblectando glorior,
	Dum meminit,		Dum iaceo
	Non desinit		Gramineo
	—Sic imperat natura—		Sub arbore frondosa
	Recenter conqueri		Riparum margine
	De veteri		Cum virgine
	Iactura.		Formosa.

6a	Vere suo	*b*	Creber erit
	Adolescens mutuo		Nec defessus cesserit
	Respondeat amori,		Venerio labori.

7a	Veneris	*b*	Rideo,
	In asperis		Dum video
	Castris nolo militem		Virum longi temporis
	Qui iuvente limitem		Qui ad annos Nestoris
	Transierit,		Progreditur
	Perdiderit		Et sequitur
	Calorem.		Amorem.[33]

---

33. Gaselee, *The Oxford Book of Medieval Latin Verse*, 117. The poem has been published by du Méril, *Poésies populaires* (1847): 232–34, from manuscript 3719, fol. 36 recto, of the Bibliothèque Nationale in Paris, and by Werner, *Beiträge*, 62, from manuscript C58/275, fol. 16–17, of the library of the city of Zurich. The text is found also in an Oxford manuscript, Bodleian Library, Add. A 44, fol. 71. Here we designate by P the text of the Paris manuscript according to du Méril, by Z the text of the manuscript of Zurich according to Werner, and by O the text of the manuscript of Oxford which I have collated myself.

1–2 om. PO 3a5 *mirifico colore* P 3b5 *Traicio* P, *Preicio* O 3c2 *et blanditur* Z, *obauditur* O 3c5 *calore* PZ post *colore* hi versus inseruntur in O : *omnis arbor foliis decoratur floribus, et merula pennis fulgens aureis dulci gaudet canore* 4a *herba florem flos odorem, odor floris ros umoris generat, generat, generat materiam* P 4b 1–2 *sementivam redivivam* P *rident prata nobis grata* O 4b3 *cunta* P 4b4 *fruges* P 5a2 *Terea* om. Z 5a4 *et definit* Z 5a5 *natura* bis P 5a6 *conquerit* P 5b2 *oblectato* O, *oblectatur* P *gratior* P 5b7–8 om. Z 6–7 om. Z 6a om. O qui habet: *iuventutis hec lex erit: iuvenis qui subiaceat amori* 6b2 *ne* O 7b5 *ingreditur* P. On our poem depend songs 82 and 145 of the *Carmina Burana*, which the editors did not see.

All the pairs of strophes here present a total correspondence, even the third. However, in the third pair strophe 3c was added, whose first two verses have a different structure.

The sequence form was used even in some very long poems. Abelard used it in his *Planctus virginum Israel super filia Iepte Galadita,* which, in the edition of Vecchi, comprises 156 verses, divided into several groups of strophes.[34] Roughly, the metrical and musical structure of the groups of strophes could be rendered by the scheme: A BB CC D EE FF G HH AA.[35]

But the sequence was not only lengthened, it was also shortened, which allowed an entire sequence to be taken as a single strophe, which, in combination with other strophes could form a song. We have an example of this in song 47 of the *Carmina Burana,* which is composed of three strophes, of which this is the first:[36]

A	Crucifigat omnes
	Domini crux altera,
	Nova Christi vulnera!
	Arbor salutifera
	Perditur; sepulcrum
	Gens evertit extera
B	Violente; plena gente
	Sola sedet civitas;
B	Agni fedus rapit hedus;
	Plorat dotes perditas
C	Sponsa Sion; immolatur
D	Ananias; incurvatur
	Cornu David; flagellatur
	Mundus;
D	Ab iniustis abdicatur,
	Per quem iuste iudicatur
	Mundus.

If one studies the melody, one notices that the structure can be described schematically by the formula A BB C DD. As a sequence form, this structure

---

34. Abelard, *Planctus,* ed. Vecchi.

35. See the analysis of the melody and the text in Vecchi's edition of Abelard and Gennrich, *Grundriss,* 157.

36. Spanke treated this song in "Der Codex Buranus als Liederbuch," 243. The melody has been published by Gennrich, *Grundriss,* 180–81.

is simple; as a strophic form, it is rather complicated. This song also contains two strophes constructed in the same way:

O quam dignos luctus!	Quisquis es signatus
Exulat rex omnium,	Fidei charactere,
Baculus fidelium	Fidem factis assere,
Sustinet opprobrium	Rugientes contere
Gentis infidelis;	Catulos leonum,
Cedit parti gentium	Miserans intuere
Pars totalis; iam regalis	Corde tristi damnum Christi!
In luto et latere	Longus Cedar incola,
Elaborat tellus, plorat	Surge, vide, ne de fide
Moysen fatiscere.	Reproberis frivola!
Homo, Dei miserere!	Suda martyr in agone
Fili, patris ius tuere!	Spe mercedis et corone!
In incerto certum quere,	Derelicta Babylone
Ducis	Pugna
Ducum dona promerere	Pro celesti regione,
Et lucrare lucem vere	Aqua vite! Te compone
Lucis!	Pugna!

The sequence form is not limited to Latin poetry. It was taken up again in the French *lai* and the German *Leich* and was developed further in a certain number of poetic forms that are more or less complicated and that have been given various names.[37]

But let us return to liturgical poetry. There were still some parts of the Mass besides the *Alleluia* before the Gospel that were susceptible of enrichment by the addition of newly composed poems that were given the name *tropes*. "The tropes" according to Léon Gautier,[38] "can sometimes precede the pre-existing texts of the real liturgy, can sometimes follow them, can sometimes slip between all their phrases and hold a place between all their words." Even the liturgical texts of the canonical hours had to be made the object of such an enrichment, although in a limited way.[39]

37. See Gennrich, *Lateinische Kontrafacta altfranzösischer Lieder,* and *Grundriss,* 96–140; Spanke, *Beziehungen zwischen romanischer und mittellateinischer Lyrik,* 74–103.

38. Gautier, *Histoire de la poésie liturgique,* 2.

39. See Young, *The Drama of the Medieval Church,* 1:178–97; Gautier, *Histoire de la poésie liturgique*; P. Wagner, *Einführung,* 1:277–99; Blume in *AH,* 47 and 49; and Frere, *The Winchester Troper.*

If the birth of the sequence remains to a great extent enveloped in obscurity, it is even more the case for the tropes. The word *tropos* originally means "melody," but like *sequentia,* the term passed from the musical to the literary domain. The melody was also often fundamental. Thus we have some good reasons for assuming that the melismas added to the syllable *-e* of *Kyrie* and of *Christe* are originally from the composition of the following trope:[40]

1a   *Kyrie,* rex, genitor
Ingenite,
Vera essentia,
Eleison.

b   *Kyrie,* qui nos tuae
Imaginis
Signasti specie,
Eleison.

c   *Kyrie,* luminis fons
Et rerum conditor,
Eleison.

2a   *Christe,* qui perfecta
Es sapientia,
Eleison.

b   *Christe,* lux oriens,
Per quem sunt omnia,
Eleison.

c   *Christe,* Dei forma,
Humanae particeps,
Eleison.

3a   *Kyrie,*
Spiritus vivifice,
Vitae vis, *eleison.*

b   *Kyrie,*
Utriusque vapor, in
Quo cuncta, *eleison.*

c   *Kyrie*
Expurgator scelerum
Et largitor gratiae,

d   Quaesumus
Propter nostras offensas
Noli nos relinquere,

e   O consolator
Dolentis animae,
Eleison.

In this case, the trope is inserted into the liturgical text. Sometimes it follows it. The offertory of the first Sunday of Advent ended in the Middle Ages with the following verse: *Respice in me et miserere mei Domine; custodi animam*

40. *AH,* 47: no. 15; Vecchi, *Poesia latina medievale,* 369.

meam et eripe me; non confundar, quoniam invocavi te. For the long vocalizations that were sung on the final syllable a trope was constructed which had the ordinary structure of a sequence:[41]

1   Invocavi

2a	*Te,* altissime,	b	Gloria, laus et
	Venturum quem		Honor, Christe,
	Longe cecinere prophetae.		Sic dicitur tibi, rex pie,
3a	Qui venis salvare me	b	Ipse blande suscepi te
	Ad te vera fide.		Devote te volente.

The final rhyme in *-e* echoes the final vowel of the liturgical text *(invocavi te).*

The trope often has a dramatic form, for example, in the famous song that was sung before the Introit during the Easter Day Mass. Its original form is as follows:[42]

1   Quem quaeritis in sepulchro
Christicolae?

2   Iesum Nazarenum crucifixum,
O caelicolae.

3   Non est hic,
Surrexit sicut praedixerat,
Ite, nuntiate
Quia surrexit de sepulchro.

Then comes the Introit: *Resurrexi et adhuc tecum sum,* and so on. There, the trope has been placed before the official liturgical text as an independent text. The sharing of the dialogue among several singers was the beginning of a development which would eventually become the religious drama of the Middle Ages.

Scholars have hardly studied the problems posed by the musical and metrical form of the trope.[43] The last trope that I quoted is an example of a poem in prose; in the first two cases, the principle of repetition, familiar to us from

41. *AH,* 49: no. 597.
42. *AH,* 49:9; Young, *The Drama of the Medieval Church,* 1:201–5.
43. Gautier gives a survey of these forms in *Histoire de la poésie liturgique,* 147–93.

the sequence, prevails. But there are also tropes written in hexameters or in other classical verses,[44] as well as in rhythmic verses.[45]

Particularly intriguing from the formal point of view are tropes in which the liturgical text is intermingled with the new song in such a way that we must assume that two soloists or one soloist and a choir sang the two texts at the same time. One of the oldest collections of tropes that we have, dating from the beginning of the tenth century, already contains a few songs of this type. A typical example is the trope of the Alleluia verse that was sung in the Mass for a confessor. Here is the verse: *Iustus germinabit sicut lilium et florebit in aeternum ante dominum.* It is entirely mixed with the following trope:[46]

1   Laetetur alma
Fidelium ecclesia,
Per Christi corpus redempta
Felix permanet in saecula,
Regnat in gloria
Perpetua,
Retinens caelica
In caelestibus praemia,
Alleluia.

2a	*Iustus*	*b*	*Germina*
	Et probitate dignus		Pacis et vitae dona
			Heredita*bit*

c   *Sicut lilium*
Et gloria rosarum.

3a	*Et flore* gratiae	*b*	Ditatus munere
	Cum lampade		Iustitiae
	Lucis perpetuae		Virtutum meritis
	Fulgebit feliciter,		Flore*bit in aeternum*

---

44. In the two volumes of *Analecta Hymnica* that contain tropes, 47 and 49, one finds hexameters passim, catalectic dactylic tetrameters 47:174, Sapphic verses 210, Adonics 209, to give only a few examples.

45. See, for example, the Ambrosian rhythmic verses (8pp) *AH*, 47: no. 71; the Adonics (5p), no. 52; the iambic trimeters (5p + 7pp), no. 120; the Sapphic verses (5p + 6p), no. 169; the Asclepiads (6pp + 6pp), no. 311; the decasyllables (4 + 6pp), nos. 50, 200, and 422; the Goliardic verses (7pp + 6p), no. 319; the strophe of *Stabat mater* (8p, 8p, 7pp), no. 317. New strophes are found, for example, *AH*, 47: nos. 111 (8, 8, 6, 5), 115 (6, 5, 3, 6), 118 (7, 6, 3, 6).

46. *AH*, 49: no. 499.

4   *Ante Dominum,*
Qui Dominus est omnium,
Qui salvat omne saeculum,
Qui fert omnium subsidium,
Qui condolens nostrum
Interitum
Pro nobis tribuit
sui sanguinis pretium.

We do not know exactly how this poem was sung. It is, however, interesting to see that the official liturgical text and the trope must have been sung together since certain vowels of the official text have been lengthened by long melismas. While, for example, one of the soloists sang *germina . . . bit* from the official text, the other sang the words *Germina pacis et vitae dona hereditabit.* This also explains the rhymes. In the first strophe, all the verses end with *-a* as if echoing the *Alleluia* that they precede; in strophe 2a they end in *-us* as an echo of *iustus,* in strophe 2b in *-a* because of *germina,* and so on.

We find again the same technique of composition in the polyphonic songs of the twelfth and thirteenth centuries that are called motets.[47] While, for example, the bass voice sang the word *docebit* from the official text, the high voice sang the following song which was new:[48]

Doce nos optime,
Vitae fons, salus animae,
Mundo nos adime,
Rex unigenite,
Vena divite
Cor imbue,
Os instrue,
Opus restitue
Manus strenuae,
Vitam distribue,
Sint ut assiduae
Duae manus Liae,
Mens Mariae,

47. See Meyer, *Ges. Abh.,* 2:303–41; Ludwig, *Repertorium,* 3; Handschin, "Über den Ursprung der Motette."
48. *AH,* 21: no. 198. See Ludwig, *Repertorium,* 105.

> Sint mutuae
> Plebi tuae,
> Perpetuae
> Vitae spem tribue,
> Quae nos doce*bit.*

In this case, we have a motet for two voices *(duplum).* There are also some triples and some quadruples where three or four different texts were sung at the same time.

If the polyphonic song is not constructed on a liturgical melody and instead all the parts are devised freely by the composer, one no longer speaks of a motet but of a *conductus.*[49] Among the *conducti* is listed, for example, the famous satire of Philip the Chancellor (d. 1236) of which this is the first strophe:[50]

> Bulla fulminante
> Sub iudice tonante,
> Reo appellante,
> Sententiam gravante,
> Veritas opprimitur,
> Distrahitur
> Et venditur
> Iustitia prostante;
> Itur et recurritur
> Ad curiam, nec ante
> Quid consequitur,
> Quam exuitur quadrante.

The principle of adding words to a given melody had already been realized in the sequences and the tropes. In this respect, the motets and the *conducti* present nothing new. But they contributed to the free composition of verses and strophes in a time period when the forms of sequences and tropes were on the way to becoming petrified.

The strophic forms that were used for songs accompanying dances have less importance for Latin poetry, for in this case the Latin poetry depended

---

49. See Chailley, 161–65. *Conductus* originally referred to the song that the choir sang when the deacon was going to read the Gospel; but, at the end of the Middle Ages, this term means, in general, a song in Latin for several voices.

50. *Carmina Burana,* 131a; *AH,* 21: no. 182.

on poetry in the vulgar language. Even so, there are Latin rondeaux, and the short song that I quote here can give the reader some idea of their form:[51]

Christo psallat ecclesia,
Mitis misericordia,
Redempta Sion filia
   Det laudem regi gloriae,
Mitis misericordia
   Mortem destruxit hodie.

Quanta Dei potentia,
Mitis misericordia,
Mortem mactat victoria
   Caesae pro nobis hostiae,
Mitis misericordia
   Mortem destruxit hodie.

Laus, honor, virtus, gloria,
Mitis misericordia,
Deo cuius nos gratia
   Emancipat miseriae,
Mitis misericordia
   Mortem destruxit hodie.

Verses 1, 3, and 4 of each strophe were sung by the soloist; the others form a refrain that the choir sang. The structure can be described with this formula: a A ab AB.[52]

51. *AH*, 21: no. 54. Besseler published the melody, 117.
52. See Gennrich, *Grundriss*, 61–62, and "Refrain-Studien"; Spanke, "Das lateinische Rondeau," and *Beziehungen zwischen romanischer und mittellateinischer Lyrik*, 104–41.

NINE ▨ CONCLUSION

The Latin versification of the Middle Ages was entirely dependent on school teaching. Because the medieval school continued the traditions of late antiquity, there was no break in the evolution of versification. Throughout the entire Middle Ages, poets continued to write ancient quantitative verses according to the model of Virgil or Sedulius, of Horace or Prudentius. Certain versifiers appropriated a purely classical technique; most of them, however, followed models which were, for them, more modern.

As early as the period of the Empire, rhetoric exercised considerable influence on poetry. From rhetoric poets inherited the taste for rhyme, assonance, and other figures, as well as for the plays on words and other devices which were sometimes cultivated to the point of exaggeration and at the cost of good taste.

Among classical verse forms the hexameter and the dactylic distich were dominant. This predominance was especially evident at the time of the Carolingian Renaissance, when Virgil and, in a general way, ancient epic were at the center of interest for the learned world. But even in the twelfth century the hexameter remained the principal verse form in the epic genre and in didactic poetry. At the end of this same century Walter of Châtillon succeeded in creating with his *Alexandreis* an epic that was a formidable rival of the works of antiquity for first place in school teaching.

In contrast, during the first centuries of the Middle Ages, few poets attempted to imitate the ancient forms of lyric verses. But, as technical ability grew, these forms gained importance; and in the eleventh century several poets, such as Alphanus of Salerno, demonstrated a remarkable talent in the art of imitating Horace, Prudentius, and Boethius. It is, therefore, somewhat surprising that about the year 1100, when the Latin literature of the Middle

Ages was at its apogee, poets generally abandoned the classical tradition in the field of lyric poetry. This is because they had succeeded in creating some entirely new forms in this field, forms of a particular character and beauty to which antiquity could not produce anything equivalent. One of the essential goals of this work has been to show precisely how the poets freed themselves, step by step, from the shackles in which the ancient tradition had chained lyric poetry and bound it to traditional forms that no longer provided poets with expressions adapted to the new conditions.

We recognize already in the hymns of St. Ambrose the beginning of this evolution. These hymns entirely follow the rules of contemporary classical metrics and do not show any rhythmic construction. But they provide evidence of a remarkable independence from the turgid rhetoric that characterized the metrical poetry of his time. St. Ambrose also moves away from more artful classical versification, of which Prudentius, for example, provides us a sample. Simplicity of style and verse is for St. Ambrose a stylistic procedure thanks to which he succeeds in creating a new, more vigorous literary genre which is a strong contrast to the artifice at the end of antiquity. It is not because of the Christian content that he succeeds but because of the song. Through St. Ambrose, the Romans obtained what they had lacked for a long time: a poetry in lyric strophes intended to be sung.[1]

The second step in the evolution toward a new lyric versification was taken when poets freed themselves from the quantity of the verse. We do not know when and how this happened. Too many phases of this evolution are unfortunately lost to us. But song probably played a certain role, as in the genesis of rhythmic poetry. It has been assumed that the most ancient rhythmic poetry that has been preserved in Latin, that is, the psalm of St. Augustine against the Donatists, in 393, would have been written to a precise melody. This is not impossible, but it is also conceivable that St. Augustine borrowed the form of his poem from now-lost songs of his Donatist adversaries.

However that may be, we cannot point out any quantitative form that could have been the immediate model for St. Augustine. We can, however, do that when it comes to the rhythmic hymns preserved since the fifth and sixth

---

1. I tried to analyze the characteristic traits of the poetry of St. Ambrose in *L'hymne ambrosien.*

centuries. In fact, it seems to be obvious that the iambic dimeter, the iambic trimeter, and the trochaic septenarius were their main models; and when we compare the models to their new rhythmic imitations, we get a precise idea of the technique used. I have formulated the result of my research in the following way: poets read ancient quantitative verses while respecting the ordinary accents as if the verses were prose and while taking note of the breaks and the arrangement of words in the verse; they then imitated the rhythmic pattern obtained in this way, without caring about the quantity. This imitation of the structure of ancient verse remained, during the entire Middle Ages, the essential way of rhythmically imitating ancient verse. But in the first centuries of the Middle Ages, there also appeared a certain number of other versification systems. In some poems, the poet contented himself with counting the number of words or the principal accents. This system, however, was not used much. What was more common was to count the syllables of a verse without taking account of the structure. Poets obtained in this way a verse that could be sung to a given melody. However, the possible variations of the melody yielded the possibility of varying the verses: one could add or remove an anacrusis and add or remove some syllables in the interior of the verse. In quite a few cases, we would understand these systems more clearly if we knew the melodies better and if we knew how the verses were sung in the different countries and in different time periods. In Italy in the eighth century, it became common practice to write verses while following a system of regular accentuation. The technique of rhythmic poetry, therefore, offers us an astonishing wealth of variants; and it is impossible to give a general formula for them.

It is also through song that the last step was taken toward liberation from the formal rigor of ancient verses. Since the most remote time of the Christian Church, people had sung, during religious services, psalms, hymns, and spiritual odes which from the Greco-Roman point of view were not in verse but in literary prose. We have seen how certain simple rhythms of this poetry in prose were used in refrains and how these, at the time of the Visigoths in Spain, gave birth to new forms of strophes and new verses. Some vestiges belonging to other countries allow us to assume that the limitation to Spain comes, in part at least, from gaps in the tradition. However, thanks above all to the sequences and to the tropes, then later to the motets and the *conducti*, this new poetry reaches its full flowering. At the apogee of the Middle Ages, the length and rhythm of verses and the construction of strophes are often as varied as the periods of the literary prose. We cannot, therefore, give a complete inventory of all these forms.[2] I will be satisfied here with adding a few points of view on their principles of construction.

The classical quantitative verse was already bound to a precise structure because of the fixed alternation between long and short syllables; and poets had controlled the versification even more by allowing only certain combinations of words before the break and at the end of the verse. These rules were taken up again in rhythmic verse, which imitated the structure of quantitative verse. But poets were not at first concerned about these rules in the new lyric verses that had originated independently of the doctrines of ancient metrics. According to the prescriptions of classical metrics, for example, a verse was not supposed to end with a monosyllable. In the small trope of the offertory that I quoted in the preceding chapter, we find, however, the words *quem, et, me,* and *te* at the ends of verses; and it is almost the same in some other tropes and sequences. To give another example: we have emphasized that in quantitative poetry, one could place a proparoxytone only at certain precise places in the verse and that rhythmic poetry had imitated this rule. In a rhythmic iambic dimeter, one normally would avoid, for example, verses of the type *Cónditor alme siderum.* In free lyric verses there was no restriction in this respect. Notker Balbulus writes in this way, *Secum múnera déferunt párvulo ófferant ut regi caeli,* in one of his sequences.[3]

But when, starting about the year 1000, a rapprochement occurred between the new free verse and the rhythmic ancient verse, this implied that poets had begun to apply the rhythmic laws of ancient verse to the new verse. Goliardic verse (7pp + 6p), for example, which was, in the twelfth century and later, one of the most popular forms of poetry, did not have any direct connection with any quantitative verse. But its construction was regulated following the models of rhythmic poetry which imitated the structure of quantitative verse. Goliardic verse most often had a system of regular accentuation:

Ánni párte flóridà,   caélo púrióre.

2. Spanke gave a general idea of the different forms of strophes in *Beziehungen zwischen romanisch und mittellateinisch Lyrik.*
3. Von den Steinen, *Notker der Dichter,* 2 [Editionsband]:22, v. 5.

But one also often finds verses such as these:

> Nec stírpe nec fáciè   néc ornátu víles,
> Dixísti de cléricò   quod indulget sibi,

in which the 7 syllables before the break have the rhythmic form ~ ́~ ~ ǀ ~ ́~
~ ́~ . I emphasized previously that the hemistich of 7 syllables that ends the
trochaic septenarius and the iambic trimeter presents the same forms. The
metrical form ＿＿＿ ǀ ◡＿◡◡ , common in the Middle Ages, had in this
way given birth to the rhythmic form ~ ́~ ~ ǀ ~ ́~ ~ ́~ . Poets regulated the
Goliardic verse according to this model. This is why even the most meticulous of them often used hemistichs of the type *Nec stírpe nec fáciè* and *Dixísti
de cléricò*.[4] But it is impossible to find in the quantitative trochaic septenarius
or in the quantitative iambic trimeter the structure ~ ́~ ~ ~ ǀ ́~ ~ `~ . Thus
poets avoided this structure in their rhythmic imitations of these verses. This
is why it is very rare to find Goliardic verses of the type:

> Sed quóniam scríptitàt   mundus universus.

An analogous rule even took root in the second hemistich of the Goliardic
verse so that poets avoided there the structure ~ ́~ ~ ~ ǀ ́~ ~ , while they per-
mitted this structure: ~ ́~ ~ ǀ ~ ́~ ~ .

Nor does the decasyllable that appeared in the middle of the eleventh century seem to have any direct connections to a quantitative verse. Nonethe-
less, the form of this verse was also regulated. Poets ordinarily fixed the break
after the fourth syllable; the verse was composed, therefore, of 4 + 6 syllables
with a final proparoxytone. In general, however, they did not go so far as to
fix the rhythmic cadence before the break. Thus in the work of Abelard, we
find the form

> Déi pátris   et mátris únicus

as well as

> Angústiàs praesépis sústinet.

The second part of this verse can have the rhythmic forms ́~ ~ ~ ́~ ~ ~ and ~
́~ ~ ́~ ~ ~ . In the first rhythmic form, certain poets avoided proparoxytone

---

4. There are, however, poets who admit the structure *nec stirpe* but avoid *dixisti*; see Meyer, *Ges. Abh.*, 1:264.

trisyllables at the beginning of this part of the verse. Therefore, they wrote, for example, *Te requirunt* ‖ *vota fidélium;* but they avoided the structure *Gaude virgo* ‖ *virginum glória.* Even in these verses, the fear of proparoxytone words had been taken up again from the older rhythmic verse.

The problem concerning the connection between Latin verses and Germanic and Romance verses is an important one. For example, I emphasized previously that the technique of alliteration practiced in Latin verse in England had probably been influenced by Germanic verse. In Germany, the form that Goliardic verse took came, without any doubt, from the fact that it resembled the four-beat verse of Middle High German. This is what Langosch emphasized in his important study of the verse technique of the work of Hugh of Trimberg.[5] The two hemistichs of Goliardic verse in Hugh's work, *Quóniàm scolárium* ‖ *àd instrúctiónèm,* correspond, for example, to *Dó huop sich ir ámbet án* and *Bí dem stúont ein láchè.* In a German verse, there was often an anacrusis. That is why one often finds an anacrusis in the Latin Goliardic verse composed in Germany, while in the other countries poets avoided it in the twelfth and thirteenth centuries. In Hugh's work, for example, the first hemistich can have the form *Ad* | *laúdes érgo vírginis.* In yet another respect the imitation of German verse appears clearly: German versification allowed for the addition of one unaccented syllable to the end of a verse ("Kadenzerweiterung" [cadence expansion]). As an illustration Langosch quotes, among others, the verses *Swénne die wúrzeln ín der érden Dúrre sínt, daz dánne wérden.* In conformity with this, Hugh of Trimberg writes Goliardic verses of the type

Héc in géstis Ròmanórum   pléniùs legúntur,
Séd pleríque dòminórum   hís non ìnstruúntur.

In Latin poetry, an extension of the final cadence such as this one is evident only in the Goliardic verses of Hugh of Trimberg and in a few poems composed in the same time period in Germany.[6]

It is quite obvious that Latin verse was influenced by other linguistic domains than England or Germany. There are occasional connections with

5. Langosch, 103–10. See also Meyer, *Ges. Abh.,* 1:250–56, and Schreiber, *Die Vaganten-Strophe der mittellateinischen Dichtung.*

Three Goliardic verses, followed by a hexameter or a pentameter borrowed from a classical author, often formed one strophe that was called the Goliardic strophe with *auctoritas.*

6. *Carmina Burana,* 193, and *Vita Marie rhythmica.* See Langosch, op. cit.

Byzantine poetry.[7] There is, as we might expect, a much greater influence from poetry of the Romance languages. Latin rondeaux, for example, which I mentioned in the preceding chapter, were created on the model of Romance rondeaux.

Yet, although it borrowed much, Latin verse itself was, above all, a creditor. Latin poetry was the point of departure for all of Romance versification. Scholars are not yet in agreement on the details.[8] But we can see already the general contours. Hymns, sequences, tropes, and other forms of liturgical poems marked an important time in Western literature. When medieval Latin versification has been better studied and is better known, it will also be possible to clarify the connections with Romance versification.

7. See Meyer, *Ges. Abh.*, 3:310–15.

8. This book was already nearly finished when I became acquainted with the remarkable work of Michel Burger, *Recherches sur la structure et l'origine des vers romans* (Geneva and Paris, 1957). I am delighted to find that we are generally in agreement about the origin of Latin rhythmic versification. But with regard to its evolution, we have arrived at quite different conclusions.

A GLOSSARY OF TERMS

Abecedarian. An acrostic poem in which the first letters of each strophe or of each verse reproduce the alphabet.

Acrostic. A poem in which the first letters of each verse or strophe form a word or words. See also *abecedarian, mesostich, telestich.*

Adonic. A dactyl followed by a spondee. See p. 72.

Adonic hexameter. A rare hymnic meter in which each dactylic hexameter is composed of three Adonics, with all three spondees in each verse rhyming. See p. 61.

Anacrusis. The placement of one or more syllables at the beginning of a verse before the normal verse pattern begins (in Norberg, *mesure d'attaque,* lit. "measure of attack" cp. Fr. *attaque,* the "striking up" of music).

Aphaeresis. Also known as prodelision. The suppression of the initial vowel of a word when this word is preceded by a word which ends in a vowel. Compare *elision.*

Bucolic (diaeresis). A diaeresis after the fourth foot in a dactylic hexameter, especially common in pastoral (bucolic) poetry. See *diaeresis,* 2, below.

Caesura. A break within a metron or foot where word ending is demanded or recommended.

Cento. A composition made up of quotations from other authors.

Diaeresis. (1) the division of one syllable into two, especially by resolution of a diphthong into two simple vowels (also the sign above a vowel to indicate this phenomenon), see chapter 2; (2) the place in a verse where a word ending is demanded or recommended to coincide with the end of a metrical unit (Gr. "taking apart").

Dipody. Two feet which together make a single metron (Gr. "two-footer").

Elision. The omission of a sound, or, specifically, the omission of a final vowel or a vowel with -*m* in one word before an initial vowel or an initial *h*- followed by a vowel in another (from Lat. *elidere* "to crush out"). Compare *aphaeresis*.

Epanalepsis. The repetition at the end of a line, sentence, or strophe of the word or phrase with which it began (Gr. "resumption, repetition").

Hephthemimer. The first part of a hexameter line preceding the caesura when this caesura occurs in the middle of the fourth foot (Gr. "consisting of seven halves," that is, seven half feet). Compare *penthemimer, trihemimeris*.

Hiatus. A break between two vowels or diphthongs which come together without an intervening consonant in successive words or syllables (Lat. "gap").

Ictus. Meter may be understood as a pattern of marked and unmarked positions. The term *ictus* designates the marked position, particularly in classical Greek and Latin poetry. Which positions would have been so marked in Latin is controversial, as is how they would have been marked (in accent, pitch, length or duration, or a combination of the foregoing (Lat. "blow, stroke").

Leonine hexameter. A dactylic hexameter with internal rhyme between a word just before the strong caesura and a word at the end of the line (the name is derived from the prose rhythm associated with Pope Leo I).

Mesostich. A poem in which letters in the middle of the lines are used to spell a word or words.

Oxytone. A word with an accent on the last syllable (Gr. "sharp-toned"). Compare *paroxytone, proparoxytone*.

Paromœon. Sustained alliteration in which a series of two or more words— sometimes every word in a phrase or sentence—begins with the same letter (Gr. "closely resembling").

Paroxytone. A word with an accent on the penultimate syllable. Compare *oxytone, proparoxytone*.

Penthemimer. The first part of a hexameter line preceding the caesura when this caesura occurs in the middle of the third foot (Gr. "consisting of five halves," that is, five half feet). Compare *hephthemimer, trihemimeris*.

Proparoxytone. A word with an accent on the antepenultimate syllable. Compare *oxytone, paroxytone*.

Prosthesis. The addition of a letter or syllable at the beginning of a word (Gr. *pros*- "toward, in addition" + *thesis* "putting").

Syllaba anceps. A place in a metrical scheme which can be occupied by a long or short syllable (Lat. "two-headed syllable").

Synaeresis. The contraction of two or more adjacent syllables into one, especially the contraction of two vowels within a single word into a diphthong or a simple vowel (Gr. "drawing together, contraction").

Syncope. The shortening of a word by omission of one or more syllables in the middle (Gr. "together" + "cutting").

Telestich. A short poem in which the final letters of the lines, taken in order, spell a word or words.

Tmesis. The separation of the elements of a word by the interposition of another word or words (Gr. "cutting").

Trihemimeris. The first part of a hexameter line preceding the caesura when this caesura occurs in the middle of the second foot (Gr. "consisting of three halves," that is, three half feet). Compare *hephthemimer, penthemimer.*

Tripertitus dactylicus. A dactylic verse without a conventional caesura, but instead divided into three parts with the second and fourth feet rhyming together. In addition the ends of successive verses rhyme, forming a couplet. See p. 61.

Versus citocadus. A rare form of hexameter in which the third foot and the sixth foot are rhymed. (The adjective seems to refer to the "swift" way in which the two parts "fall.") See pp. 61–62.

Versus rhopalicus. A verse in which each word contains one more syllable than the previous word, for example, a verse composed of one, two, three, four, and five syllables (Gr. "a cudgel thicker at one end"). See p. 54.

Versus spondiacus. A dactylic hexameter verse but with a spondee as the fifth foot. See p. 58.

Versus trinini salientes. Hexameter verses with trihemimeral and penthemimeral caesuras, in the middle of the second and third feet respectively (Lat. "verses of three leaps"). See pp. 60–61.

BIBLIOGRAPHY

Abelard, Peter. *Planctus.* Ed. Giuseppe Vecchi. Istituto di filologia romanza della Università di Roma, Collezione di testi e manuali, no. 35. Modena: Società tipografica modenese, 1951.

Adam of St. Victor. *Sämtliche Sequenzen.* Ed. and trans. Franz Wellner. 2nd ed. Munich: Kosel-Verlag, 1955.

AH = Analecta hymnica medii aevi. Ed. Guido Maria Dreves, Clemens Blume, and Henry Marriott Bannister. 55 vols. Leipzig: O. R. Reisland, 1886–1922.

Anthologia latina: sive poesis latinae supplementum. Ed. Franz Bücheler and Alexander Riese. 2nd ed. Leipzig: B. G. Teubner, 1894–1926.

Archpoet: in *Hymnen und Vagantenlieder: lateinische Lyrik des Mittelalters mit deutschen Versen.* Comp. and trans. Karl Langosch. Basel: B. Schwabe, [1954]. Reprint, Darmstadt: Wissenschaftliche Buchgesellschaft, 1958 (pp. 219–77).

Bartsch, Karl. *Die lateinischen Sequenzen des Mittelalters in musikalischer und rhythmischer Beziehung.* Rostock: Stiller'sche Hofbuchhandlung (H. Schmidt), 1868.

Baudri of Bourgueil. *Les oeuvres poétiques.* Ed. Phyllis Abrahams. Paris: H. Champion, 1926.

Becker, Philipp August. "Der gepaarte Achtsilber in der französischen Dichtung." *Abhandlungen der philologisch-historischen Klasse der sächsischen Akademie der Wissenschaften zu Leipzig* 43/1 (1934): 1–117.

Besseler, Heinrich. *Die Musik des Mittelalters und der Renaissance.* Ed. Ernst Bücken. Handbuch der Musikwissenschaft. Potsdam: Akademische Verlagsgesellschaft Athenaion, 1931–34.

Bieler, Ludwig, trans. and ed. *The Works of St. Patrick. Hymn on St. Patrick [by] St. Secundinus.* Westminster, MD: Newman Press, 1953.

———. *The Life and Legend of Saint Patrick: Problems of Modern Scholarship.* Dublin: Clonmore & Reynolds, 1949.

Bittinger, Werner. "Fünfzig Jahre Musikwissenschaft als Hilfswissenschaft der rom. Philologie." *Zeitschrift für romanische Philologie* 69 (1953): 161–94.

Boucherie, Anatole. "Mélanges latins et bas-latins." *Revue des langues romanes* 7 (1875): 5–41.

Bourciez, Edouard. *Éléments de linguistique romane.* 4th ed. Paris: C. Klincksieck, 1946.

Brandes, Wilhelm. *Des Auspicius von Toul rhythmische Epistel an Arbogastes von Trier.* Wissenschaftliche Beilage zum Jahresbericht des herzoglichen Gymnasiums zu Wolfenbüttel, Programm 840. Wolfenbüttel: Heckner, 1905.

———. "Die Epistel des Auspicius und die Anfänge der lateinischen Rhythmik." *Rheinisches Museum für Philologie,* n.s., 64 (1909): 57–97.

Brinkmann, Hennig. *Geschichte der lateinischen Liebesdichtung im Mittelater.* 2nd ed. Darmstadt: Wissenschaftliche Buchgesellshaft, 1979. (See especially "Die Form," pp. 96–102.)

Bulst, Walther. "Eine Sequenz auf Otto II." *Nachrichten von der Gesellschaft der Wissenschaften zu Göttingen, Philologisch-historische Klasse.* Fachgruppe 4, n.s. 2/3 (1937): 67–85.

———. "Studien zu Marbods Carmina varia und Liber decem capitulorum." *Nachrichten von der Gesellschaft der Wissenschaften zu Göttingen, Philologisch-historische Klasse.* Fachgruppe 4, n.s. 2/10 (1939): 173–241.

Burger, André. "De Virgile à Guillaume IX. Histoire d'un mètre." *Bibliothèque d'humanisme et renaissance* 13 (1951): 7–25.

Burger, Michel. *Recherches sur la structure et l'origine des vers romans.* Geneva: Droz, 1957.

Carmina Burana. Ed. Alfons Hilka and Otto Schumann. I Band, text volumes 1–2. Heidelberg: C. Winter, 1930–41. (Still incomplete. An additional volume I/3 appeared in 1970.)

Carmina Cantabrigiensia. Die Cambridger Lieder. Ed. Karl Strecker. MGH, Scriptores rerum germanicarum in usum scholarum separatim editi 40. Berlin: Weidmann, 1926.

Carmina Latina Epigraphica. Ed. Franz Bücheler. 2 vols. *Anthologia latina,* vol. 2/1–2. Leipzig: Teubner, 1895–97.

Chailley, Jacques. *Histoire musicale du Moyen Âge.* Paris: Presses Universitaires de France, 1950.

Christensen, Heinrich Jens Carl. *Das Alexanderlied Walters von Chatillon.* Halle an der Saale: Verlag der Buchhandlung des Waisenhauses, 1905.

Corona quernea. Festgabe Karl Strecker zum 80. Geburtstage dargebracht. Schriften des Reichsinstituts für ältere deutsche Geschichtskunde (MGH) 6. Leipzig: K. W. Hiersemann, 1941.

CSEL = Corpus Scriptorum Ecclesiasticorum Latinorum. Vienna 1866–.

Curtius, Ernst Robert. *Europäische Literatur und lateinisches Mittelalter.* Bern: A. Francke, 1948. [English translation: *European Literature and the Late Middle Ages,* trans. Willard R. Trask, Bollingen Series 36 (New York: Pantheon, 1953)]

Descroix, J. *De versu leonino.* Lyons: M. Audin, 1931.

Dihle, Albrecht. "Die Anfänge der griechischen akzentuierenden Verskunst." *Hermes* 82 (1954): 182–99.

Dingeldein, Otto. *Der Reim bei den Griechen und Römern, Ein Beitrag zur Geschichte des Reims.* Leipzig: B. G. Teubner, 1892.

Dreves, Guido Maria. *Ein Jahrtausend lateinischer Hymnendichtung, Eine Blütenlese aus den Analecta hymnica mit literarhistorischen Erläuterungen.* 2 vols. Leipzig: O. R. Reisland, 1909.

Dümmler, Ernst. "Lateinische Gedichte des neunten bis elften Jahrhunderts." *Neues Archiv der Gesellschaft für ältere deutsche Geschichtskunde* 10 (1885): 333–57.

Ebel, Basilius. *Das älteste alemannische Hymnar mit Noten, Kodex 366 (472) Einsiedeln (XII. Jahrhundert) mit neun Faksimile-Kunsttafeln.* Einsiedeln: Benziger, [1930].

Erdmann, Carl. "Leonitas. Zur mittelalterlichen Lehre von Kursus, Rhythmus und Reim," in *Corona quernea,* 15–28.

Eskuche, Gustav. "Die Elisionen in den zwei letzten Füssen des lateinischen Hexameters." *Rheinisches Museum* 45 (1890): 236–65, 385–418.

Faral, Edmond. *Les arts poétiques du XIIe et du XIIIe siècle, recherches et documents sur la technique littéraire du Moyen Âge.* Bibliothèque de l'École des hautes études, Sciences historiques et philologiques, 238. Paris: H. Champion, 1924.

Fickermann, Norbert. "Zu den alten Rhythmen." *Revue bénédictine* 43 (1931): 313–22.

Gaselee, Stephen, ed. *The Oxford Book of Medieval Latin Verse*. Oxford: Clarendon Press, 1928.

Gautier, Léon. *Histoire de la poésie liturgique au Moyen Âge—les Tropes. I.* Paris: V. Palme, A. Picard, 1886.

Gennrich, Friedrich. *Grundriss einer Formenlehre des mittelalterlichen Liedes als Grundlage einer musikalischen Formenlehre des Liedes*. Halle an der Saale: M. Niemeyer, 1932.

———. "Lateinische Kontrafakta altfranzösischer Lieder." *Zeitschrift für romanische Philologie* 50 (1930): 187–207.

———. *Musikwissenschaft und romanische Philologie. Ein Beitrag zur Bewertung der Musik als Hilfswissenschaft der romanischen Philologie*. Halle an der Saale: M. Niemeyer, 1918.

———. "Refrain-Studien." *Zeitschrift für romanische Philologie* 71 (1955): 365–90.

———. ed. *Rondeaux, Virelais und Balladen, aus dem Ende des XII., dem XIII. und dem ersten Drittel des XIV. Jahrhunderts mit den überlieferten Melodien*. Gesellschaft für romanische Literatur, vols. 43, 47. Dresden: Gedruckt für die Gesellschaft für romanische Literatur, 1921–1927.

Gérold, Théodore. *Histoire de la musique des origines à la fin du XIVᵉ siècle*. Manuels d'histoire de l'art. Paris: H. Laurens, 1936.

Gladysz, Bronislaw. *De extremis quibus Seduliana carmina ornantur verborum syllabis inter se consonantibus*. Eus supplementa, vol. 17. Lwów, Poland: apud Societatem philologam polonorum, 1931.

Grimm, Wilhelm. *Kleinere Schriften*. Ed. Gustav Hinrichs. 4 vols. Berlin: Ferd. Dümmler and Gütersloh: C. Bertelsmann, 1881–87. (See especially, "Zur Geschichte des Reims," vol. 4, pp. 125–336.)

Handschin, Jacques. "Über den Ursprung der Motette." In *Bericht über den musikwissenschaftlichen Kongress in Basel. Veranstaltet anlässlich der Feier des 25-jährigen Bestehens der Ortsgruppe Basel der Neuen Schweizerischen Musikgesellschaft, Basel vom 26. bis 29. September 1924*. Leipzig: Breitkopf & Hartel, 1925.

———. "Über Estampie und Sequenz, I–II." *Zeitschrift für Musikwissenschaft* 12 (1929–30): 1–20; 13 (1930–31): 113–32.

Hugo von Trimberg. *Das "Registrum multorum auctorum."* Ed. Karl Langosch. Germanische Studien, no. 235. Berlin: E. Ebering, 1942.

Huemer, Johann. *Untersuchungen über den iambischen Dimeter bei den christlich-lateinischen Hymnendichtern der vorkarolingischen Zeit*. Vienna: Selbstverlag der Lehranstalt, 1876.

———. *Untersuchungen über die ältesten lateinisch-christlichen Rhythmen*. Vienna: Selbstverlag der Lehranstalt, 1879.

Jungmann, Josef A. *Missarum sollemnia: Explication génétique de la messe romaine*. 2 vols. Paris: Aubier, 1950–52.

Keil, Heinrich, ed. *Grammatici Latini*. 7 vols. Leipzig: B. G. Teubner, 1857–80.

Kunz, L. "Die Textgestalt der Sequenz 'Congaudent angelorum chori.'" *Deutsche Vierteljahrsschrift für Literaturwissenschaft und Geistesgeschichte* 28 (1954): 273–86.

———. "Rhythmik und formaler Aufbau der frühen Sequenz." *Zeitschrift für deutsches Altertum und deutsche Literatur* 79 (1942): 1–20.

———. "Textrhythmus und Zahlenkomposition in frühen Sequenzen." *Die Musikforschung* 8 (1955): 403–44.

Die lateinischen Bearbeitungen der Acta Andreae et Mattiae apud anthropophagos. Ed. Franz Blatt. Beihefte zur Zeitschrift für die neutestamentliche Wissenschaft und die Kunde der älteren Kirche 12. Giessen: A. Topelmann, 1930.

Lejay, Paul. "Le grammairien Virgile et les rythmes latines." *Revue de philologie,* n.s., 19 (1895): 45–64.

Leo, Friedrich, ed. *Venanti Fortunati Opera poetica.* Vol. 4, pt. 1 of MGH, *Auctores antiquissimi.* Berlin: Weidmann, 1881. (See especially "Index rei metricae," pp. 422–27.)

Lind, Levi Robert. "Reginald of Canterbury and the Rhyming Hexameter." *Neophilologus* 25 (1940): 273–75.

———, ed. *The Vita sancti Malchi of Reginald of Canterbury: A Critical Edition with Introduction, Apparatus Criticus, Notes, and Indices.* Illinois Studies in Language and Literature, vol. 27, nos. 3–4. Urbana : University of Illinois Press, 1942.

Ludwig, Friedrich. "Die geistliche nichtliturgische und weltliche einstimmige und die mehrstimmige Musik des Mittelalters bis zum Anfang des 15. Jahrhunderts." In *Handbuch der Musikgeschichte,* 2nd ed. Ed. Guido Adler, 157–295. Berlin–Wilmersdorf: H. Keller, 1930.

———, ed. *Repertorium organorum recentioris et motetorum vetustissimi stili.* Halle an der Saale: M. Niemeyer, 1910.

Maas, Paul. "Kurz- und Langzeile in der Auspicianischen Strophe." *Philologus* 68 (1909): 157–60.

Mariné Bigorra, Sebastian. *Inscripciones hispanas en verso.* Publicaciones de la Escuela de Filologia de Barcelona, Filologia clasica, vol. 11. Barcelona: Escuela de Filologia, 1952.

Marouzeau, Jules. *Traité de stylistique latine.* Collection d'études latines, publiée par la Société des études latines, Série scientifique, 12. Paris: Société d'édition "Les Belles lettres," 1946.

du Méril, Édélestand. *Poésies inédites du Moyen Âge, précedées d'une histoire de la fable ésopique.* Paris: Franck, 1854.

———. *Poésies populaires latines antérieures au douzième siècle.* Paris: Brockhaus et Avenarius, 1843.

———. *Poésies populaires latines du Moyen Âge.* Paris: F. Didot; Leipzig: A. Franck, 1847.

Meyer, Wilhelm. *Die Arundel-Sammlung mittellateinischer Lieder.* Abhandlungen der königlichen Gesellschaft der Wissenschaften zu Göttingen, Philologisch-historische Klasse. n.s. 11/2 (1908) 1–52. Reprint, Darmstadt: Wissenschaftliche Buchgesellschaft, 1970.

———. *Ges. Abh.* = Meyer, Wilhelm. *Gesammelte Abhandlungen zur mittellateinischen Rythmik.* 3 vols. Berlin: Weidmann, 1905–36. Reprint, Hildesheim and New York: Georg Olms Verlag, 1970.

———. *Die Oxforder Gedichte des Primas. Nachrichten von der königlichen Gesellschaft der Wissenschaften zu Göttingen, Philologisch-historische Klasse.* 1 (1907) 75–111 and 2 (1907) 113–75 and 231–34. Reprint, Libelli 288. Darmstadt: Wissenschaftliche Buchgesellschaft, 1970

———. *Die Preces der mozarabischen Liturgie, Abhandlungen der königlichen Gesellschaft der Wissenschaften zu Göttingen.* Philologisch-historische Klasse, n.s., 15/3. Berlin, 1914–17.

Meyer-Lübke, Wilhelm. *Grammaire des langues romanes.* Trans. Eugène Rabiet. 4 vols. Paris: H. Welter, 1890–1906.

MGH = *Monumenta Germaniae Historica.* Leipzig and Hanover, 1826–.

Epist. = *Epistulae.*

Libelli de lite.

PLAC = *Poetae Latini Aevi Carolini.*

MGH Poetae = *Monumenta Germaniae Historica, Poetae Latini Medii Aevi:* 1 (Berlin, 1881), ed. Ernest Dümmler; 2 (1884), ed. Ernst Dümmler; 3 (1886), ed. Ludwig Traube; 4, fascicle

1 (1899), ed. Paul von Winterfeld; 4, fascicles 2–3 (1923), ed. Karl Strecker; 5, fascicles 1–2 (1937–39), ed. Karl Strecker; 6, fascicle 1 (1951), ed. Karl Strecker.

Miltner-Zurunić, Helene. "De carmine ad Flavium Felicem misso quod inscribitur De resurrectione mortuorum." *Wiener Studien* 48 (1930): 82–97.

Mone, Franz Joseph. *Lateinische Hymnen des Mittelalters*. 3 vols. Freiburg im Breisgau: Herder, 1853–55.

Müller, Lucian. *De re metrica poetarum latinorum praeter Plautum et Terentium*. 2nd ed. St. Petersburg and Leipzig: C. Ricker, 1894.

Muratori, Lodovico Antonio. *Dissertatio de rhythmica veterum poesi*. In *Patrologiae Cursus Completus, Series Latina*, ed. Jacques Paul Migne, vol. 151, col. 755–84.

Neff, Karl. *Die Gedichte des Paulus Diaconus*. Quellen und Untersuchungen zur lateinischen Philologie des Mittelalters, vol. 3, no. 4. Munich: C. H. Beck, 1908.

Nicolau, Mathieu G. "Les deux sources de la versification latine accentuelle." *Bulletin du Cange, Archivum Latinitatis Medii Aevi* 9 (1935): 55–87.

———. *L'origine du "cursus" rhythmique et les débuts de l'accent d'intensité en latin*. Collection d'études latines, 5. Paris: Société d'édition "Les Belles lettres," 1930.

Nilsson, Nils Ola. *Metrische Stildifferenzen in den Satiren des Horaz*. Studia Latina Holmiensia, 1. Uppsala: Almqvist & Wiksell, 1952

Norberg, Dag. "Ad Sancti Augustini Psalmum abecedarium adnotationes." *Studi Italiani di Filologia Classica* 27–28 (1956): 315–17.

———. "Contributions à l'étude du latin vulgaire." In *Hommages à Max Niedermann*, Collection Latomus, vol. 23, 251–57 . Brussels: Latomus, Revue d'études latines, 1956.

———. "L'hymne ambrosien." *Kungl. Humanistiska Vetenskapsamfundet i Uppsala Årsbok*, 1953. Pp. 5–20.

———. "Notes sur quelques poèmes du haut Moyen Âge." *Latomus* 15 (1956): 353–58.

———. *La poésie latine rythmique du haut Moyen Âge*. Studia Latina Holmiensia, 2. Stockholm: Almqvist & Wiksell, 1954.

———. "L'origine de la versification latine rythmique." *Eranos* 50 (1952): 83–90.

Norden, Eduard. "Über die Geschichte des Reims." In *Die antike Kunstprosa vom VI. Jahrhundert v. Chr. bis in die Zeit der Renaissance*, 2nd ed., vol. 2, pp. 810–908. Stuttgart: B. G. Teubner, 1958.

Nougaret, Louis. *Traité de métrique latine classique*. Nouvelle collection à l'usage des classes, vol. 36. Paris: C. Klincksieck, 1948.

Pannenborg, Albert. "Über den Ligurinus." *Forschungen zur deutschen Geschichte* 11 (1871): 161–300.

Paris, Gaston. "Lettre à Léon Gautier sur la versification latine rythmique." *Bibliothèque de l'École des Chartes* 27 (1866), series 6, no. 2, pp. 578–610. Reprint, Paris: Franck, 1866.

PLAC = *Monumenta Germaniae Historica, Poetae Latini Aevi Carolini*, 1–4.

Polheim, Karl. *Die lateinische Reimprosa*. Berlin: Weidmann, 1925.

Reichert, Georg. "Strukturprobleme der älteren Sequenz." *Deutsche Vierteljahrsschrift für Literaturwissenschaft und Geistesgeschichte* 33 (1949): 227–51. Reprinted in George Reichert, *Ausgewählte Aufsätze*, ed. Martin Just (Tutzing: Schneider, 1977), pp. 77–98.

Ruodlieb, der älteste Roman des Mittelalters, nebst Epigrammen. Mit Einleitung, Anmerkungen und Glossar. Ed. Friedrich Seiler. Halle an der Salle: Buchhandlung des Waisenhauses, 1882. (See especially, "Die metrische Form," 143–59.)

Schlicher, John Jacob. "The Origin of Rhythmical Verse in Late Latin." Ph.D. thesis, University of Chicago, 1900.

Scholz, Richard. "Metrisches." In Conrad of Megenberg, *Planctus ecclesiae in Germaniam*, rev. Richard Scholz, *MGH* C2: Staatsschriften des späteren Mittelalters 2/1, 101–2. Leipzig: K. W. Hiersemann, 1941.

Schreiber, Jakob. *Die Vaganten-Strophe der mittellateinischen Dichtung und das Verhältnis derselben zu mittelhochdeutschen Strophenformen; ein Beitrag zur Carmina-Burana-Frage.* Strasbourg: Ch. Müh & Cie, 1894.

Schubiger, Anselm. *Die Sängerschule St. Gallens vom achten bis zwölften Jahrhundert. Ein Beitrag zur Gesanggeschichte des Mittelalters.* Einsiedeln: K. und N. Benziger, 1858. Reprint, Hildesheim: Georg Olms, 1966.

Sedgwick, W. B. "The Bellum Troianum of Joseph of Exeter." *Speculum* 5 (1930): 49–76.

———. "The Origin of Rhyme." *Revue bénédictine* 36 (1924): 330–46.

———. "The Style and Vocabulary of the Latin Arts of Poetry of the Twelfth and Thirteenth Centuries." *Speculum* 3 (1928): 349–81.

Seelmann, Emil Paul. *Die Aussprache des Latein nach physiologisch-historischen Grundsätzen.* Heilbronn: Gebr. Henninger, 1885.

Sessini, Ugo. *Poesia e musica nella latinità cristiana dal III al X secolo.* Ed. Giuseppe Vecchi. Torino: Società editrice internazionale, [1949].

Simonetti, Manlio. *Studi sull'innologia popolare cristiana dei primi secoli.* Atti della Accademia nazionale dei Lincei; anno CCCXLIX, Memorie, Classe di scienze morali, storiche e filologiche, ser. 8, vol. 4, fasc. 6. [Roma, 1952], pp. 341–484.

Spanke, Hans. "Aus der Vorgeschichte und Frühgeschichte der Sequenz." *Zeitschrift für deutsches Altertum und deutsche Literatur* 71 (1934): 1–39. Reprinted in Hans Spanke, *Studien zu Sequenz, Lai und Leich,* ed. Ursula Aarburg (Darmstadt: Wissenschaftliche Buchgesellschaft, 1977), pp. 107–45.

———. *Beziehungen zwischen romanischer und mittellateinischer Lyrik: mit besonderer Berücksichtigung der Metrik und Musik.* Abhandlungen der Gesellschaft der Wissenschaften zu Göttingen, Philologisch-historische Klasse; ser. 3, no. 18. Berlin: Weidmannsche Buchhandlung, 1936.

———. "Das lateinische Rondeau." *Zeitschrift für französische Sprache und Literatur* 53 (1930): 113–48.

———. "Der Codex Buranus als Liederbuch." *Zeitschrift für Musikwissenschaft* 13 (1930–31): 241–51.

———. "Die Kompositionskunst der Sequenzen Adams von St. Victor." *Studi Medievali*, n. s., 14 (1941): 1–29. Reprinted in Hans Spanke, *Studien zu Sequenz, Lai und Leich,* ed. Ursula Aarburg (Darmstadt: Wissenschaftliche Buchgesellschaft, 1977), pp. 203–31.

———. "Ein lateinisches Liederbuch des 11. Jahrhunderts." *Studi Medievali*, n. s., 15 (1942): 111–42.

———. "Rhythmen- und Sequenzenstudien." *Studi Medievali*, n.s., 4 (1931): 286–320. Reprinted in Hans Spanke, *Studien zu Sequenz, Lai und Leich,* ed. Ursula Aarburg (Darmstadt: Wissenschaftliche Buchgesellschaft, 1977), pp. 1–35.

———. "St. Martial-Studien." *Zeitschrift für französische Sprache und Literatur* 54 (1931): 282–317, 385–422; 56 (1932): 450–78.

———. "Zur Geschichte der lateinischen nicht-liturgischen Sequenz." *Speculum* 7 (1932): 367–82. Reprinted in Hans Spanke, *Studien zu Sequenz, Lai und Leich,* ed. Ursula Aarburg (Darmstadt: Wissenschaftliche Buchgesellschaft, 1977), pp. 91–106.

Spiegel, Nic. *Untersuchungen über die ältere christliche Hymnenpoesie.* Part 1, *Reimverwendung und Taktwechsel.* Würzburg: Druck der kgl. Universitätsdruckerei von H. Sturtz, 1896–97.

Steinen, Wolfram von den. "Die Anfänge der Sequenzendichtung." *Zeitschrift für schweizerische Kirchengeschichte* 40 (1946): 190–212, 241–68; 41 (1947): 19–48, 122–62.

———. *Notker der Dichter und seine geistige Welt.* 2 vols. Bern: A. Francke, 1948.

Strecker, Karl. "Index metricus et rhythmicus." In *Poetae Latini Aevi Carolini.* Ed. Ernst Dümmler, *MGH, Poetae Latini Medii Aevi,* vol. 4, fasc. 3, ed. Karl Strecker, pp. 1161–64. Berlin: Weidmann, 1923.

———. "Prosodie und Metrik." In *Ecbasis cuiusdam captivi per tropologiam,* ed. Karl Strecker, Scriptores rerum germanicarum in usum scholarum ex Monumentis Germaniae historicis separatim editi, no. 52. Hanover: Hahn, 1935.

———. "Studien zu karolingischen Dichtern, V. Leoninische Hexameter und Pentameter im 9. Jh." *Neues Archiv der Gesellschaft für ältere deutsche Geschichte* 44 (1922): 209–51.

———. "Die zweite Beichte des Erzpoeten. Mittelalterliche Handschriften." In *Mittelalterliche Handschriften: Paläographische, kunsthistorische, literarische und bibliotheksgeschichtliche Untersuchungen. Festgabe zum 60 Geburtstage von Hermann Degering,* 244–52. Leipzig: K. W. Hiersemann, 1926.

———. See also Walter of Châtillon.

Studien zur lateinischen Dichtung des Mittelalters. Ehrengabe für Karl Strecker zum 4. September 1931. Ed. Walter Stach und Hans Walther. Schriftenreihe zur Historischen Vierteljahrschrift, no. 1. Dresden: Buchdruckerei der Wilhelm und Bertha von Baensch Stiftung, 1931.

Suchier, Walther. *Französische Verslehre auf historischer Grundlage.* Sammlung kurzer Lehrbücher der romanischen Sprachen und Literaturen, no. 14. Tübingen: Niemeyer, 1952.

Thalhofer, Valentin. *Handbuch der katholischen Liturgik.* 2nd ed. by Ludwig Eisenhofer. 2 vols. Theologische Bibliothek. Freiburg im Breisgau: Herder, 1932–33. [The revised edition was first published in 1912.]

Thurot, Charles. *Notices et extraits de divers manuscrits latins pour servir à l'histoire des doctrines grammaticales au Moyen Âge.* Notices et extraits des manuscripts de la Bibliothèque impériale [nationale], no. 22. Paris: Imprimerie impériale [nationale], 1868.

Traube, Ludwig. *Karolingische Dichtungen.* Schriften zur germanischen Philologie, no. 1. Berlin: Weidmann, 1888.

———. "O Roma nobilis. Philologische Untersuchungen aus dem Mittelalter." *Abhandlungen der philosophisch-philologischen Classe der königlichen bayerischen Akademie,* 19 (1891): 299–395. Separately printed, Munich: Verlag der k. Akademie, 1891. Pp. 1–99.

———. *Poetae Latini Aevi Carolini.* 6 vols. Monumenta Germaniae Historica inde ab anno Christi quingentesimo usque ad annum millesimum et quingentesimum, Poetae Latini Medii Aevi. Berlin: Weidmann, 1881–1923. (See especially, "Index metricus et rhythmicus," vol. 3, pp. 815–18.)

Tréhorel, E. "Le psaume abécédaire de saint Augustin." *Revue des études latines* 17 (1939): 309–29.

Valerius, Marcus. *Bucoliche* [Bucolica]. Ed. Franco Munari. Florence: F. Le Monnier, 1970.

Valous, Guy de. "La poésie amoureuse en langue latine au Moyen Âge." *Classica et Mediaevalia* 13 (1952): 285–345 and 14 (1953): 156–204.

Vecchi, Giuseppe, ed. and trans. *Poesia latina medievale.* Collezione Fenice, Edizione fuori serie, 17. Parma: Guanda, 1952 [2nd ed. 1958].

———, Giuseppe. See Abelard.

Verrier, Paul Isadore. *Le vers français, formes primitives: développement—diffusion.* 3 vols. Bibliothèque de la Société des amis de l'Université de Paris, nos. 1–3. Paris: H. Didier, 1931–32.

Voigt, Ernst, ed. *Ysengrimus*. Halle an der Salle: Buchhandlung des Waisenhauses, 1884. (See especially "Prosodie und Metrik," pp. xxvi–xxxviii.)

Vossler, Karl. *Die Dichtungsformen der Romanen*. Ed. Andreas Bauer. Stuttgart: K. F. Koehler, 1951.

Vroom, Hermanus Bernardus. *Le psaume abécédaire de saint Augustin et la poésie latine rhythmique*. Latinitas Christianorum primaeva, 4. Nijmegen: Dekker & van de Vegt en J. W. van Leeuwen, 1933.

Wagner, Johannes Kurt. *Quaestiones neotericae imprimis ad Ausonium pertinentes*. Leipzig: R. Noske, 1907.

Wagner, Peter. *Einführung in die gregorianischen Melodien: ein Handbuch der Choralwissenschaft*. 3 vols. Leipzig: Breitkopf & Hartel, 1911–21.

Walpole, Arthur S. *Early Latin Hymns, with Introduction and Notes*. Cambridge Patristic Texts. Cambridge: University Press, 1922.

Walter of Châtillon. *Moralisch-satirische Gedichte Walters von Chatillon aus deutschen, englischen, franzosischen und italienischen Handschriften*. Ed. Karl Strecker. Heidelberg: C. Winter, 1929.

Wattenbach, Wilhelm. "Lateinische Gedichte aus Frankreich im elften Jahrhundert," *Sitzungsberichte der Akademie der Wissenschaften zu Berlin* 1 (1891): 97–144.

Weinmann, Karl, ed. *Hymnarium Parisiense, Das Hymnar der Zisterzienser-Abtei Pairis im Elsass, Aus zwei Codices des 12. und 13. Jahrhunderts*. Regensburg: Druck von F. Pustet, 1904.

Wellesz, Egon. *Eastern Elements in Western Chant, Studies in the Early History of Ecclesiastical Music*. Monumenta Musicae Byzantinae, Subsidia, vol. 2, American series, no. 1. Oxford: Byzantine Institute, 1947. Reprint, Copenhagen: Munksgaard, 1967.

Werner, Jakob. *Beiträge zur Kunde der lateinischen Literatur des Mittelalters*. Aarua: H. R. Sauerlander, 1905. Reprint, Hildesheim: Georg Olms, 1949.

The Winchester Troper, from MSS. of the Xth and XIth Centuries, with Other Documents Illustrating the History of Tropes in England and France. Ed. Walter Howard Frere. London: [Harrison and sons, printers], 1894.

Winterfeld, Paul von. "Die lateinische Eulaliensequenz und ihre Sippe." *Zeitschrift für deutsches Altertum und deutsche Literatur* 45 (1901): 133–49.

———, ed. *Hrotsvithae opera*. MGH, Scriptores rerum germanicarum in usum scholarum ex Monumentis Germaniae historicis separatim editi, no. 34. Berlin: Weidmann, 1902. (See especially "Index metricus" pp. 543–48.)

Wölfflin, Eduard von. "Der Reim im Lateinischen." *Archiv für lateinische Lexikographie und Grammatik mit Einschluss des älteren Mittellateins* 1 (1884): 350–89

———. "Über die allitterierenden Verbindungen der lateinischen Sprache." *Sitzungsberichte der philolosophischen und historischen Klasse der Bayerischen Akademie der Wissenschaften zu München* 2 (1881): 1–94.

Wright, Thomas. *The Anglo-Latin Satirical Poets and Epigrammatists of the Twelfth Century*. 2 vols. Rolls Series. London: Longman, 1872.

Young, Karl. *The Drama of the Medieval Church*. 2 vols. Oxford: Clarendon Press, 1933.

INDEX OF WORDS

INDEX OF NAMES

French spellings of names (in Norberg) appear in italics.

Porphyrius, Publilius Optatianus; *Porfyre Optatien*, 50
Primas. *See* Hugh of Orléans
Probus; *Probus*, 103
Prosper of Aquitaine; *Prosper d' Aquitaine*, 67
Prudentius; *Prudence*, 7–8, 46, 57, 63–67, 69, 71, 74–78, 107, 109–10, 148, 180–81

Quiricus of Barcelona; *Quiricus de Barcelone*, 67, 69

Rabanus Maurus; *Raban Maur*, 33, 67, 71, 73
Radbod; *Radbode*, 78
Rahewin; *Rahewin*, 17, 30
Ratpert; *Ratpert*, 142
Reginald of Canterbury; *Réginald de Cantorbéry*, 43, 63, 116
Robert of Anjou; *Robert d'Anjou*, 60, 62
Ronto, Matthaeus; *Matthaeus Ronto*, 5
Rumold; *Romoldus*, 118
Rupert of Deutz; *Rupert de Deutz*, 65, 72, 74–76, 78

Saxo Grammaticus; *Saxo Grammaticus*, 72, 74, 76–78
Sechnall; *Sechnall*, 107
Secundinus (*Latin name for* Sechnall; *see* Sechnall)
Sedulius; *Sedulius*, 1–3, 26–27, 31–32, 50, 56, 63–65, 67, 102–3, 112, 133, 180
Sedulius Scottus; *Sedulius Scotus*, 71, 73
Sergius III; *Sergius III*, 50
Sisebert of Toledo; *Sisbert de Tolède*, 9, 11, 15, 97–99, 110–11
Smaragdus of St. Mihiel; *Smaragde de Saint-Mihiel*, 67, 114
Statius; *Stace*, 5
Stephen, Master; *Étienne, Maître (Étienne de Pavie)*, 86, 88, 96, 106
Stöcklin, Ulrich (von Rottach); *Ulrich Stöcklin*, 50
Suintharic; *Suintharic*, 49, 143
Symphosius; *Symphosius*, 15

Terentianus Maurus; *Térentianus*, 73
Theoderich of Trier; *Thierry de Trèves*, 25

Theodulf of Orléans; *Théodulphe d' Orléans*, 33, 89
Theofrid of Corbie; *Théofride de Corbie*, 32, 106, 111
Thomas Aquinas; *Thomas d'Aquin*, 40, 94, 169
Thomas à Kempis; *Thomas a Kempis*, 93, 118, 145
Thomas of Milan; *Thomas de Milan*, 97, 99
Tisserand, Jean; *Tisserant, Jean*, 41, 121

Udalschalk of Augsburg; *Udalschalk de Maissach*, 115
Ulrich Stöcklin. *See* Stöcklin, Ulrich

Valerius; *Valerius*, 3
Venantius Fortunatus; *Venance Fortunat*, 2–3, 5–7, 12, 18, 24, 32, 46, 50, 56, 64, 69
Vigila of St. Martin of Albelda; *Vigila de San Martin de Albelda*, 122, 124
Virgil the Grammarian (Virgilius Maro Grammaticus); *Virgile le Grammairien*, 53, 113, 127
Virgil; *Virgil*, 1, 23, 27, 43, 59, 96, 180
Virgin Mary; *Vierge*, 37, 48, 52, 83, 112

Walafrid Strabo; *Walafrid Strabon*, 33, 49, 64, 67–68, 71, 74, 76–77
Waldrammus; *Waldrammus*, 122
Walter of Châtillon; *Gauthier de Châtillon*, 11, 14–15, 17–18, 20–21, 23, 26, 46, 63, 180
Walter of Speyer; *Gauthier de Spire*, 43
Walter of Wimbourne; *Gauthier Wiburn*, 18, 116
Wandalbert of Prüm; *Wandalbert de Prüm*, 71, 73, 77
Wido of Ivrea; *Wido d'Ivrea*, 5, 116
William Longsword; *Guillaume Longue-Epée*, 148
William of Deguilleville; *Guillaume de Deguilleville*, 49, 52, 57, 121
Willibald; *Willibald*, 92
Winwallus; *Guénolé*, 120
Wipo; *Wipon*, 36, 121, 124, 168

Yrieix, St.; *saint Yrieix*, 127

INDEX OF ANONYMOUS TEXTS

Italics indicate conventional titles; regular typeface indicates incipits.

GENERAL PROSODIC INDEX

Songs with glosses (borrowed verses), 57
Syllaba anceps, 62–63, 73
Synaeresis (synezesis), 23–24, 29, 83, 97, 99, 115, 132, 136–37, 146
Syncope, 25–26

Telestichs, 50
Tmesis, 52
Tropes, 158, 173–78, 181, 183, 186

Versus anadiplositi, 56
    dirupti, 52
    ianuarii, 55
    rapportati, 54
    recurrentes, 55
    retrogradi or reciproci, 55
    rhopalici, 54
Versification, metrical (and rhythmic imitations), 58–80
    Adonic, 45, 72–74, 79, 91–92, 128, 141, 149–150, 176
    Adonic hexameter, 61–62
    Adonici, 61–62
    Alcaic, 75, 76–78, 95
    Anacreontic meter, 67
    anapestic, 78, 125
    archaic iambic verses, 66
    Archilochian, 78
    Asclepiad, 2, 9, 35, 73–75, 92–95, 119, 176
    caudati, collaterales, cruciferi, unisoni, 62
    choriambic, 78
    citocadi, 61–62
    dactylic catalectic tetrameter, 77–79, 125, 147, 176
    dactylic hexameter, 58–61
    Glyconic, 75–76, 78–80, 94–95
    iambic dimeter, catalectic, 66–67, 105, 121–22, 140
    iambic dimeter, 2, 19, 27, 31, 63–67, 75, 78, 100, 119–22, 133, 135, 137, 140, 182–83
    iambic trimeter, 65–66, 75, 105, 111, 122, 128, 148, 176, 182, 184
    Leonine hexameter *(Leonini),* 30, 32–34, 40–41, 43, 55, 59, 62–63

minor ionics, 78
new strophes, 78–79
pentameter, 24, 33, 56, 63, 96
Phalaecian verse, 71, 75
Pherecratean, 75–76, 79, 95, 122
Sapphic verse, 5–7, 35, 52, 57, 71–72, 75, 79–80, 89–91, 118, 143, 149, 176
Terentianean (versus Terentianeus: *Squalent arva soli pulvere multo*), 73
trinini salientes, 60, 62
tripertiti dactylici, 61
trochaic septenarius, 67–71
trochaic septenarius, archaic type, 69
use of two short syllables for a long, 66
Versification, rhythmic, 81–155, 160, 165–66, 168, 176, 181–86
    entire imitation of the structure, 89–113
    free verses written to a given melody and without any connection to classical rapprochement of free verse and the old rhythmic verse, 167–68, 183–185; versification, 159–60, 182–83
    imitation of the number of syllables, 118–25; of Byzantine verse, 142; of the number of words, 125–27; of the quantity, 127–29; of the structure of quantitative verses, 88
    influence of German verse, 141–42, 185
    new rhythmic verses formed from prosaic refrains, 143–48; after the model of biblical poetry, 156
    partial imitation, 90–93, 95, 99, 104–7, 109–12, 131–33
    regular alternation of accents, 113–18
    theories of scholars, 82–86
    variation of the number of syllables, 136–42

Wordplay with letters, 48–53; with long words, 54; with monosyllabic words, 53–54; with vowels, 47
Words, metrical. *See* Metrical Words

RHYTHMIC VERSES

Abbreviations: p = with final paroxytone cadence, pp = with final proparoxytone cadence, R = regular alternation of accents

VERSES OF 1 SYLLABLE:
1: for example *Das,* 39

VERSE OF 2 SYLLABLES:
2: *Suave,* 39

VERSES OF 3 SYLLABLES:
3p: *Calorem,* 171
3pp: *Veneris,* 171

VERSES OF 4 SYLLABLES:
4p: *Terra floret,* 170
4pp: *Progreditur,* 170

VERSES OF 5 SYLLABLES:
5p (imitation of Adonic): *Cuncta precatur,* 89
5pp: *Rex altissime,* 152

VERSES OF 6 SYLLABLES:
6p: *Ave maris stella,* 145
6pp: *De terre gremio,* 170
6: 139–40, 153

VERSES OF 7 SYLLABLES:
7p (imitation of catalectic iambic dimeter): *Quieti tempus adest,* 105
7pp (imitation of second hemistich of the trochaic septenarius): *Inest quibus caritas,*111–12
7: 121–23

VERSES OF 8 SYLLABLES:

8p (imitation of trochaic dimeter): *Qui signati estis Christo,* 112–13

R 8p: 116

4p + 4p: *Sancte sator suffragator,* 113

8pp (imitation of iambic dimeter): *Praecelso et spectabili,* 100–102

8pp if the final word is polysyllabic, 8p if it is disyllabic, 103

R 8pp: 117

4p + 4pp: *Quisquis videns voluerit,* 104

4pp + 4pp: *Non tumidae superbiae,* 104

2 + 2 + 4pp: *Cruci truci fles filium,* 38–39

8: 119–120

VERSES OF 9 SYLLABLES:

9p: *Audivi avem acclattire,* 153

3 + 6p: *Domine audi lacrimantes,* 147–48

9pp: *Adtende homo quod pulvis es,* 142–43

VERSES OF 10 SYLLABLES:

4p + 6p: *Bone pastor moriens pro grege,* 146

10pp: *In sanctis narratur ecclesiis,* 147

4 + 6pp: *In te loca pulcra sunt omnia,* 146–47

10 (on the model of the catalectic dactylic tetrameter): *Psallere quod docuit cytara,* 124–25

VERSES OF 11 SYLLABLES:

5p + 6p (imitation of Sapphic verse): *Terra marique victor honorande,* 89–90

5 + 6: 118

5p + 6pp (imitation of Alcaic verse): *Laüdes Deo dicam per saecula,* 95

6 + 5p (6pp if the word before the break is polysyllabic, 6p if it is disyllabic: imitation of Terentianean verse): *Ad te bona fluunt ad te recurrunt,* 92–93

6 + 5: 118–19

4p + 7pp: *Dei patris festinare maximum,* 112

7pp + 4p: *Cuius estis oculi vos prophetae,* 153–54

VERSES OF 12 SYLLABLES:

6p + 6p: *Lamentemur nostra socii peccata,* 154

6pp + 6pp (imitation of Asclepiadic verse): *En pater gloriae rutilum gaudium,* 93

6pp + 6p if the final word is disyllabic, 93–94

6 + 6: 119–120

5p + 7pp (imitation of iambic trimeter): *Aspice Deus de supernis sedibus,* 105–6.

5 + 7: 122–23

7p + 5p: *Et miseratus parce populo tuo*, 151.

4 + 8p: *Seniores iuvenes atque lactantes*, 150

R 8p + 4p: *Congregavit nos in unum Christi amor*, 148

4p + 4p + 4p: *Laxis fibris resonante plectro linguae*, 148

12: 123

VERSES OF 13 SYLLABLES:

7pp + 6p (Goliardic verse): *Miserere Domine miserere Christe*, 145–46, 183–84

6pp + 7p: *Averte Domine iram furoris tui*, 151

8p + 5p: *Lamentemur et ploremus quare tacemus*, 154

8pp + 5p: *Pie precantes supplices exaudi Christe*, 149

VERSES OF 14 SYLLABLES:

7 + 7p: *Clare sacerdos clues almo fultus decore*, 135

7 + 7pp: *Carta Christo comite per telluris spatium*, 136

7p + 7pp: *A patre missus veni perditos requirere*, 144

8p + 6p: *Per quem te semper in celis credimus regnantem*, 150–51

VERSES OF 15 SYLLABLES:

8p + 7pp (imitation of trochaic septenarius): *Audite omnes amantes Deum sancta merita*, 107–8.

8p + 7p if the final word is disyllabic, 107

4p + 4p + 7pp: *Apparebit repentina dies magna Domini*, 108

R 8p + 7pp: 113–16.

R 8p + R 7pp: 115

8 + 7: 123–24

8pp + 7pp: *Adtende rex piissime planctus hos ecclesie*, 151–52

5p + 5p + 5p: *Quidquid est tutum quidquid virtutum et honestatis*, 100

VERSES OF OF 16 SYLLABLES:

8p + 8p: *Abundantia peccatorum solet fratres conturbare*, 131–32

8 + 8pp: 133–334

8 + 8: 120–21.

VERSES OF OF 17 SYLLABLES:

6pp + 6pp + 5p: *Quidquid est floridum, nobile, lucidum, amoenitatis*, 100

VERSES OF 18 SYLLABLES:

6p + 6p + 6p: 144

VERSES OF VARIABLE SYLLABLES:

   8 to 10 (imitation of catalectic anapestic dimeter): *Iam dulcis amica venito,* 125

   5 to 7 + 8 to 10p (imitation of dactylic hexameter): 95–97.

   8pp or 7pp (Ambrosian verse without anacrusis): (~) ´~ ~ ´~ ~ ´~ ~ ´~, 137–38

   7p or 6p: (~) ´~ ~ ´~ ~ ´~ ~, 137

   8p + 7pp or 9p + 8pp: (~) ´~ ~ ´~ ~ ´~ ~ ´~ ~ || (~) ´~ ~ ´~ ~ ´~ ~ `~, 137–38

   7 to 8p + 6pp: (~) ~ ~ ´~ ~ ~ ´~ ~ || ~ ~ ~ ´~ ~ ~, 148

   4 to 7 (free Adonic): 141

   6 to 8 (free catalectic iambic dimeter): 140

   6 to 9 (Ambrosian free verse): 139–40.

VERSES OF A CERTAIN NUMBER OF WORDS:

   3 words: 126

   4 words: 127

   2 + 2 words: 126–27

   3 + 3 words: 126

RHYTHMIC STROPHES

A FEW STROPHES FORMED AFTER THE MODEL OF
QUANTITATIVE VERSIFICATION:
    3 x (5p + 6p), 5p (Sapphic strophe): 89–91
    4 x (6pp + 6pp) (asclepiadic strophe): 93
    3 x (6pp + 6pp), 8pp (asclepiadic strophe): 94–95
    2 x (6 + 6), 7, 8 (asclepiadic strophe): 119
    7 x 5p (pseudo-Sapphic strophe): 91
    4 x 8pp (Ambrosian strophe): 100–101
    2 x (8 + 8pp): 134–35
    8pp, 8pp, 8 + 8pp: 133–34
    2 or 3 or 4 or 5 x (5p + 7pp): 105–6
    2 or 3 or 4 x (8p + 7pp): 107–8, 123–24

STROPHES FORMED WITH THE AID OF A REFRAIN:
    3 x (5p + 7pp), 5p (pseudo-Sapphic strophe): 148–49
    5p + 6p, 2 x 9pp: 143
    3 x 8pp, 5p: 149
    4 x 8p, 5p: 149
    2 x (5p + 6pp), 7pp: 149–50
    2 x (8p + 6p): 150–51
    6pp + 7p, 7p + 5p: 151.
    5pp, 2 x 7pp: 152
    5pp, 2 x 7pp, 3pp: 152
    8pp, 5pp, 2 x 7pp: 152–53

OTHER NEW STROPHES:
    3 x (7pp + 6p), 1 quantitative hexameter (Goliardic hexameter strophe with
auctoritas): 183–84
    2 x 8p, 7pp (*Stabat mater* strophe): 111–12, 168–69

2 x 7p, 9p: 153

2 x 6, 8: 153

3 x R 8pp, R 7p: 116–17

2 x 7pp, 3 x (7pp + 4p): 153–54

7pp, 2 x (7pp + 4): 153–54

3 x 7pp, 4p + 7pp: 154

3 + 7pp, 7pp, 3 x (4 + 7pp): 154

2 x 8pp, 2 x 8p, 4p: 154

2 x (6p + 6p, 8p + 5p): 154

4p, 2, 4p, 2, 2, 2, 5pp, 1, 3pp, 10p: 38–39

A: 6p, 3 x 7pp, 6p, 7pp, B: 2 x (4p + 4p + 7pp), C: 8p, D: 2 x (2 x 8p, 2) = strophe with the form of a sequence: 172.

Sequence strophes pp. 169–71.: 1a, b: 2 x 4p, 9pp; 2a, b: 2 x 4p, 7pp; 3a, b: 2 x 6pp, 4pp, 7pp, 7p; 3c: 2 x 7pp, 4pp, 7pp, 7p; 4a, b: 4 x 4p, 7pp; 5a, b: 2 x 7pp, 2 x 4pp, 7p, 6pp, 4pp, 3p; 6a, b: 4p, 7pp, 7p; 7a, b: 3pp, 4pp, 2 x 7pp, 2 x 4pp, 3p.

An Introduction to the Study of Medieval Latin Versification was designed and composed in Minion with Hiroshige Sans display type by Kachergis Book Design, Pittsboro, North Carolina; and printed on 60-pound Glatfelter and bound by Edwards Brothers, Inc., Lillington, North Carolina.